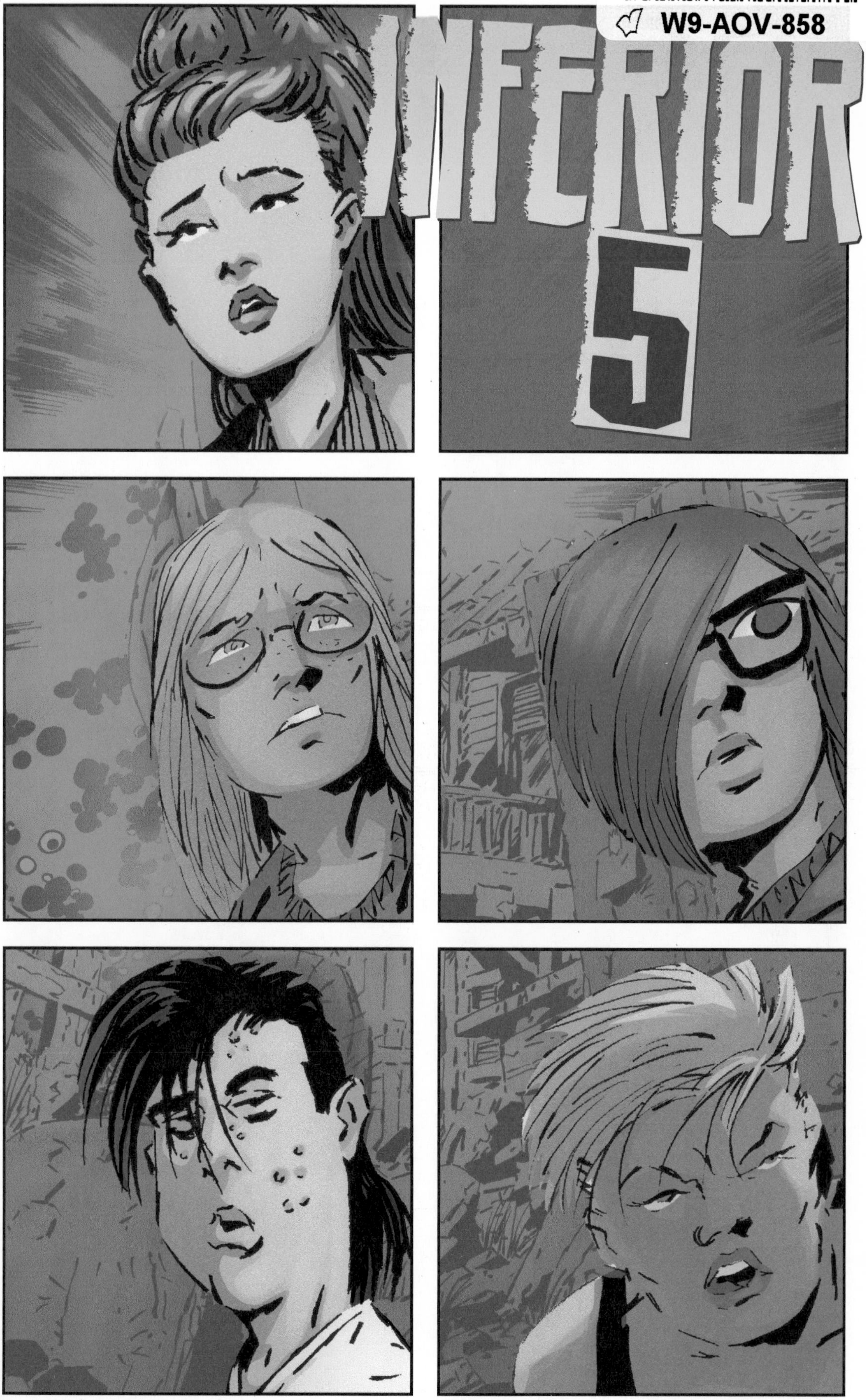
INFERIOR
5

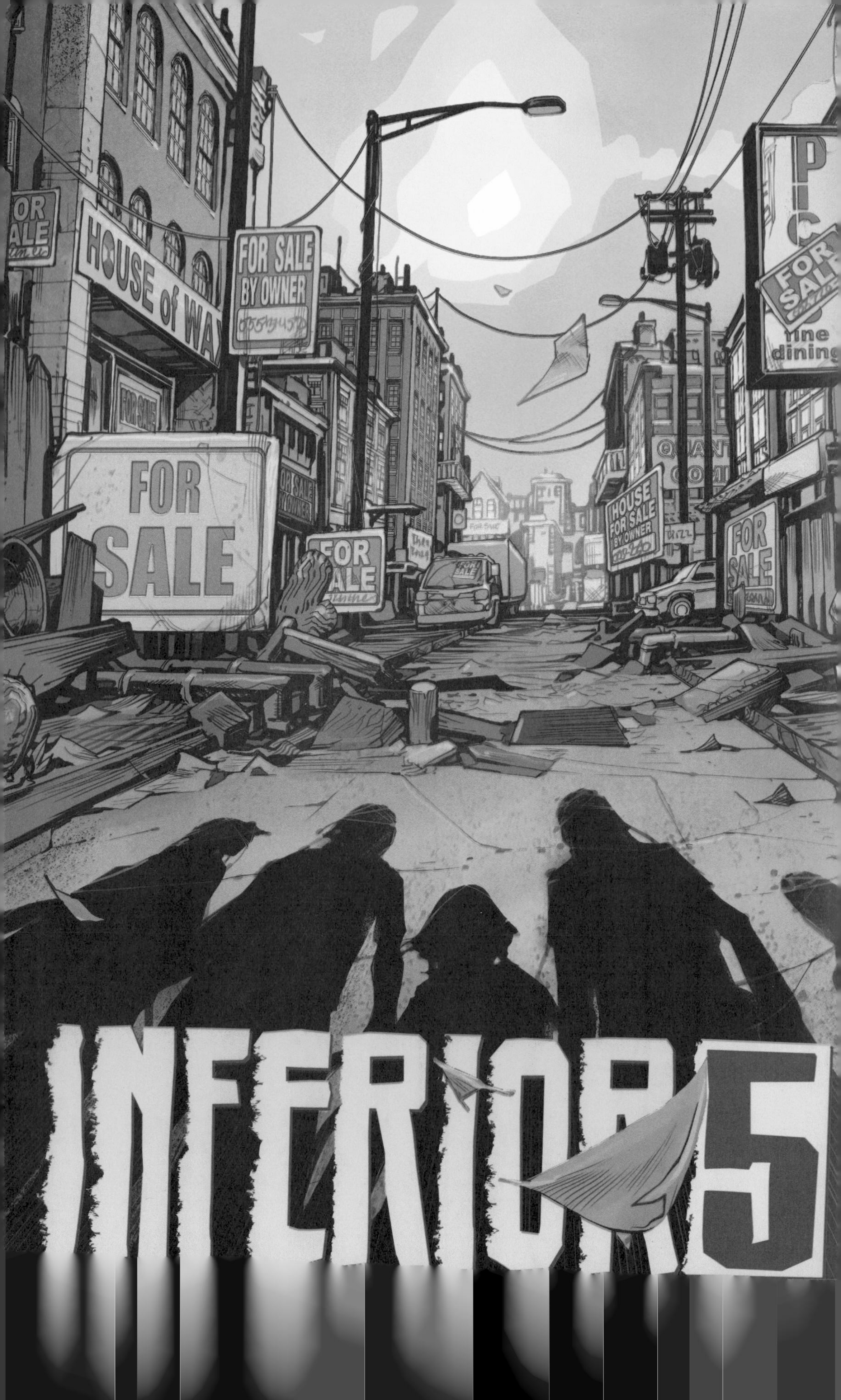

FOR SALE
HOUSE of WAX
FOR SALE BY OWNER
FOR SALE
FOR SALE
HOUSE FOR SALE BY OWNER
FOR SALE
FOR SALE
fine dining
INFERIOR 5

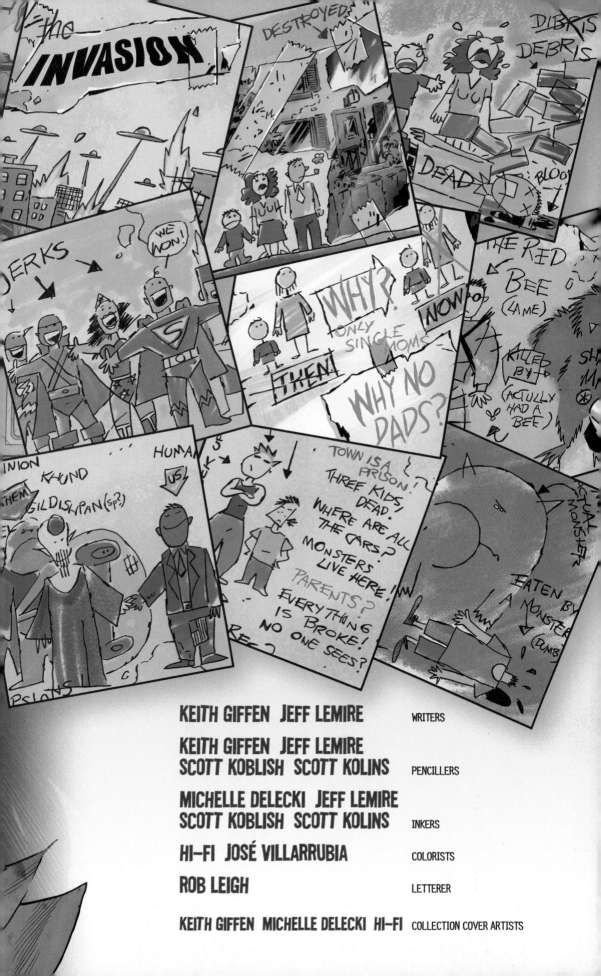

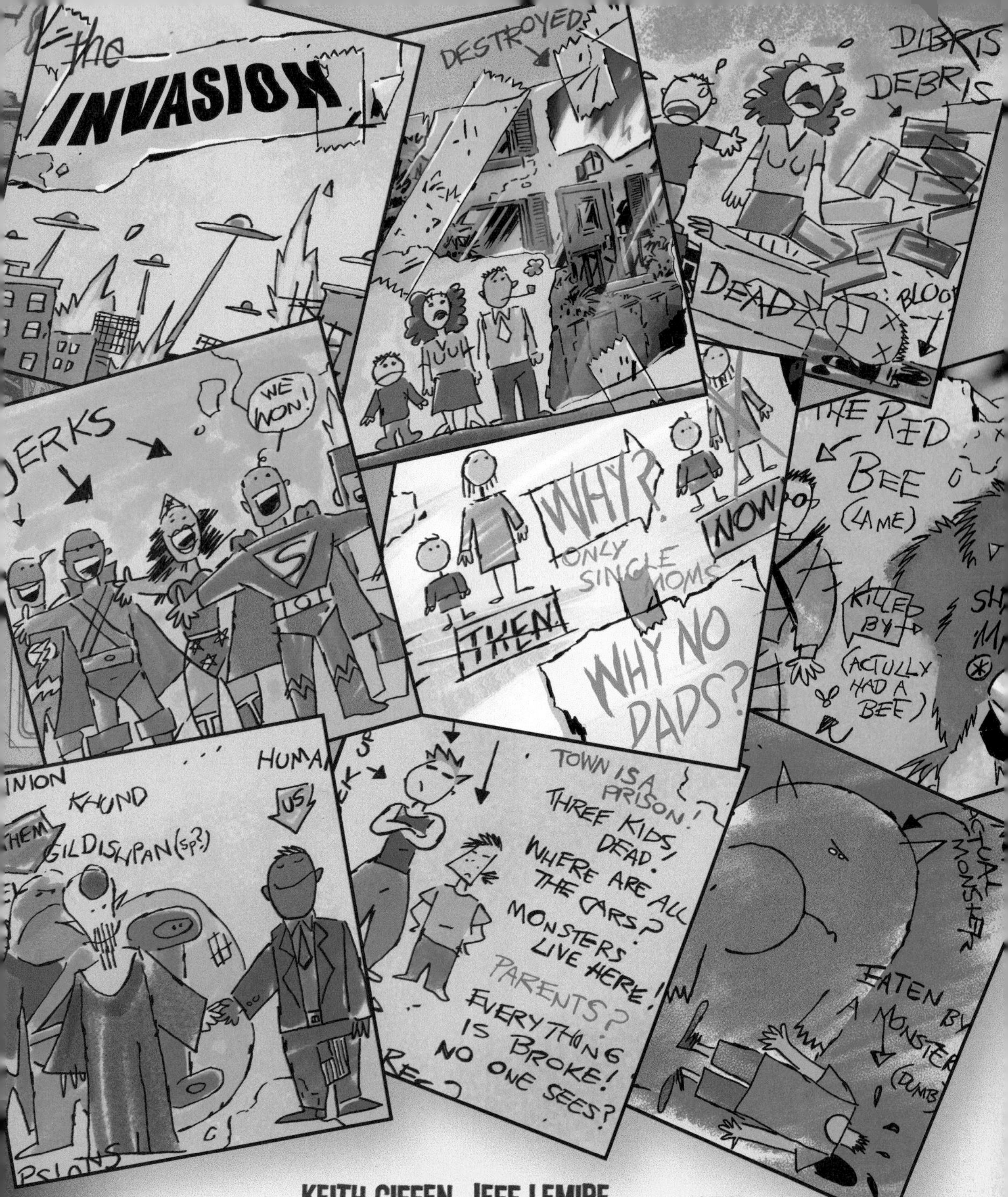
the
INVASION
DESTROYED
DIBRIS
DEBRIS
DEAD
JERKS
WE WON!
WHY?
ONLY SINGLE MOMS
NOW
THEN
WHY NO DADS?
THE RED BEE
(LAME)
KILLED BY
(ACTULLY HAD A BEE)
US
KHUND
THEM
GILDISHPAN (sp?)
TOWN IS A PRISON!
THREE KIDS, DEAD.
WHERE ARE ALL THE CARS?
MONSTERS LIVE HERE!
PARENTS?
EVERYTHING IS BROKE!
NO ONE SEES?
ACTUAL MONSTER
EATEN BY A MONSTER

KEITH GIFFEN JEFF LEMIRE WRITERS

KEITH GIFFEN JEFF LEMIRE
SCOTT KOBLISH SCOTT KOLINS PENCILLERS

MICHELLE DELECKI JEFF LEMIRE
SCOTT KOBLISH SCOTT KOLINS INKERS

HI-FI JOSÉ VILLARRUBIA COLORISTS

ROB LEIGH LETTERER

KEITH GIFFEN MICHELLE DELECKI HI-FI COLLECTION COVER ARTISTS

JOEY CAVALIERI Editor – Original Series
MICHAEL McCALISTER Editor – Collected Edition
STEVE COOK Design Director – Books
CURTIS KING JR. Publication Design
ERIN VANOVER Publication Production

MARIE JAVINS Editor-in-Chief, DC Comics

DANIEL CHERRY III Senior VP – General Manager
JIM LEE Publisher & Chief Creative Officer
JOEN CHOE VP – Global Brand & Creative Services
DON FALLETTI VP – Manufacturing Operations & Workflow Management
LAWRENCE GANEM VP – Talent Services
ALISON GILL Senior VP – Manufacturing & Operations
NICK J. NAPOLITANO VP – Manufacturing Administration & Design
NANCY SPEARS VP – Revenue

INFERIOR FIVE

DC Comics, 2900 West Alameda Ave., Burbank, CA 91505
Printed by LSC Communications, Owensville, MO, USA. 9/3/21. First Printing.
ISBN: 978-1-77951-347-2

Library of Congress Cataloging-in-Publication Data is available.

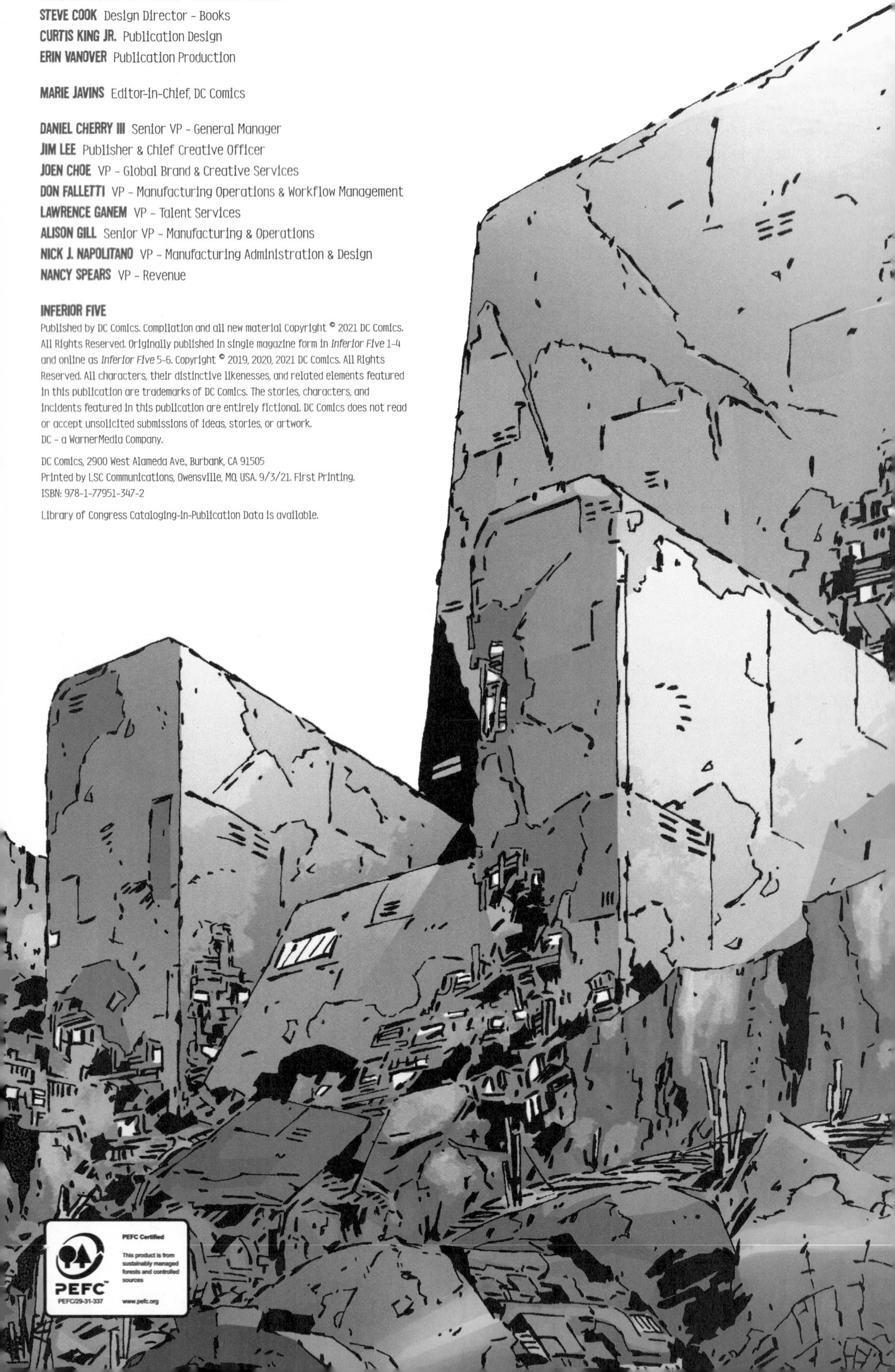

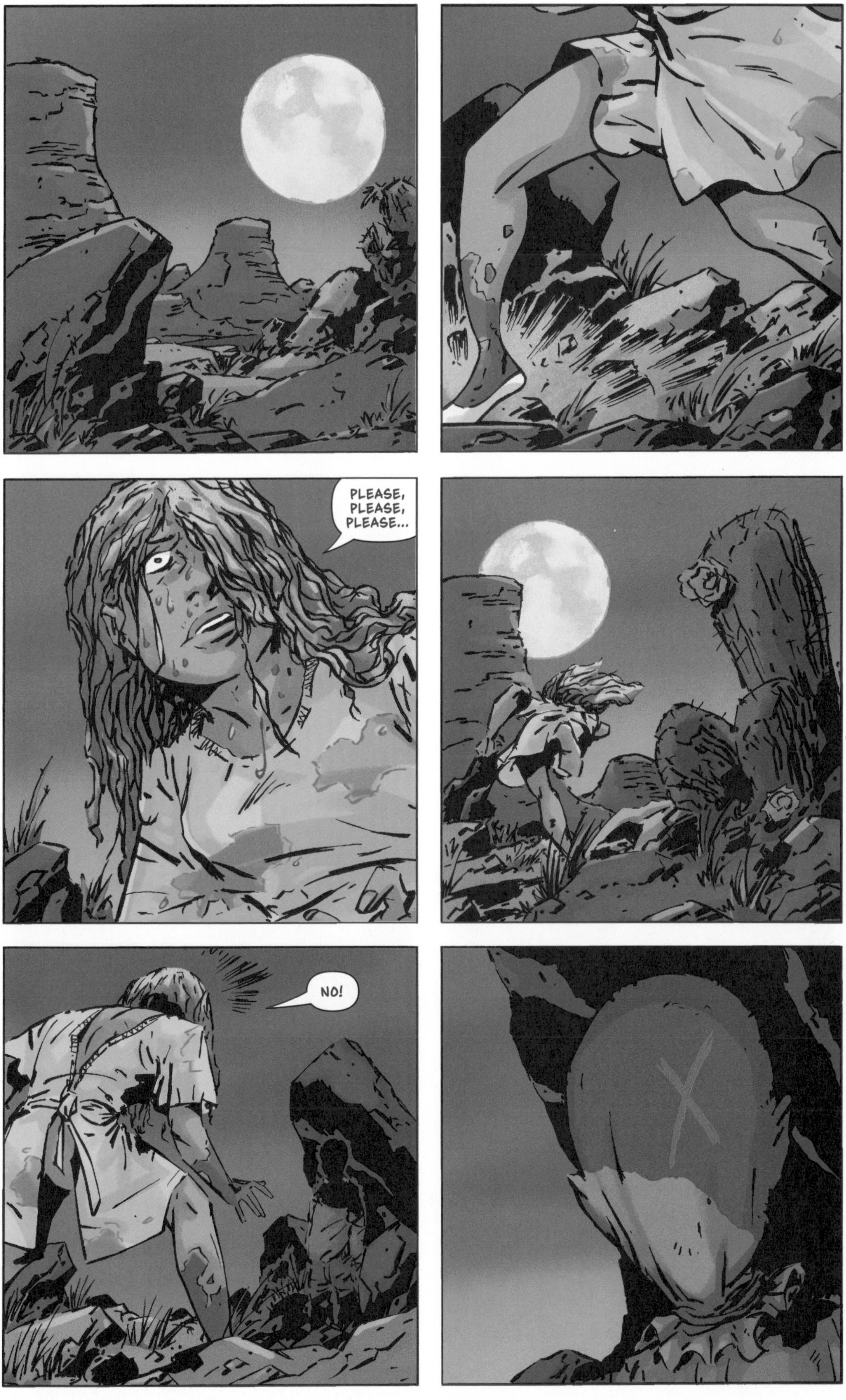
PLEASE,
PLEASE,
PLEASE...
NO!

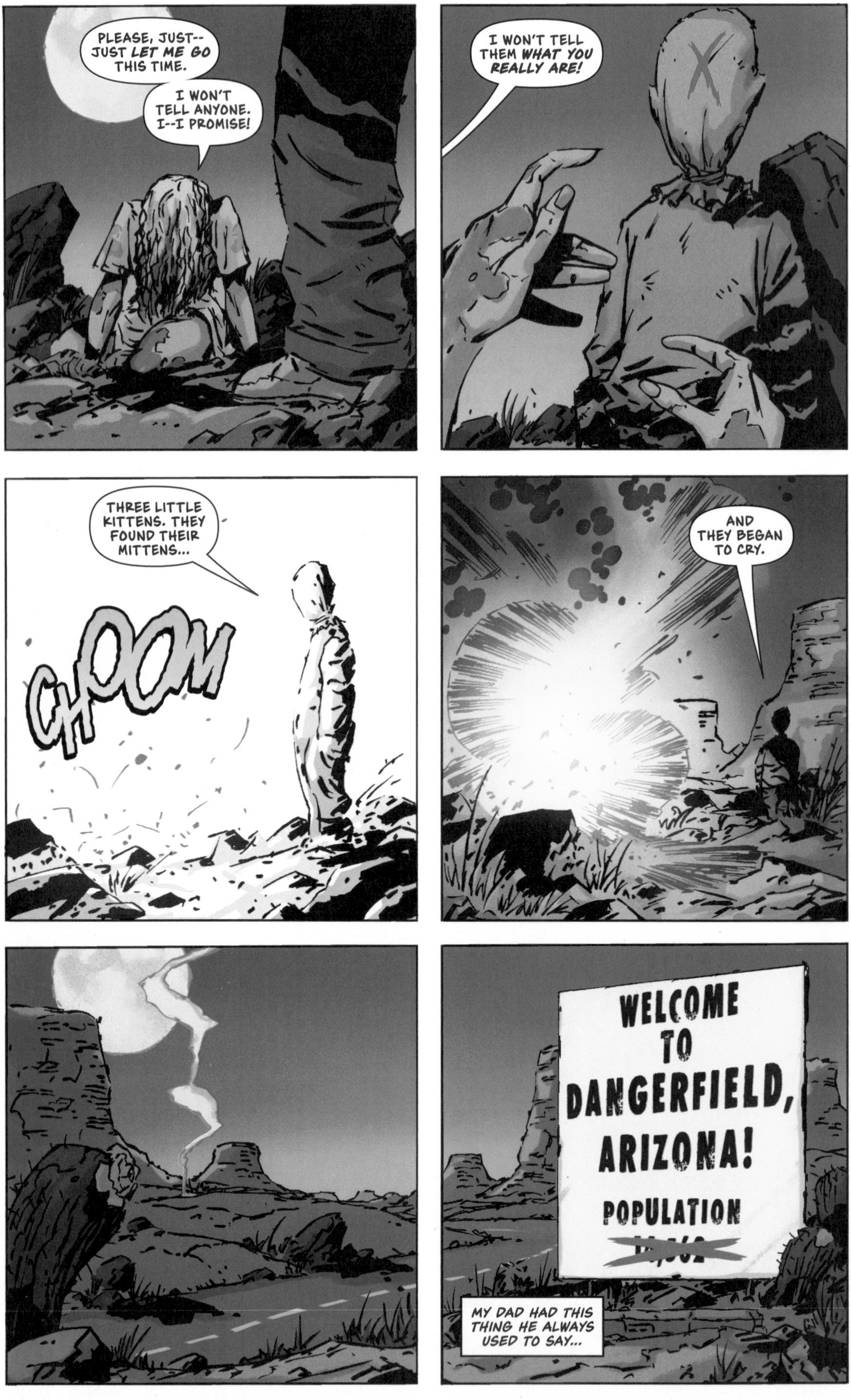
PLEASE, JUST--
JUST LET ME GO THIS TIME.
I WON'T TELL ANYONE. I--I PROMISE!
I WON'T TELL THEM WHAT YOU REALLY ARE!
THREE LITTLE KITTENS. THEY FOUND THEIR MITTENS...
CHOOM
AND THEY BEGAN TO CRY.
WELCOME TO DANGERFIELD, ARIZONA!
POPULATION
MY DAD HAD THIS THING HE ALWAYS USED TO SAY...

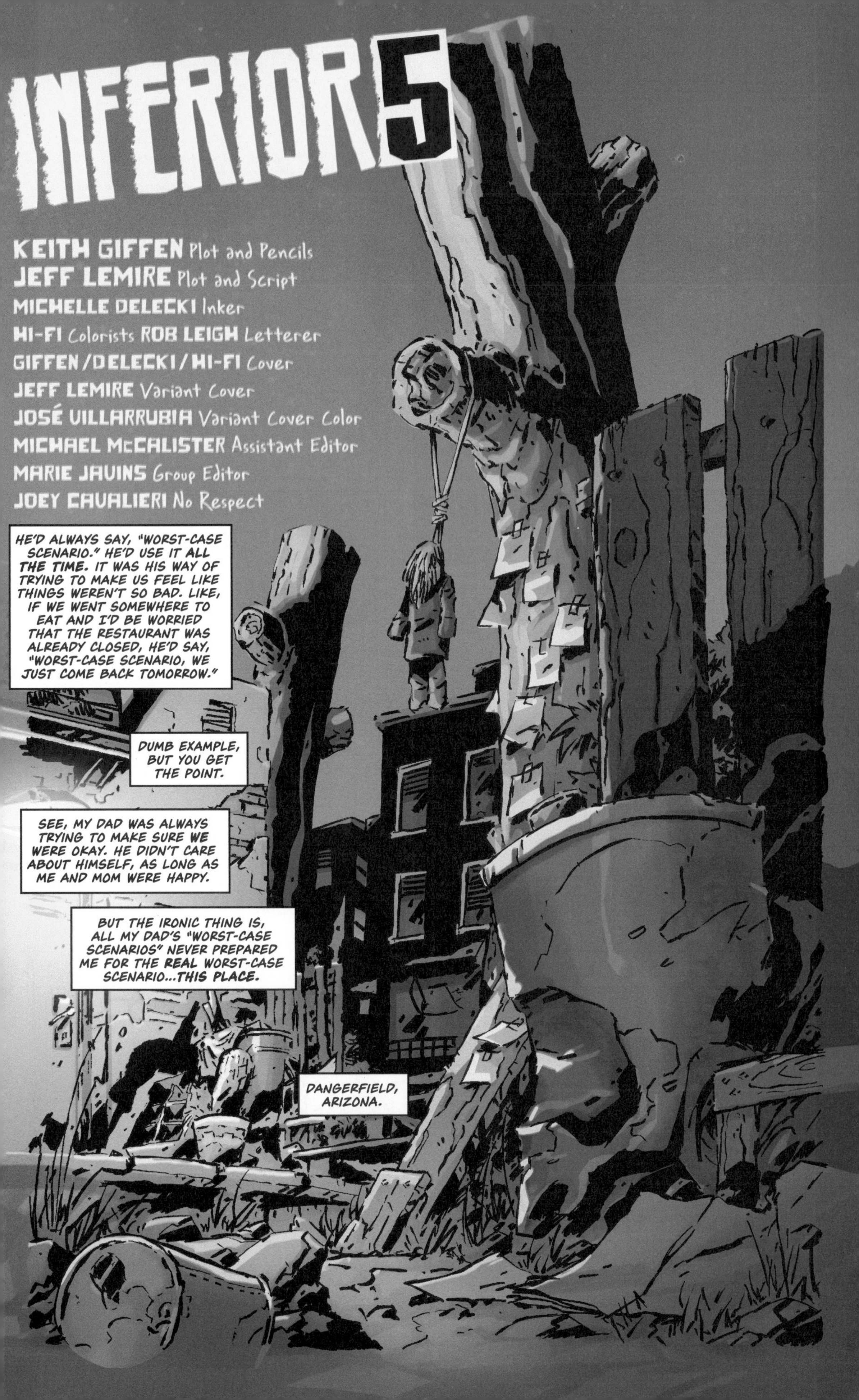
INFERIOR 5
KEITH GIFFEN Plot and Pencils
JEFF LEMIRE Plot and Script
MICHELLE DELECKI Inker
HI-FI Colorists ROB LEIGH Letterer
GIFFEN/DELECKI/HI-FI Cover
JEFF LEMIRE Variant Cover
JOSÉ VILLARRUBIA Variant Cover Color
MICHAEL McCALISTER Assistant Editor
MARIE JAVINS Group Editor
JOEY CAVALIERI No Respect
HE'D ALWAYS SAY, "WORST-CASE SCENARIO." HE'D USE IT ALL THE TIME. IT WAS HIS WAY OF TRYING TO MAKE US FEEL LIKE THINGS WEREN'T SO BAD. LIKE, IF WE WENT SOMEWHERE TO EAT AND I'D BE WORRIED THAT THE RESTAURANT WAS ALREADY CLOSED, HE'D SAY, "WORST-CASE SCENARIO, WE JUST COME BACK TOMORROW."
DUMB EXAMPLE, BUT YOU GET THE POINT.
SEE, MY DAD WAS ALWAYS TRYING TO MAKE SURE WE WERE OKAY. HE DIDN'T CARE ABOUT HIMSELF, AS LONG AS ME AND MOM WERE HAPPY.
BUT THE IRONIC THING IS, ALL MY DAD'S "WORST-CASE SCENARIOS" NEVER PREPARED ME FOR THE REAL WORST-CASE SCENARIO...THIS PLACE.
DANGERFIELD, ARIZONA.

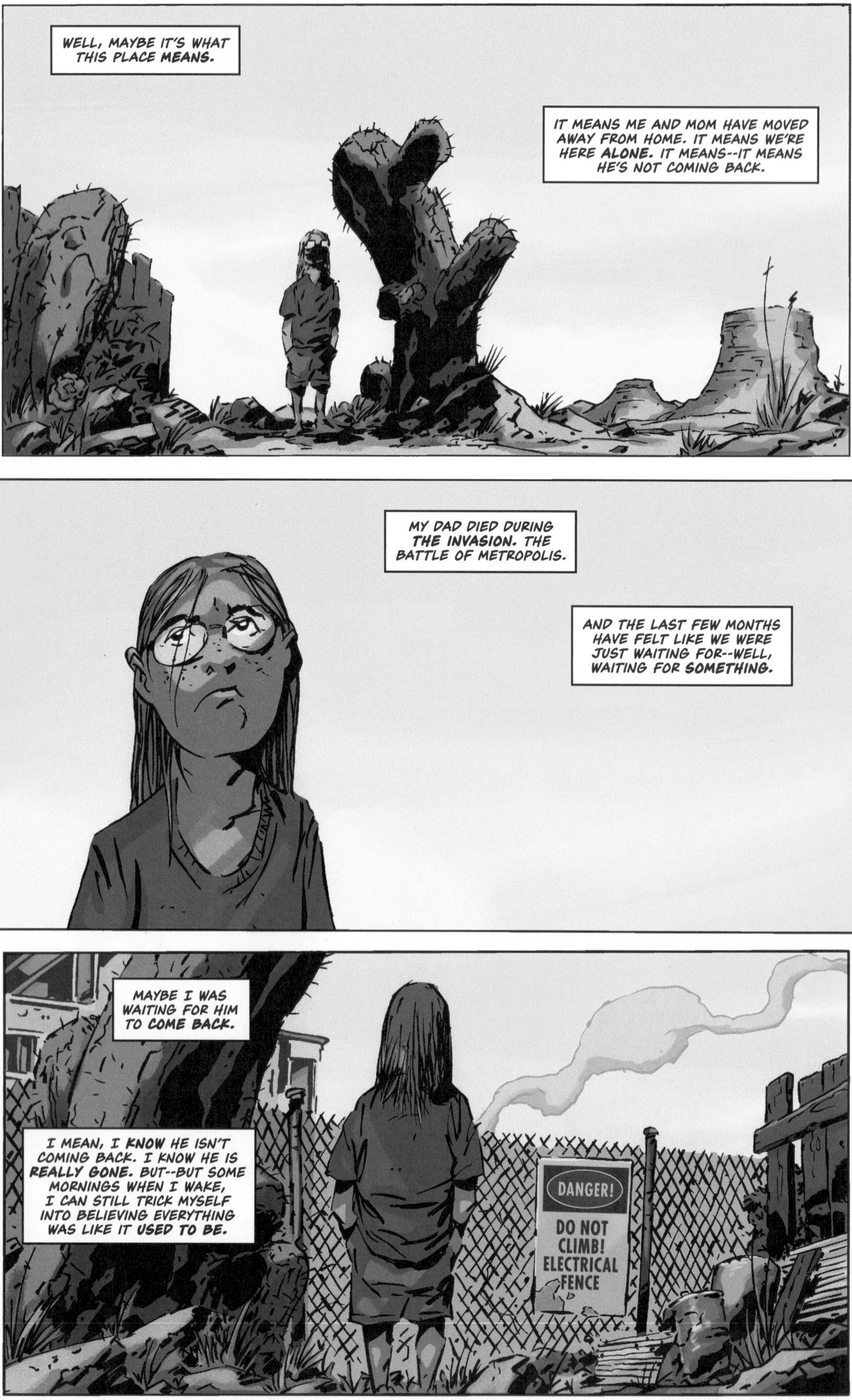
WELL, MAYBE IT'S WHAT THIS PLACE MEANS.
IT MEANS ME AND MOM HAVE MOVED AWAY FROM HOME. IT MEANS WE'RE HERE ALONE. IT MEANS--IT MEANS HE'S NOT COMING BACK.
MY DAD DIED DURING THE INVASION. THE BATTLE OF METROPOLIS.
AND THE LAST FEW MONTHS HAVE FELT LIKE WE WERE JUST WAITING FOR--WELL, WAITING FOR SOMETHING.
MAYBE I WAS WAITING FOR HIM TO COME BACK.
I MEAN, I KNOW HE ISN'T COMING BACK. I KNOW HE IS REALLY GONE. BUT--BUT SOME MORNINGS WHEN I WAKE, I CAN STILL TRICK MYSELF INTO BELIEVING EVERYTHING WAS LIKE IT USED TO BE.
DANGER!
DO NOT CLIMB! ELECTRICAL FENCE

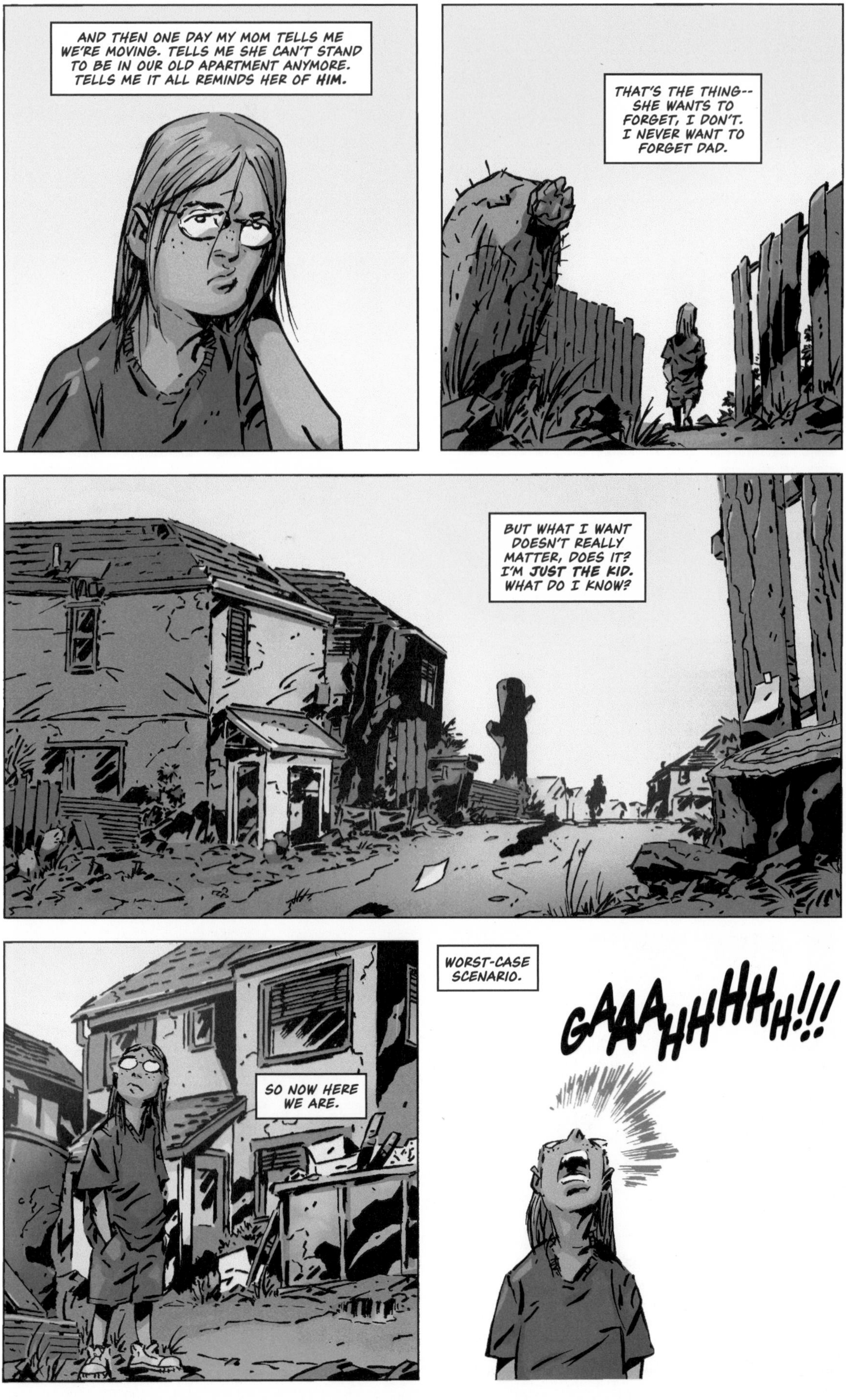
AND THEN ONE DAY MY MOM TELLS ME WE'RE MOVING. TELLS ME SHE CAN'T STAND TO BE IN OUR OLD APARTMENT ANYMORE. TELLS ME IT ALL REMINDS HER OF HIM.
THAT'S THE THING-- SHE WANTS TO FORGET, I DON'T. I NEVER WANT TO FORGET DAD.
BUT WHAT I WANT DOESN'T REALLY MATTER, DOES IT? I'M JUST THE KID. WHAT DO I KNOW?
SO NOW HERE WE ARE.
WORST-CASE SCENARIO.
GAAAHHHHH!!!

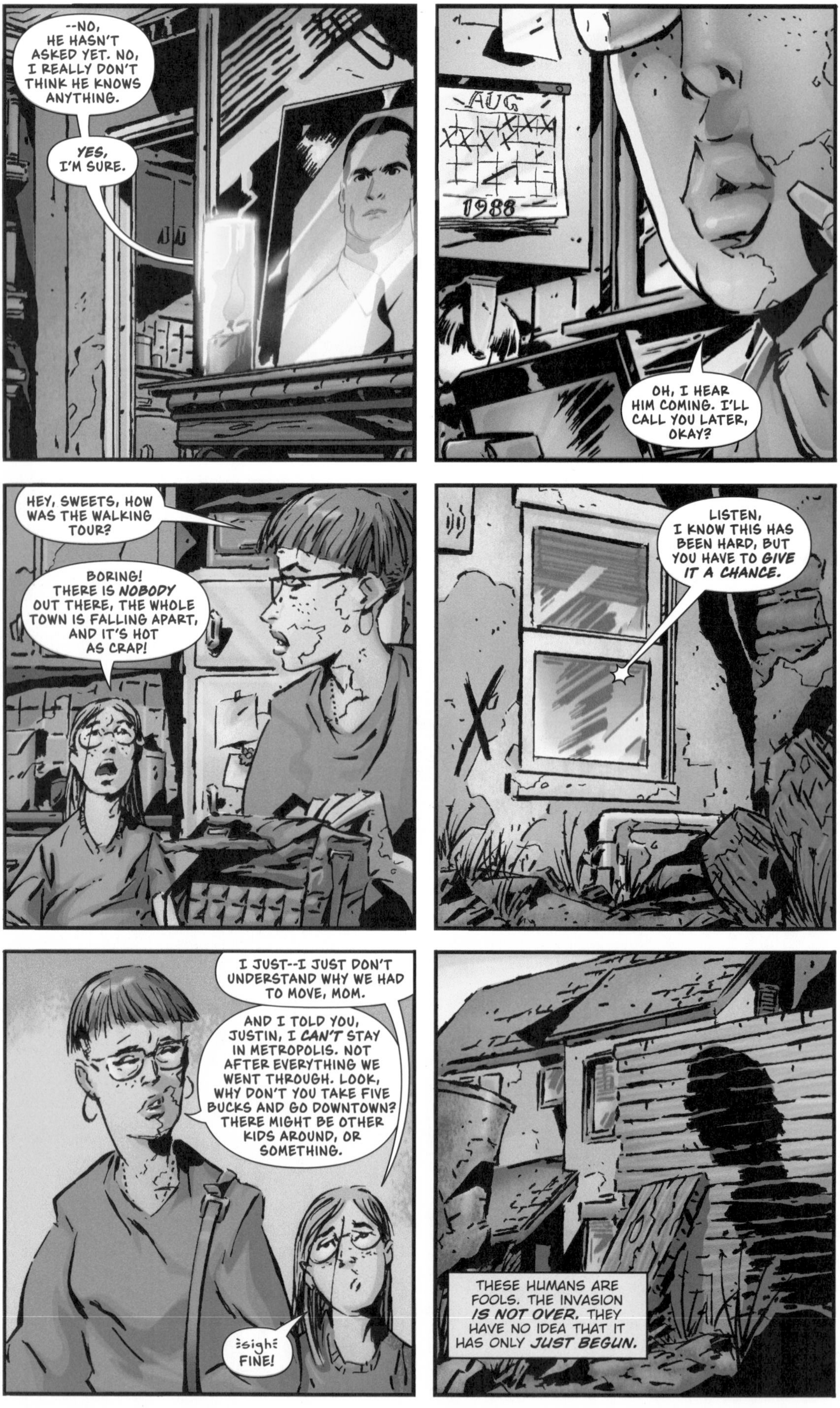
--NO, HE HASN'T ASKED YET. NO, I REALLY DON'T THINK HE KNOWS ANYTHING.
YES, I'M SURE.
AUG
1988
OH, I HEAR HIM COMING. I'LL CALL YOU LATER, OKAY?
HEY, SWEETS, HOW WAS THE WALKING TOUR?
BORING! THERE IS NOBODY OUT THERE, THE WHOLE TOWN IS FALLING APART, AND IT'S HOT AS CRAP!
LISTEN, I KNOW THIS HAS BEEN HARD, BUT YOU HAVE TO GIVE IT A CHANCE.
I JUST--I JUST DON'T UNDERSTAND WHY WE HAD TO MOVE, MOM.
AND I TOLD YOU, JUSTIN, I CAN'T STAY IN METROPOLIS. NOT AFTER EVERYTHING WE WENT THROUGH. LOOK, WHY DON'T YOU TAKE FIVE BUCKS AND GO DOWNTOWN? THERE MIGHT BE OTHER KIDS AROUND, OR SOMETHING.
sigh FINE!
THESE HUMANS ARE FOOLS. THE INVASION IS NOT OVER. THEY HAVE NO IDEA THAT IT HAS ONLY JUST BEGUN.

THINGS ARE PROCEEDING AS EXPECTED, GRAND LEADER. THE NEXT PHASE OF COLONIZATION HAS BEGUN, AND THE LAST OF EARTH'S METAHUMANS HAVE BEEN GATHERED UP AND PLACED IN THE GULAG.

WHAT ABOUT THE KRYPTONIAN AND HIS RESSSSSSISTANCE FORCE?

SUPERMAN IS DEAD, CAPTAIN ATOM HAS BEEN CONTAINED, AND THE THANAGARIANS HAVE BEEN WIPED OUT. THERE IS NO ONE LEFT TO STOP US, GRAND LEADER.

EXCELLENT, MY KHUNDIAN FRIEND.

"BRING HIM IN. HE WHO MARKSSSSS THE HOUSSSSSESSSSS."

LISSSSTEN TO ME. YOU ARE THE MOSSST IMPORTANT PIECE OF THISSSS NEW OPERATION. IF YOU FAIL, ALL OF THE DOMINION'SSS PLANSSS FAIL. DO YOU UNDERSSSSSSSTAND ME, BILLY?

THE THREE LITTLE KITTENS, THEY WASHED THEIR MITTENS, AND HUNG THEM OUT TO DRY.

EXCELLENT.

OH, MY GOD, WHO IS WRITING THIS @$%$#@?!

THEY SHOULD JUST CANCEL THIS BOOK ALREADY! I MEAN, THIS IS ISSUE 37. HOW LONG ARE THEY GOING TO DRAG THIS THING OUT FOR?!

INVASI

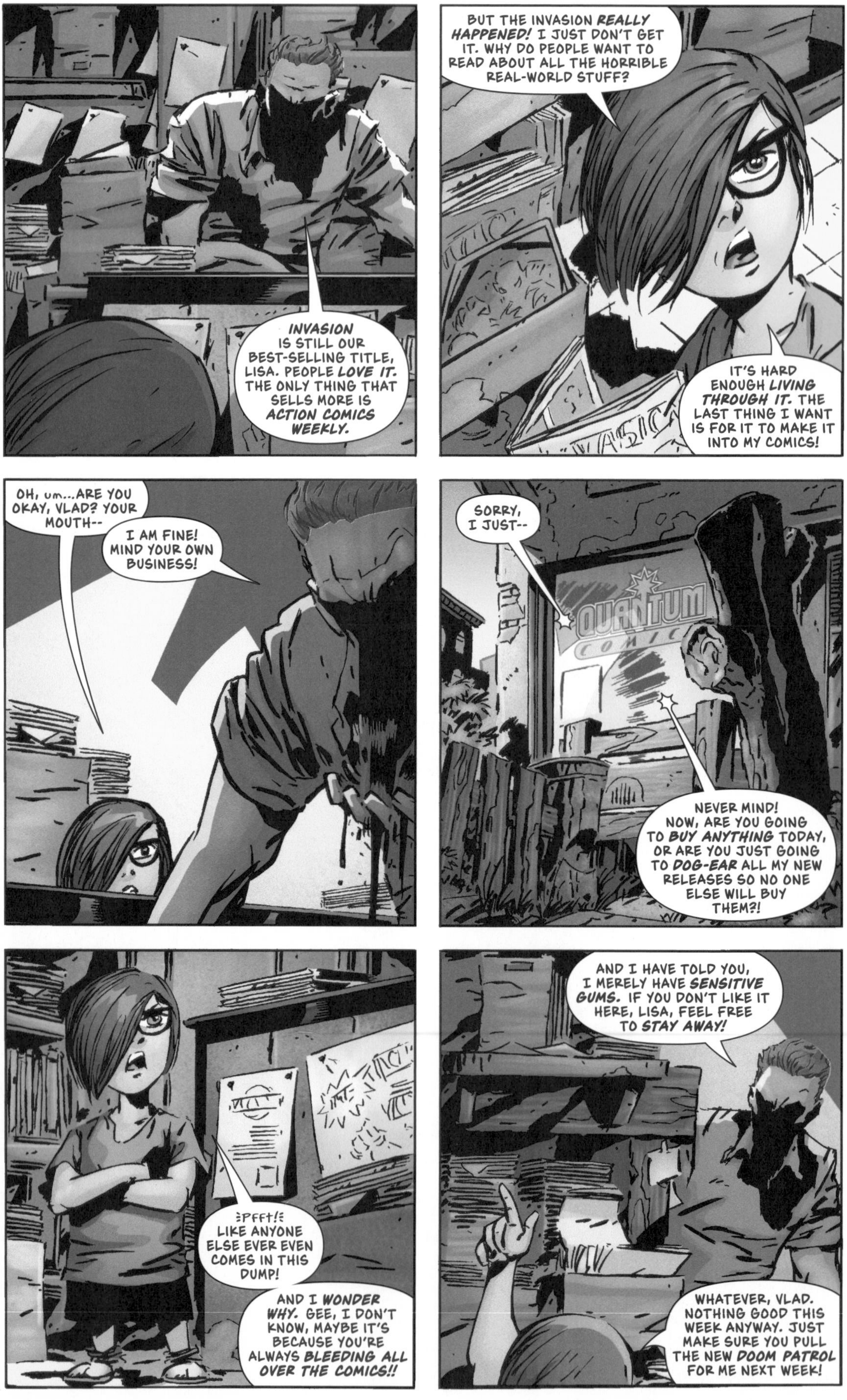
INVASION IS STILL OUR BEST-SELLING TITLE, LISA. PEOPLE LOVE IT. THE ONLY THING THAT SELLS MORE IS ACTION COMICS WEEKLY.
BUT THE INVASION REALLY HAPPENED! I JUST DON'T GET IT. WHY DO PEOPLE WANT TO READ ABOUT ALL THE HORRIBLE REAL-WORLD STUFF?
IT'S HARD ENOUGH LIVING THROUGH IT. THE LAST THING I WANT IS FOR IT TO MAKE IT INTO MY COMICS!
OH, UM...ARE YOU OKAY, VLAD? YOUR MOUTH--
I AM FINE! MIND YOUR OWN BUSINESS!
SORRY, I JUST--
QUANTUM COMICS
NEVER MIND! NOW, ARE YOU GOING TO BUY ANYTHING TODAY, OR ARE YOU JUST GOING TO DOG-EAR ALL MY NEW RELEASES SO NO ONE ELSE WILL BUY THEM?!
PFFT! LIKE ANYONE ELSE EVER EVEN COMES IN THIS DUMP!
AND I WONDER WHY. GEE, I DON'T KNOW, MAYBE IT'S BECAUSE YOU'RE ALWAYS BLEEDING ALL OVER THE COMICS!!
AND I HAVE TOLD YOU, I MERELY HAVE SENSITIVE GUMS. IF YOU DON'T LIKE IT HERE, LISA, FEEL FREE TO STAY AWAY!
WHATEVER, VLAD. NOTHING GOOD THIS WEEK ANYWAY. JUST MAKE SURE YOU PULL THE NEW DOOM PATROL FOR ME NEXT WEEK!

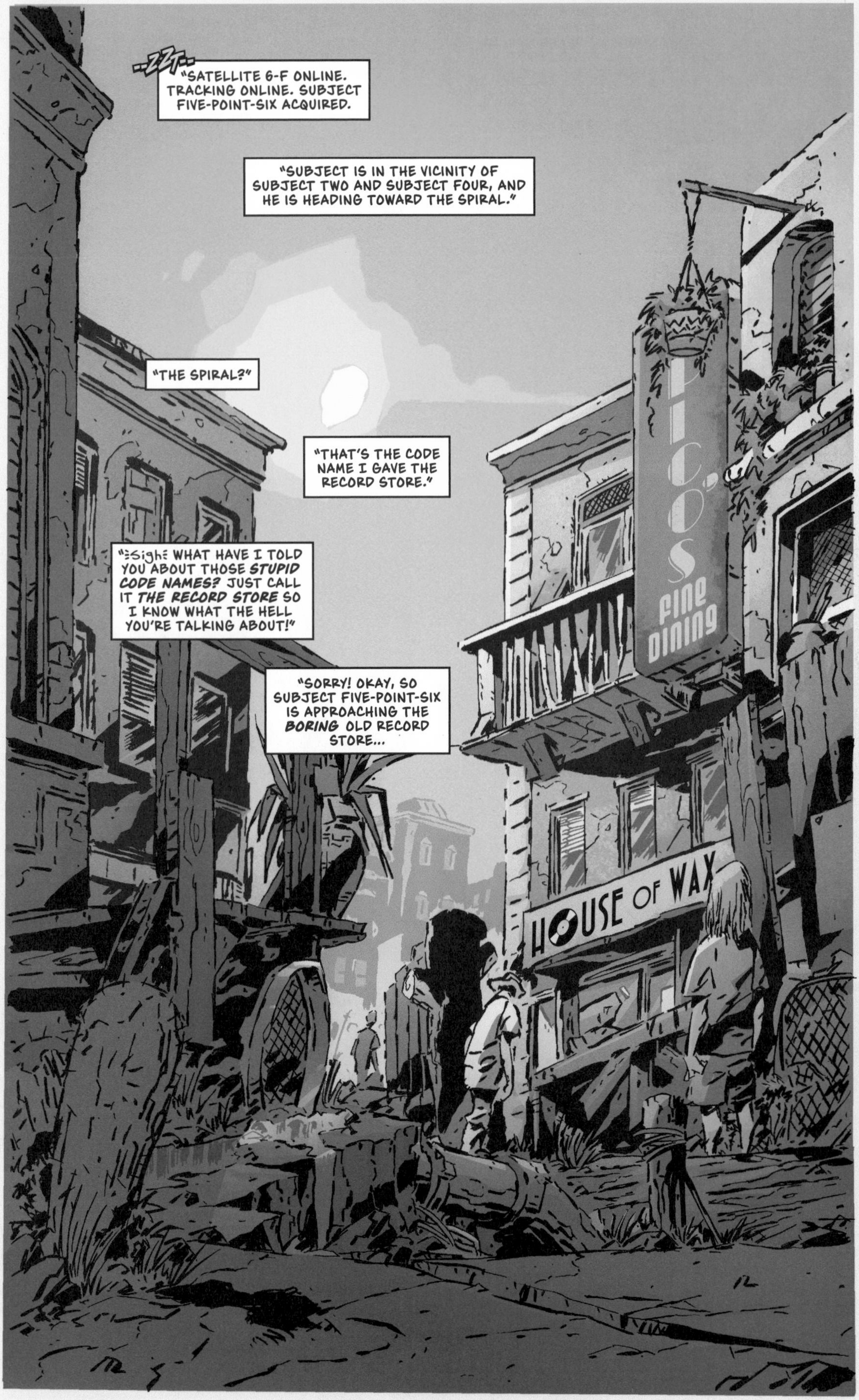
-ZZT-
"SATELLITE 6-F ONLINE. TRACKING ONLINE. SUBJECT FIVE-POINT-SIX ACQUIRED.
"SUBJECT IS IN THE VICINITY OF SUBJECT TWO AND SUBJECT FOUR, AND HE IS HEADING TOWARD THE SPIRAL."
"THE SPIRAL?"
"THAT'S THE CODE NAME I GAVE THE RECORD STORE."
"*Sigh* WHAT HAVE I TOLD YOU ABOUT THOSE STUPID CODE NAMES? JUST CALL IT THE RECORD STORE SO I KNOW WHAT THE HELL YOU'RE TALKING ABOUT!"
"SORRY! OKAY, SO SUBJECT FIVE-POINT-SIX IS APPROACHING THE BORING OLD RECORD STORE...
PICO'S fine DINING
HOUSE OF WAX

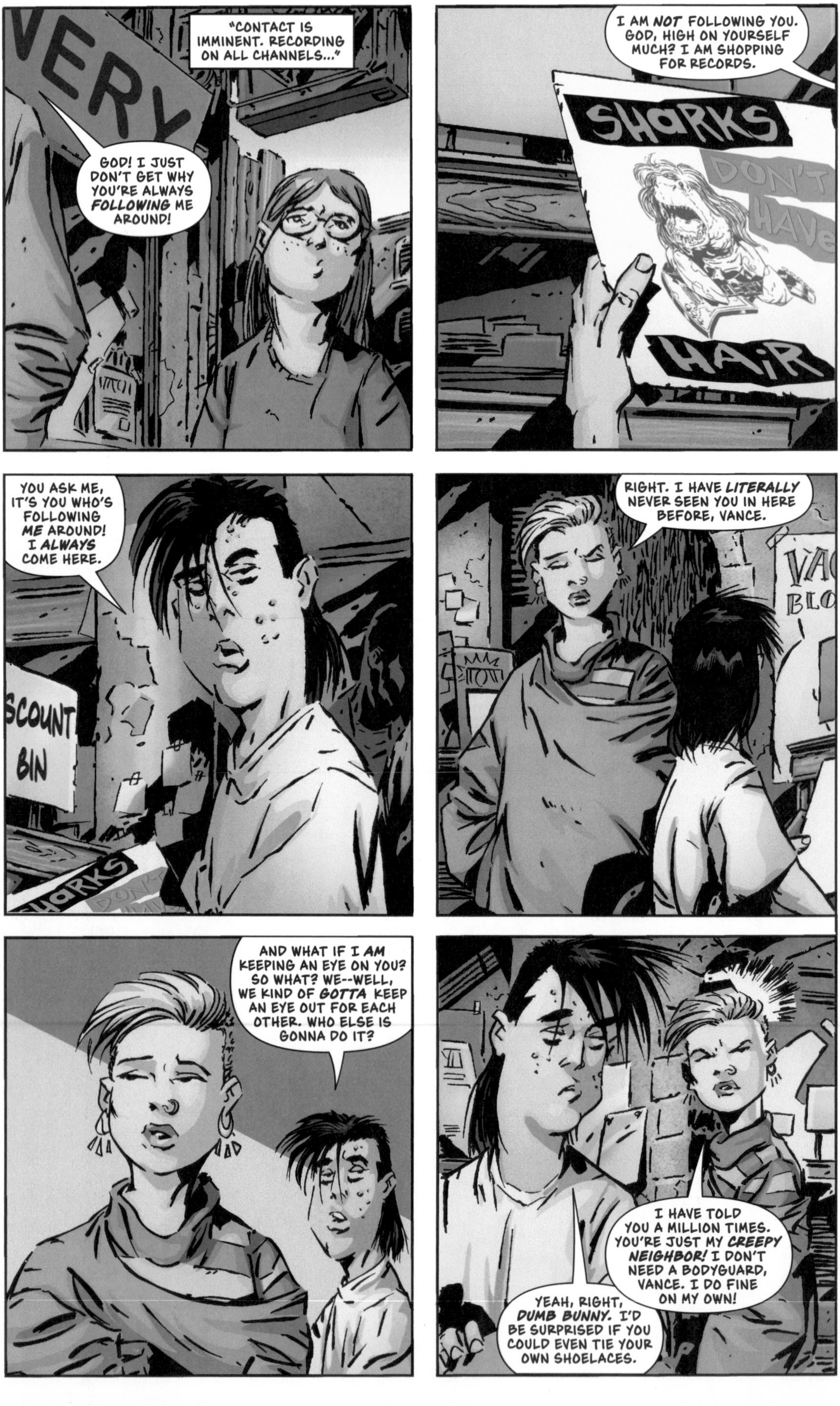
"CONTACT IS IMMINENT. RECORDING ON ALL CHANNELS..."
VERY
GOD! I JUST DON'T GET WHY YOU'RE ALWAYS FOLLOWING ME AROUND!
I AM NOT FOLLOWING YOU. GOD, HIGH ON YOURSELF MUCH? I AM SHOPPING FOR RECORDS.
SHARKS
DON'T HAVE
HAIR
YOU ASK ME, IT'S YOU WHO'S FOLLOWING ME AROUND! I ALWAYS COME HERE.
SCOUNT BIN
SHARKS
RIGHT. I HAVE LITERALLY NEVER SEEN YOU IN HERE BEFORE, VANCE.
AND WHAT IF I AM KEEPING AN EYE ON YOU? SO WHAT? WE--WELL, WE KIND OF GOTTA KEEP AN EYE OUT FOR EACH OTHER. WHO ELSE IS GONNA DO IT?
I HAVE TOLD YOU A MILLION TIMES. YOU'RE JUST MY CREEPY NEIGHBOR! I DON'T NEED A BODYGUARD, VANCE. I DO FINE ON MY OWN!
YEAH, RIGHT, DUMB BUNNY. I'D BE SURPRISED IF YOU COULD EVEN TIE YOUR OWN SHOELACES.

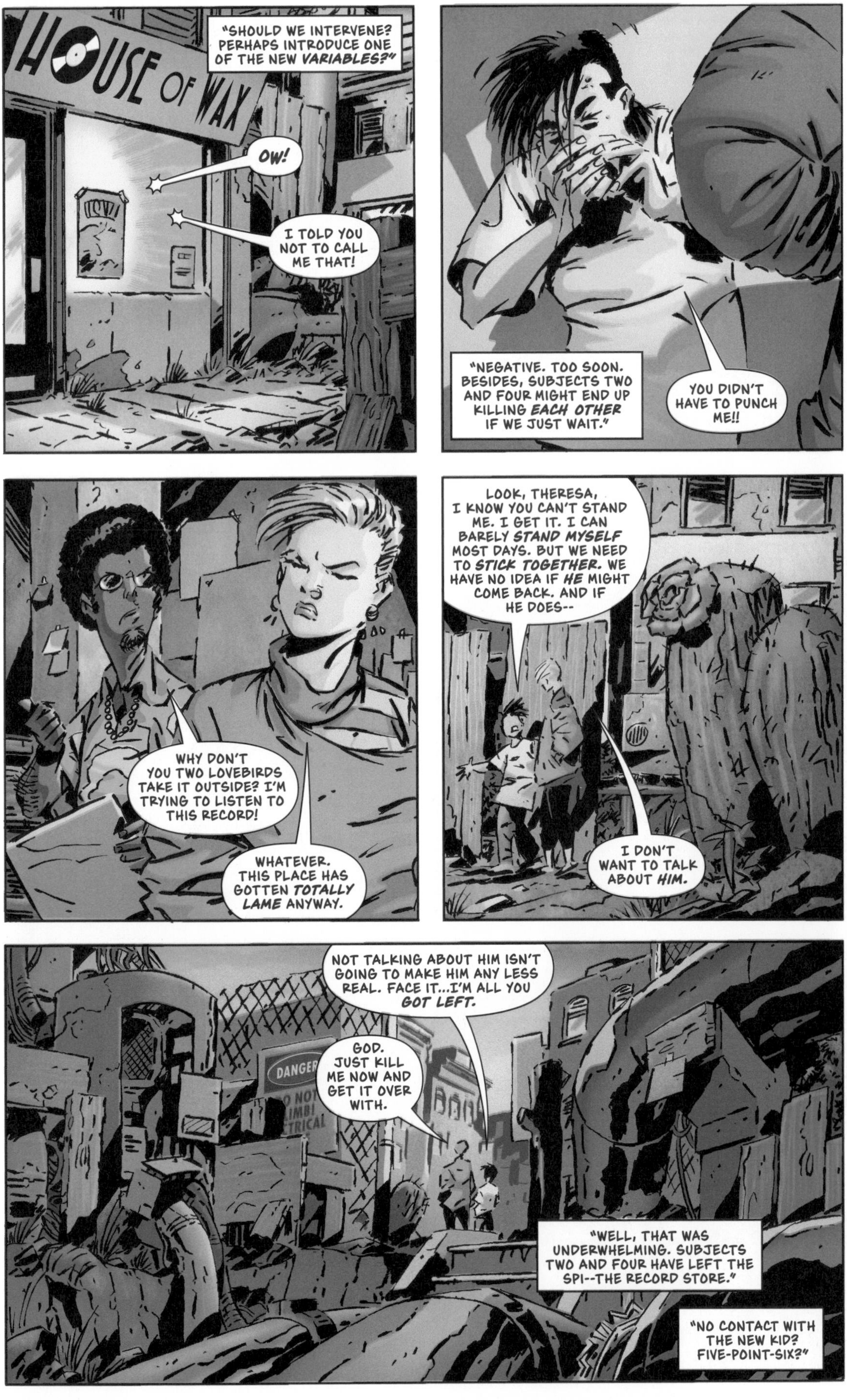
HOUSE OF WAX
"SHOULD WE INTERVENE? PERHAPS INTRODUCE ONE OF THE NEW VARIABLES?"
OW!
I TOLD YOU NOT TO CALL ME THAT!
"NEGATIVE. TOO SOON. BESIDES, SUBJECTS TWO AND FOUR MIGHT END UP KILLING EACH OTHER IF WE JUST WAIT."
YOU DIDN'T HAVE TO PUNCH ME!!
WHY DON'T YOU TWO LOVEBIRDS TAKE IT OUTSIDE? I'M TRYING TO LISTEN TO THIS RECORD!
WHATEVER. THIS PLACE HAS GOTTEN TOTALLY LAME ANYWAY.
LOOK, THERESA, I KNOW YOU CAN'T STAND ME. I GET IT. I CAN BARELY STAND MYSELF MOST DAYS. BUT WE NEED TO STICK TOGETHER. WE HAVE NO IDEA IF HE MIGHT COME BACK. AND IF HE DOES--
I DON'T WANT TO TALK ABOUT HIM.
NOT TALKING ABOUT HIM ISN'T GOING TO MAKE HIM ANY LESS REAL. FACE IT...I'M ALL YOU GOT LEFT.
GOD. JUST KILL ME NOW AND GET IT OVER WITH.
DANGER
"WELL, THAT WAS UNDERWHELMING. SUBJECTS TWO AND FOUR HAVE LEFT THE SPI--THE RECORD STORE."
"NO CONTACT WITH THE NEW KID? FIVE-POINT-SIX?"

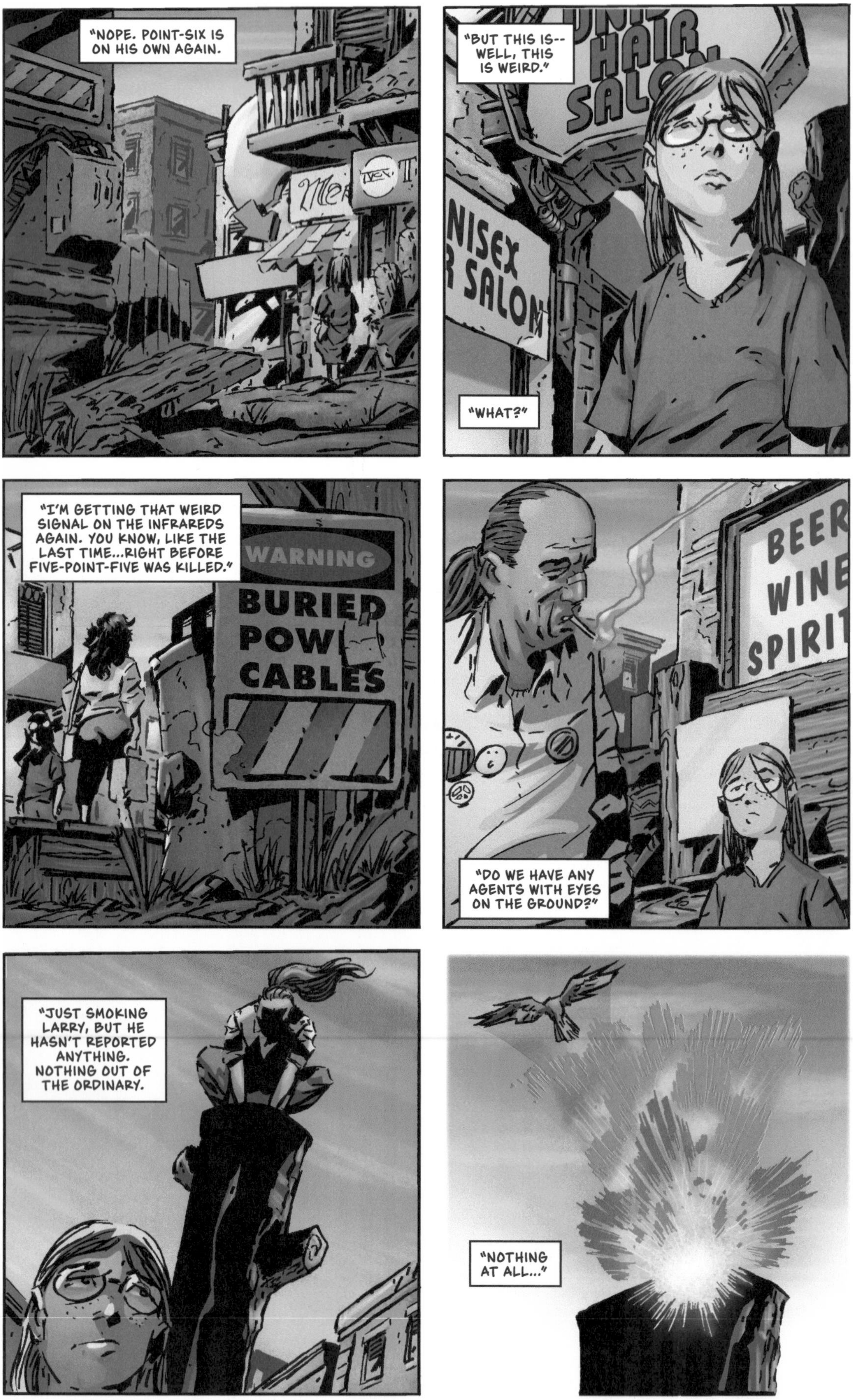
"NOPE. POINT-SIX IS ON HIS OWN AGAIN.
"BUT THIS IS-- WELL, THIS IS WEIRD."
"WHAT?"
"I'M GETTING THAT WEIRD SIGNAL ON THE INFRAREDS AGAIN. YOU KNOW, LIKE THE LAST TIME...RIGHT BEFORE FIVE-POINT-FIVE WAS KILLED."
WARNING
BURIED
CABLES
BEER
"DO WE HAVE ANY AGENTS WITH EYES ON THE GROUND?"
"JUST SMOKING LARRY, BUT HE HASN'T REPORTED ANYTHING. NOTHING OUT OF THE ORDINARY.
"NOTHING AT ALL..."

DANGER ST
LISA? ARE YOU IN THIS LOCATION?
OH! I DID NOT OBSERVE YOU CONCEALED IN THAT TINY TERRITORY. YOU STARTLED ME OUT OF MY WITS.
"TINY TERRITORY"? YOU ARE SUPER WEIRD, HELEN. YOU KNOW THAT?
I AM NOT WEIRD. I AM JUST A NORMAL HUMAN GIRL LIKE YOU, LISA.
Uh-huh. ANYWAY, LISTEN, FREAKSHOW, I'M GLAD YOU'RE HERE, BUT I AIN'T GOT TIME FOR THE CHITCHAT. I THINK I FOUND SOMETHING.
THE TOWN IS PRISON!!!
CARS
BILLY?
=GONE
WHY
JUST
CHECK IT OUT. I FOUND ANOTHER ONE OF THOSE X THINGS PAINTED ON MR. CROP'S HOUSE. OUT BACK BY HIS WORK SHED. THAT MAKES AT LEAST ONE OF THOSE ON EVERY HOUSE SO FAR.

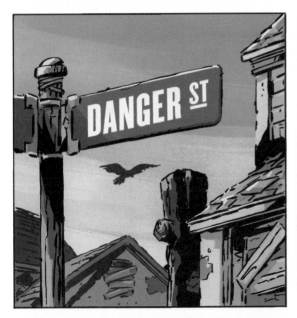

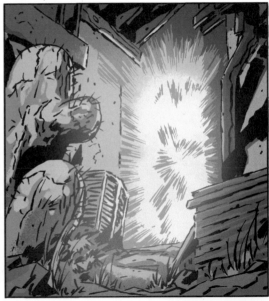

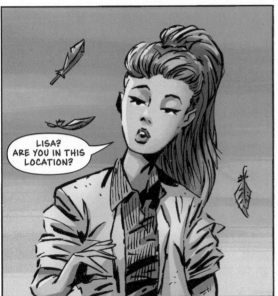

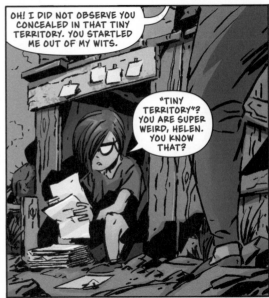

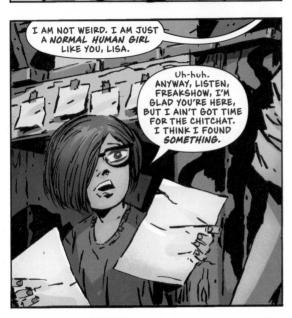

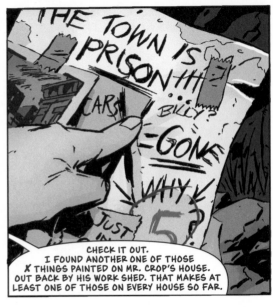

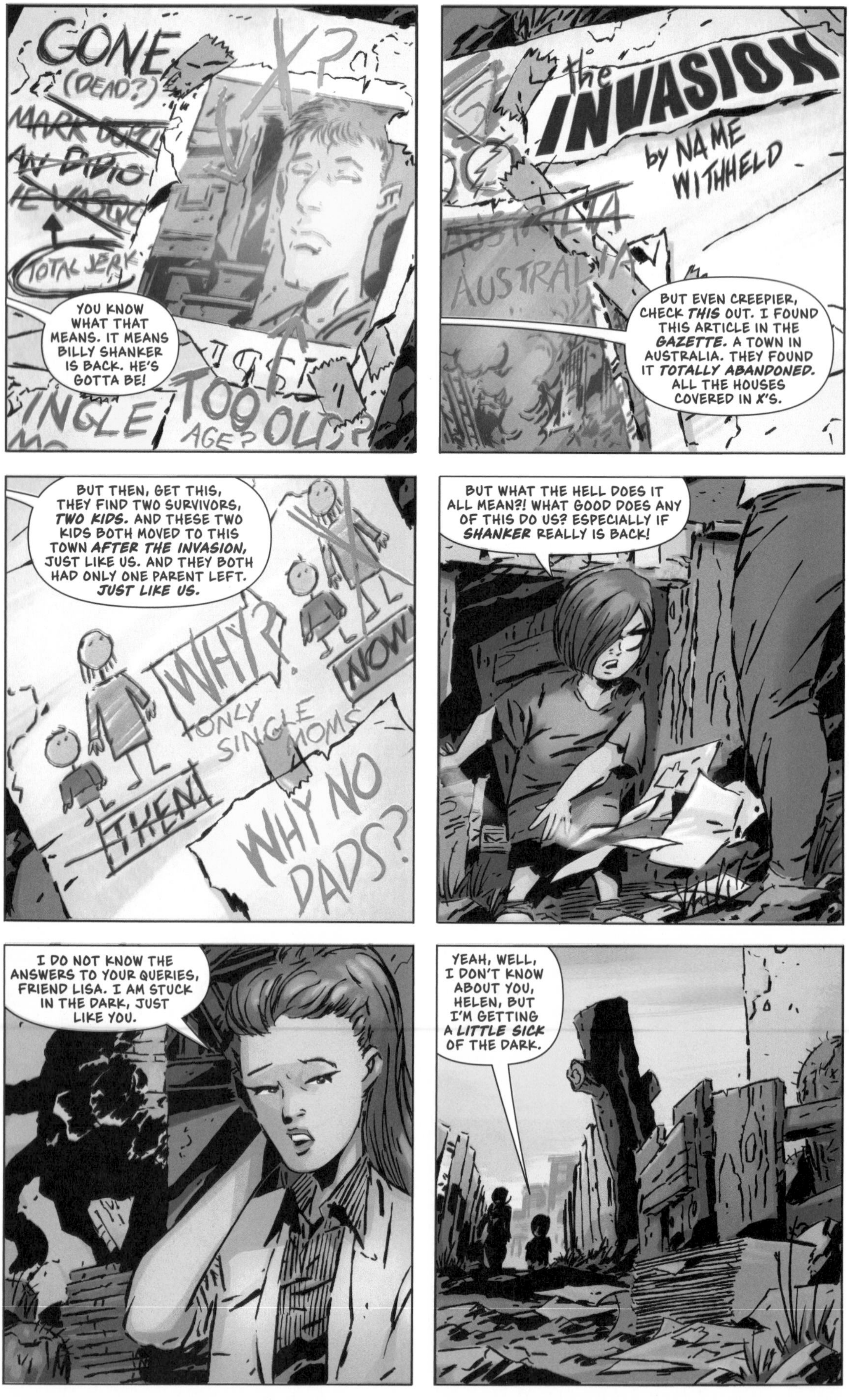
GONE
(DEAD?)
TOTAL JERK
YOU KNOW WHAT THAT MEANS. IT MEANS BILLY SHANKER IS BACK. HE'S GOTTA BE!
TOO OLD?
AGE?
the INVASION
by NAME WITHHELD
AUSTRALIA
BUT EVEN CREEPIER, CHECK *THIS* OUT. I FOUND THIS ARTICLE IN THE *GAZETTE*. A TOWN IN AUSTRALIA. THEY FOUND IT *TOTALLY ABANDONED.* ALL THE HOUSES COVERED IN X'S.
BUT THEN, GET THIS, THEY FIND TWO SURVIVORS, *TWO KIDS.* AND THESE TWO KIDS BOTH MOVED TO THIS TOWN *AFTER THE INVASION*, JUST LIKE US. AND THEY BOTH HAD ONLY ONE PARENT LEFT. *JUST LIKE US.*
WHY?
NOW
ONLY SINGLE MOMS
THEN
WHY NO DADS?
BUT WHAT THE HELL DOES IT ALL MEAN?! WHAT GOOD DOES ANY OF THIS DO US? ESPECIALLY IF *SHANKER* REALLY IS BACK!
I DO NOT KNOW THE ANSWERS TO YOUR QUERIES, FRIEND LISA. I AM STUCK IN THE DARK, JUST LIKE YOU.
YEAH, WELL, I DON'T KNOW ABOUT YOU, HELEN, BUT I'M GETTING A *LITTLE SICK* OF THE DARK.

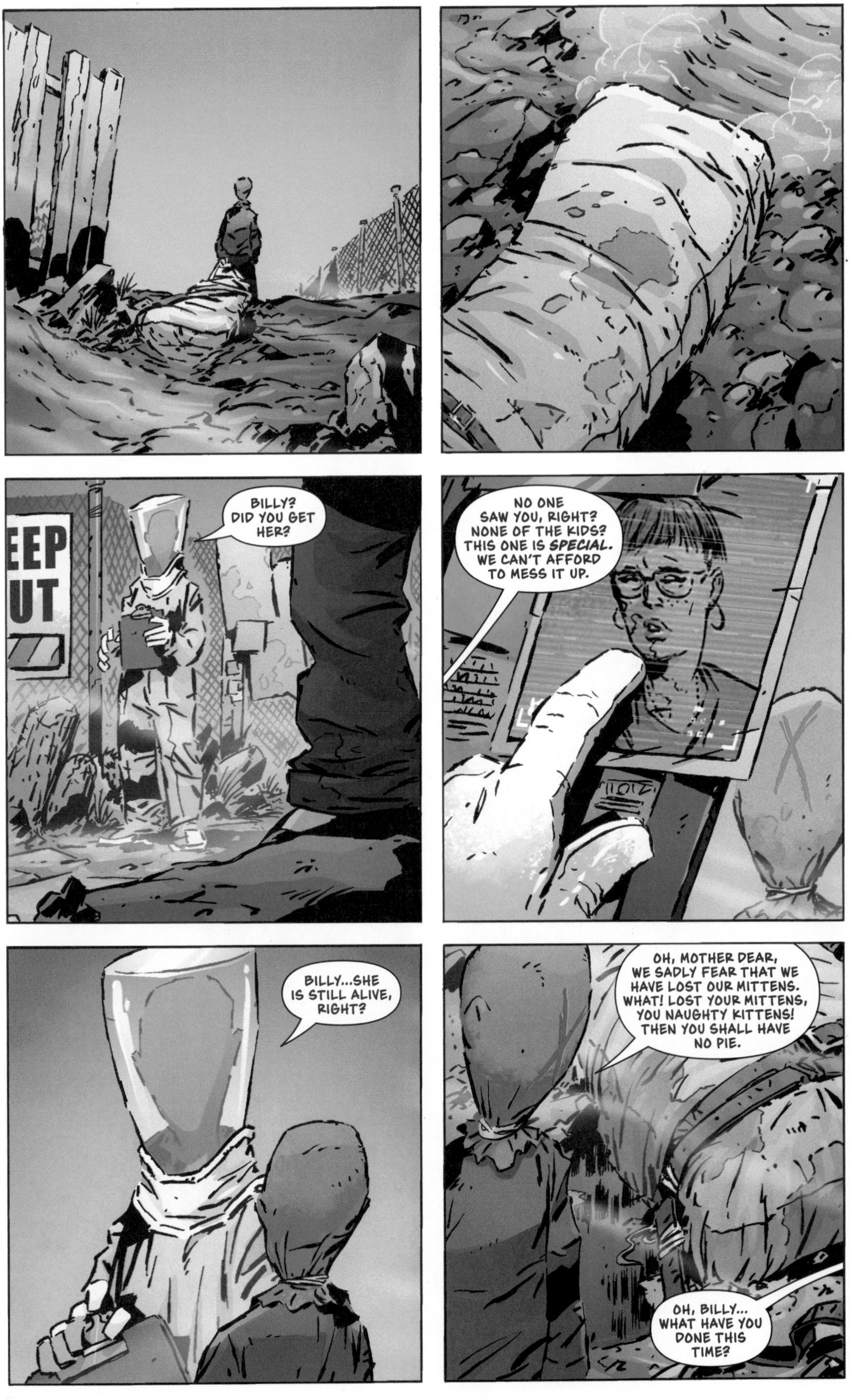
EEP
UT
BILLY? DID YOU GET HER?
NO ONE SAW YOU, RIGHT? NONE OF THE KIDS? THIS ONE IS SPECIAL. WE CAN'T AFFORD TO MESS IT UP.
BILLY...SHE IS STILL ALIVE, RIGHT?
OH, MOTHER DEAR, WE SADLY FEAR THAT WE HAVE LOST OUR MITTENS. WHAT! LOST YOUR MITTENS, YOU NAUGHTY KITTENS! THEN YOU SHALL HAVE NO PIE.
OH, BILLY... WHAT HAVE YOU DONE THIS TIME?

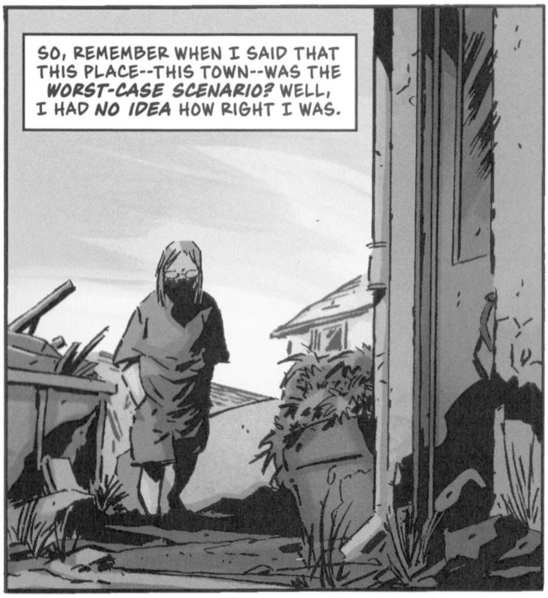
SO, REMEMBER WHEN I SAID THAT THIS PLACE--THIS TOWN--WAS THE *WORST-CASE SCENARIO?* WELL, I HAD *NO IDEA* HOW RIGHT I WAS.

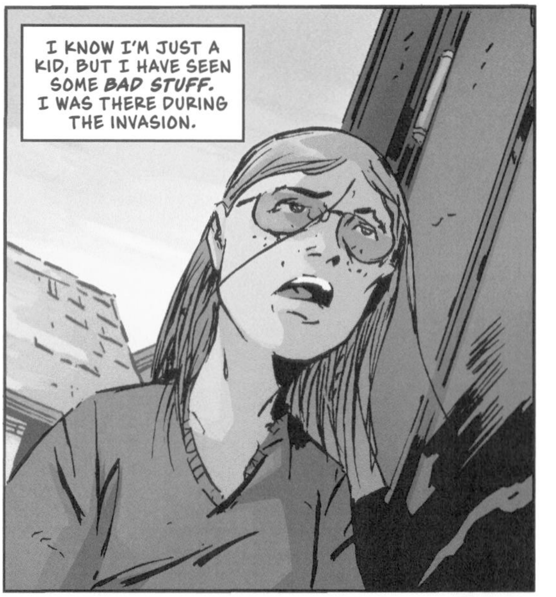
I KNOW I'M JUST A KID, BUT I HAVE SEEN SOME *BAD STUFF.* I WAS THERE DURING THE INVASION.

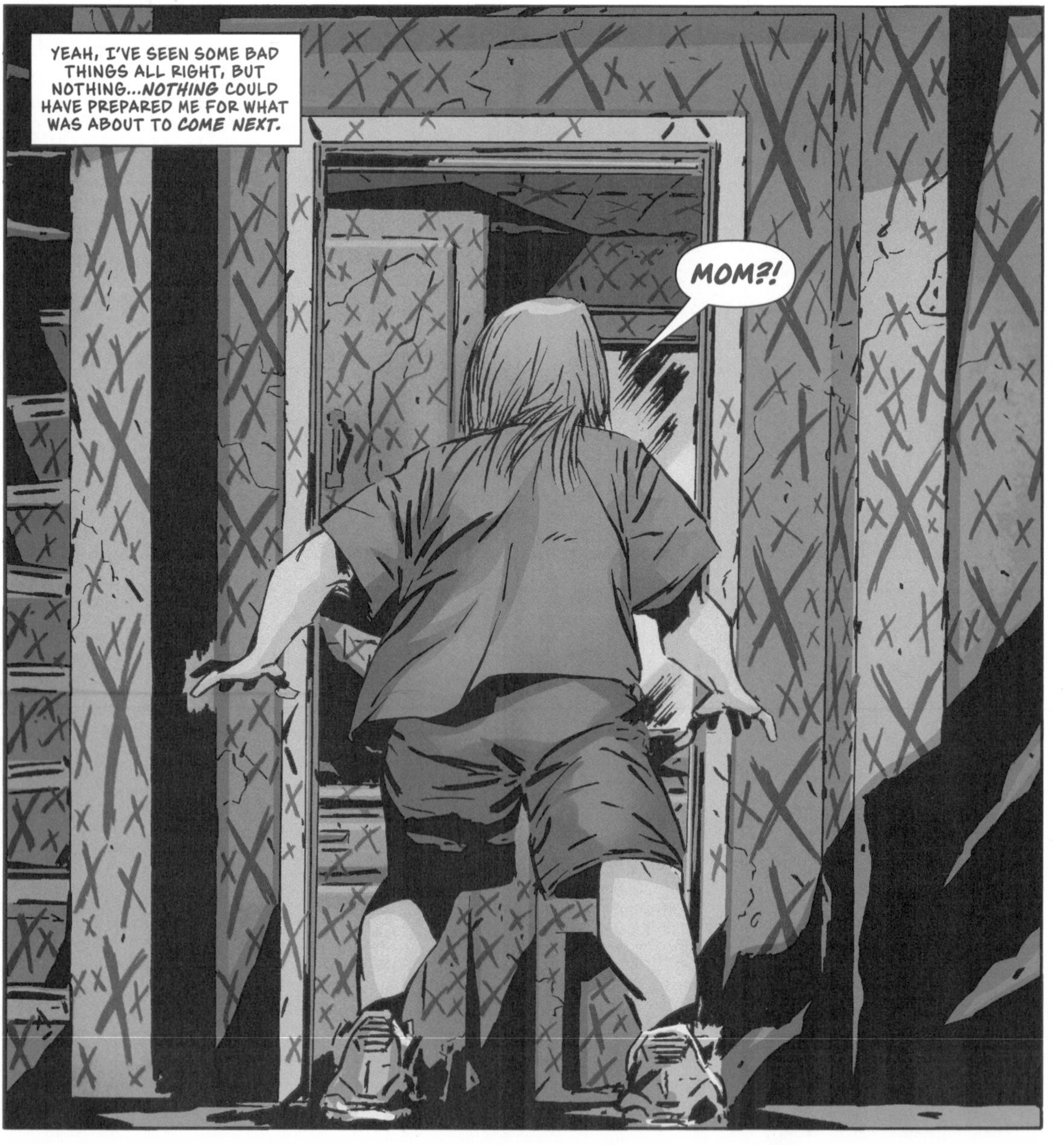
YEAH, I'VE SEEN SOME BAD THINGS ALL RIGHT, BUT NOTHING...*NOTHING* COULD HAVE PREPARED ME FOR WHAT WAS ABOUT TO *COME NEXT.*
MOM?!

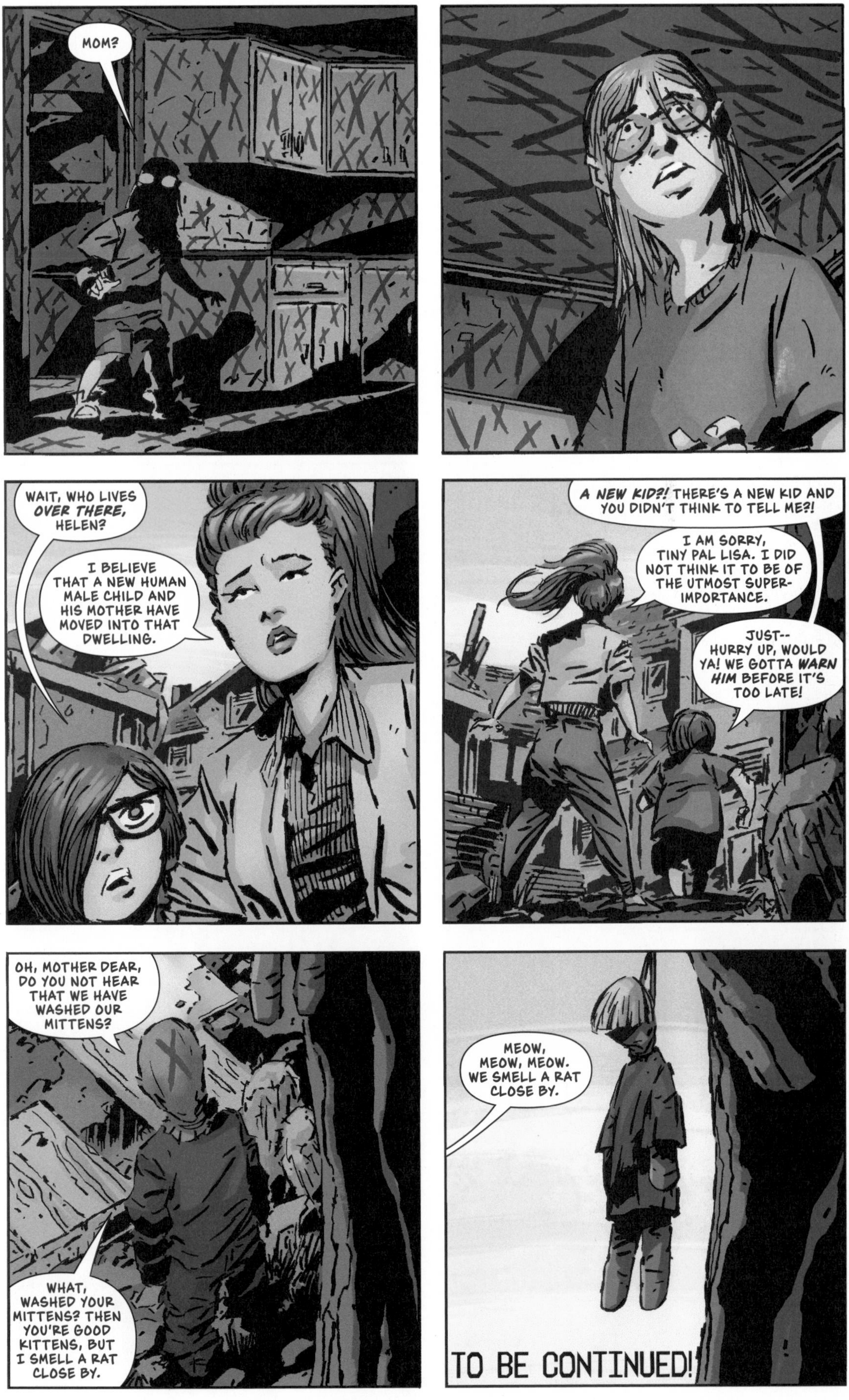
MOM?
WAIT, WHO LIVES *OVER THERE,* HELEN?
I BELIEVE THAT A NEW HUMAN MALE CHILD AND HIS MOTHER HAVE MOVED INTO THAT DWELLING.
A NEW KID?! THERE'S A NEW KID AND YOU DIDN'T THINK TO TELL ME?!
I AM SORRY, TINY PAL LISA. I DID NOT THINK IT TO BE OF THE UTMOST SUPER-IMPORTANCE.
JUST-- HURRY UP, WOULD YA! WE GOTTA *WARN HIM* BEFORE IT'S TOO LATE!
OH, MOTHER DEAR, DO YOU NOT HEAR THAT WE HAVE WASHED OUR MITTENS?
WHAT, WASHED YOUR MITTENS? THEN YOU'RE GOOD KITTENS, BUT I SMELL A RAT CLOSE BY.
MEOW, MEOW, MEOW. WE SMELL A RAT CLOSE BY.
TO BE CONTINUED!

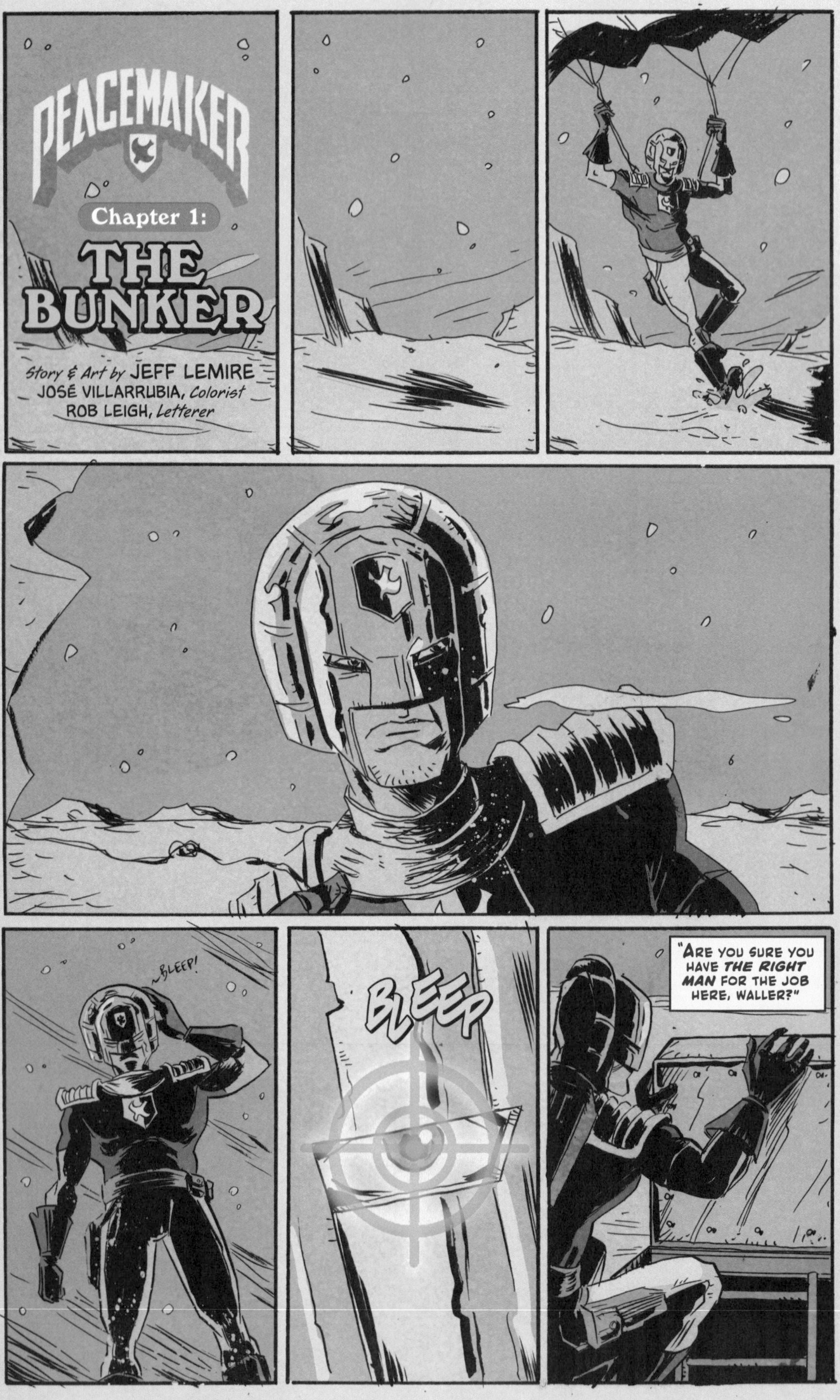
PEACEMAKER
Chapter 1:
THE BUNKER
Story & Art by JEFF LEMIRE
JOSÉ VILLARRUBIA, Colorist
ROB LEIGH, Letterer
BLEEP!
BLEEP
"ARE YOU SURE YOU HAVE THE RIGHT MAN FOR THE JOB HERE, WALLER?"

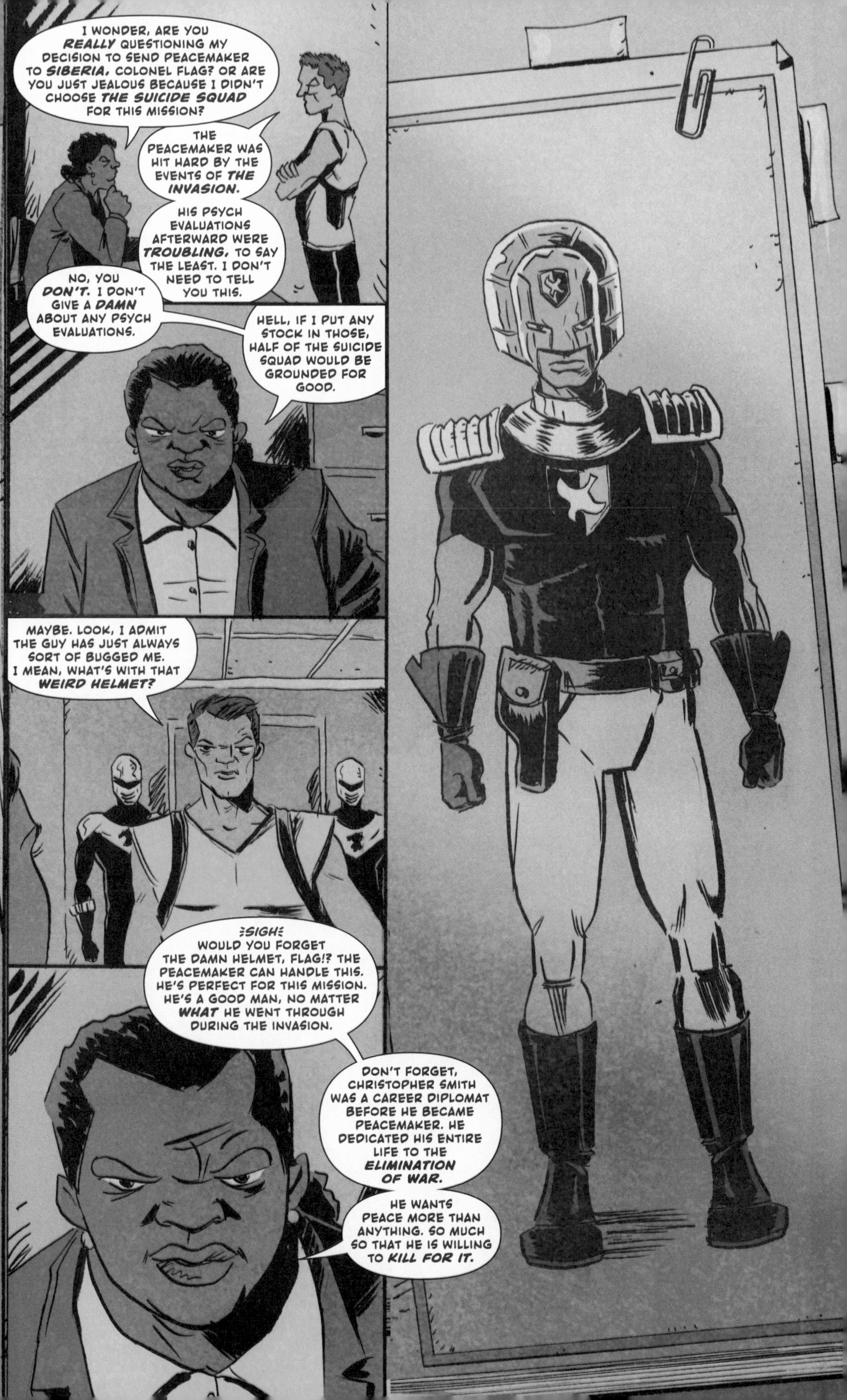
I WONDER, ARE YOU REALLY QUESTIONING MY DECISION TO SEND PEACEMAKER TO SIBERIA, COLONEL FLAG? OR ARE YOU JUST JEALOUS BECAUSE I DIDN'T CHOOSE THE SUICIDE SQUAD FOR THIS MISSION?
THE PEACEMAKER WAS HIT HARD BY THE EVENTS OF THE INVASION.
HIS PSYCH EVALUATIONS AFTERWARD WERE TROUBLING, TO SAY THE LEAST. I DON'T NEED TO TELL YOU THIS.
NO, YOU DON'T. I DON'T GIVE A DAMN ABOUT ANY PSYCH EVALUATIONS.
HELL, IF I PUT ANY STOCK IN THOSE, HALF OF THE SUICIDE SQUAD WOULD BE GROUNDED FOR GOOD.
MAYBE. LOOK, I ADMIT THE GUY HAS JUST ALWAYS SORT OF BUGGED ME. I MEAN, WHAT'S WITH THAT WEIRD HELMET?
SIGH
WOULD YOU FORGET THE DAMN HELMET, FLAG!? THE PEACEMAKER CAN HANDLE THIS. HE'S PERFECT FOR THIS MISSION. HE'S A GOOD MAN, NO MATTER WHAT HE WENT THROUGH DURING THE INVASION.
DON'T FORGET, CHRISTOPHER SMITH WAS A CAREER DIPLOMAT BEFORE HE BECAME PEACEMAKER. HE DEDICATED HIS ENTIRE LIFE TO THE ELIMINATION OF WAR.
HE WANTS PEACE MORE THAN ANYTHING. SO MUCH SO THAT HE IS WILLING TO KILL FOR IT.

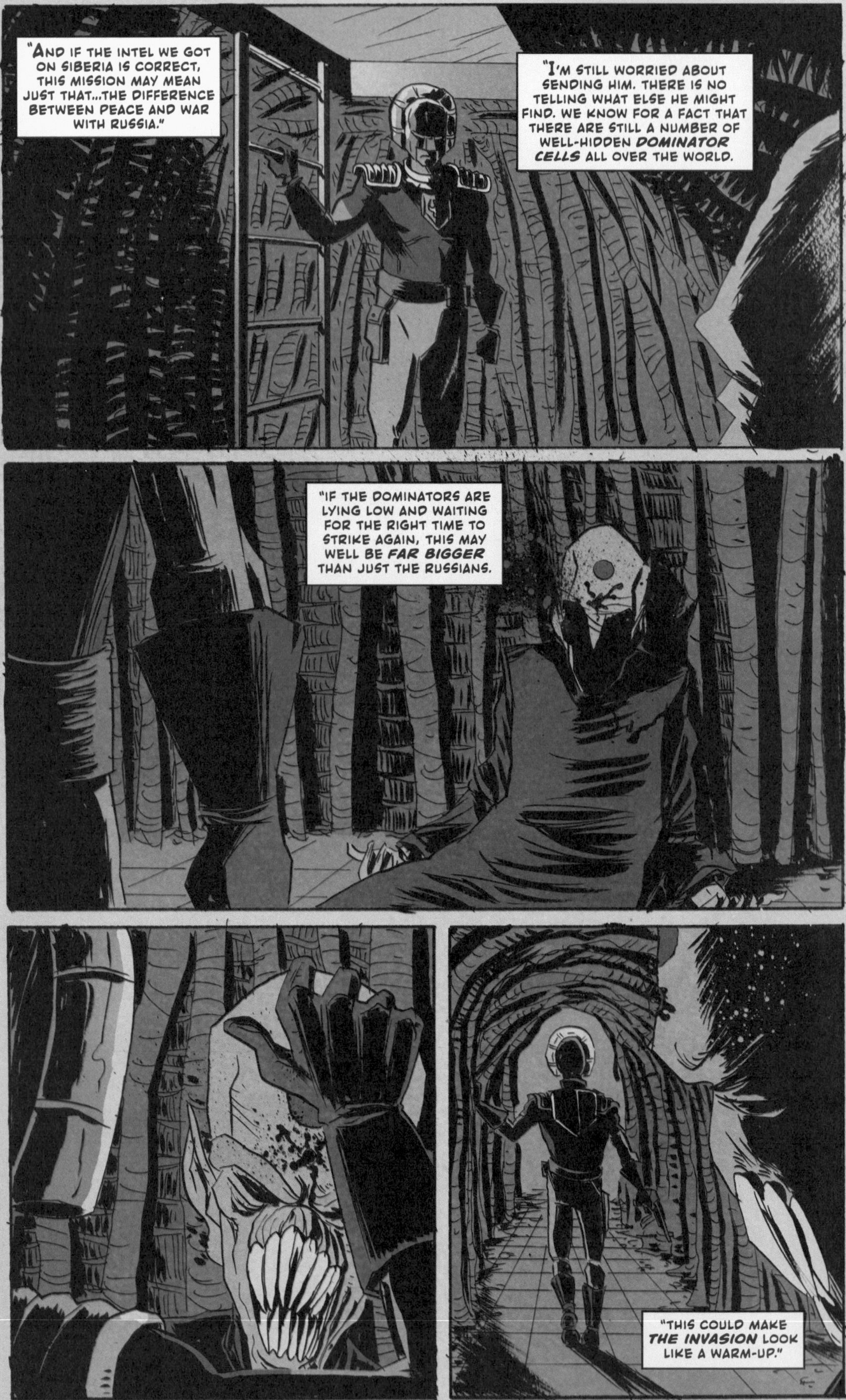
"And if the intel we got on Siberia is correct, this mission may mean just that...the difference between peace and war with Russia."
"I'm still worried about sending him. There is no telling what else he might find. We know for a fact that there are still a number of well-hidden *dominator cells* all over the world.
"If the Dominators are lying low and waiting for the right time to strike again, this may well be *far bigger* than just the Russians.
"This could make *the invasion* look like a warm-up."

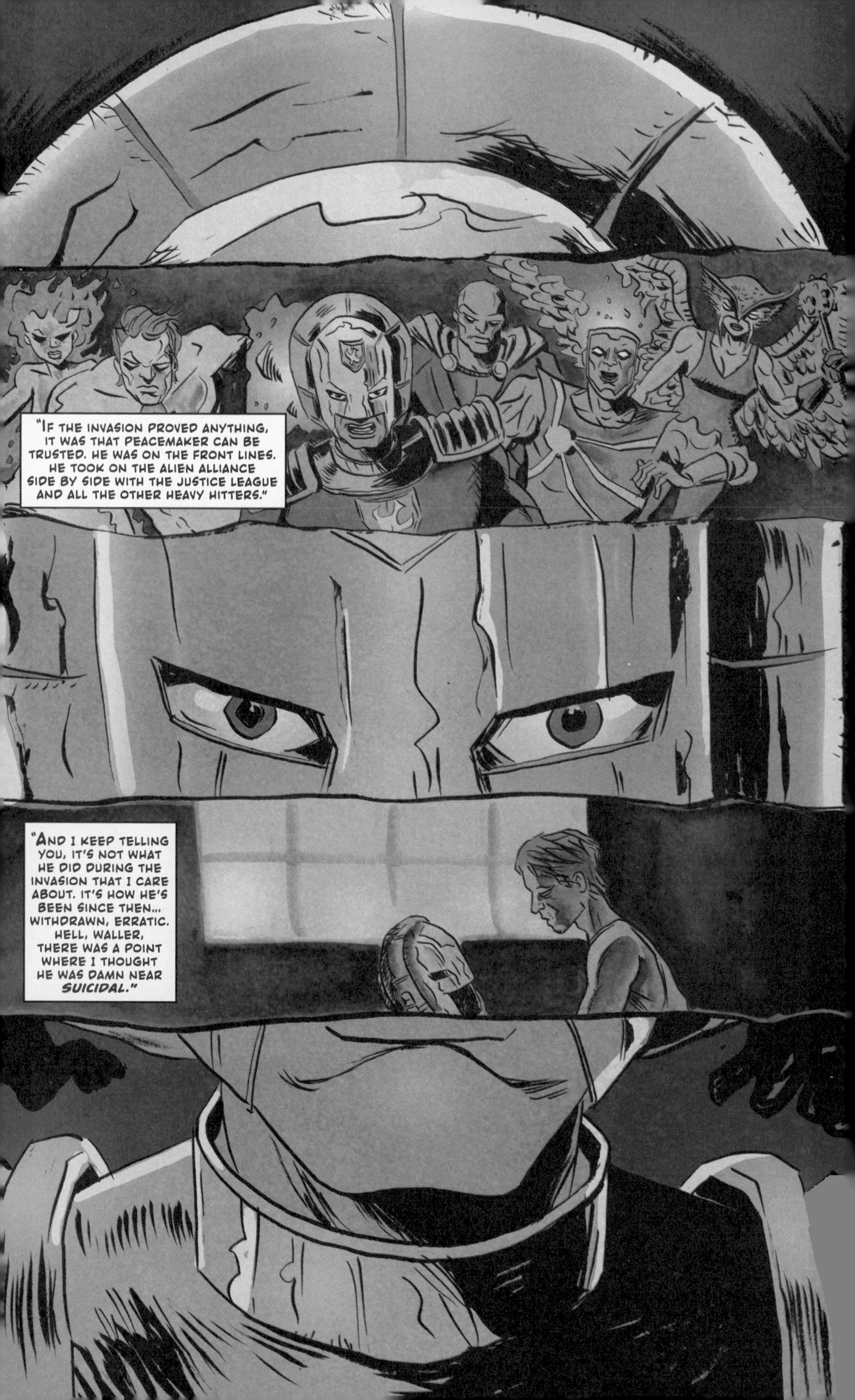
"IF THE INVASION PROVED ANYTHING, IT WAS THAT PEACEMAKER CAN BE TRUSTED. HE WAS ON THE FRONT LINES. HE TOOK ON THE ALIEN ALLIANCE SIDE BY SIDE WITH THE JUSTICE LEAGUE AND ALL THE OTHER HEAVY HITTERS."
"AND I KEEP TELLING YOU, IT'S NOT WHAT HE DID DURING THE INVASION THAT I CARE ABOUT. IT'S HOW HE'S BEEN SINCE THEN... WITHDRAWN, ERRATIC. HELL, WALLER, THERE WAS A POINT WHERE I THOUGHT HE WAS DAMN NEAR *SUICIDAL*."

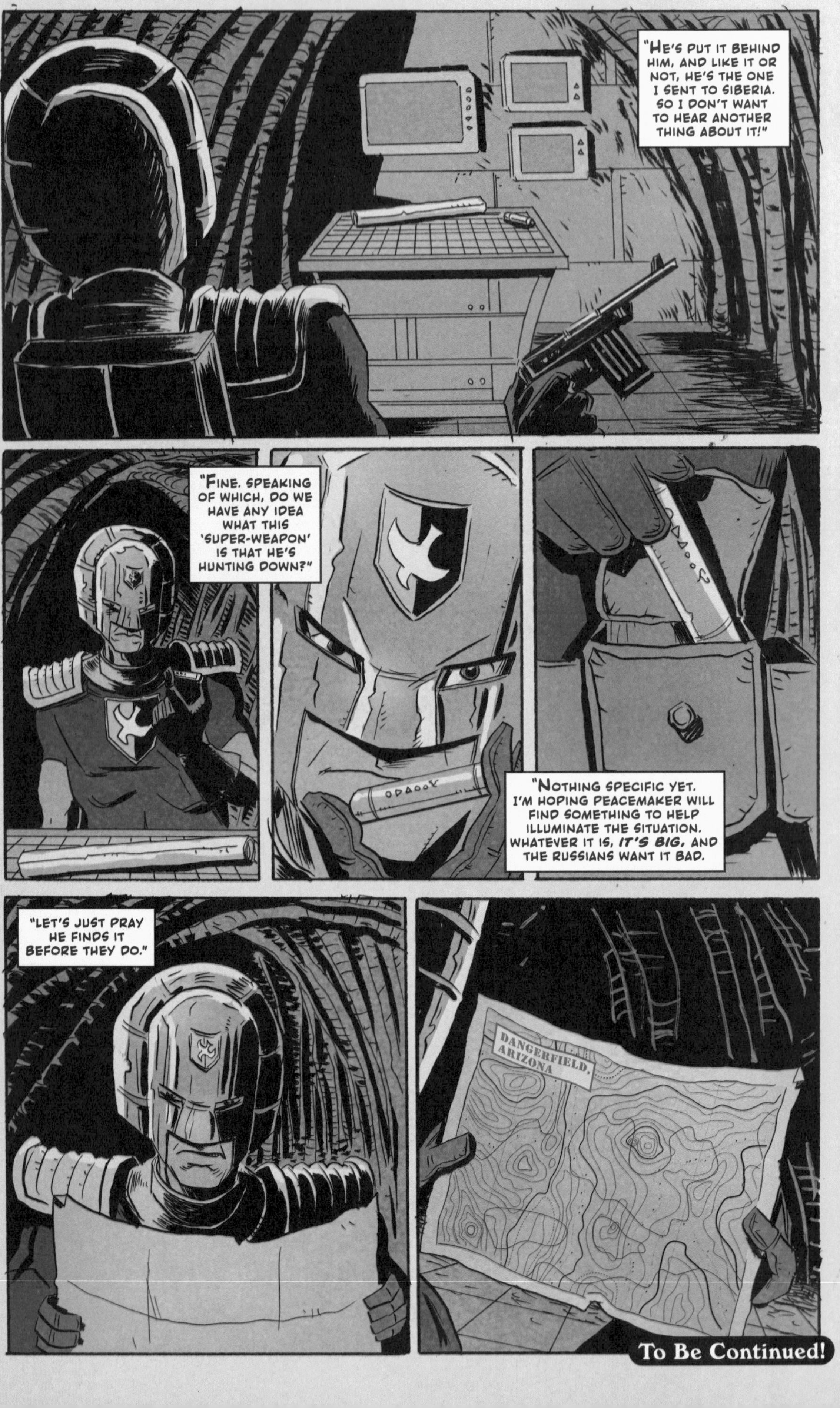
"HE'S PUT IT BEHIND HIM, AND LIKE IT OR NOT, HE'S THE ONE I SENT TO SIBERIA. SO I DON'T WANT TO HEAR ANOTHER THING ABOUT IT!"
"FINE. SPEAKING OF WHICH, DO WE HAVE ANY IDEA WHAT THIS 'SUPER-WEAPON' IS THAT HE'S HUNTING DOWN?"
"NOTHING SPECIFIC YET. I'M HOPING PEACEMAKER WILL FIND SOMETHING TO HELP ILLUMINATE THE SITUATION. WHATEVER IT IS, IT'S BIG, AND THE RUSSIANS WANT IT BAD.
"LET'S JUST PRAY HE FINDS IT BEFORE THEY DO."
DANGERFIELD, ARIZONA
To Be Continued!

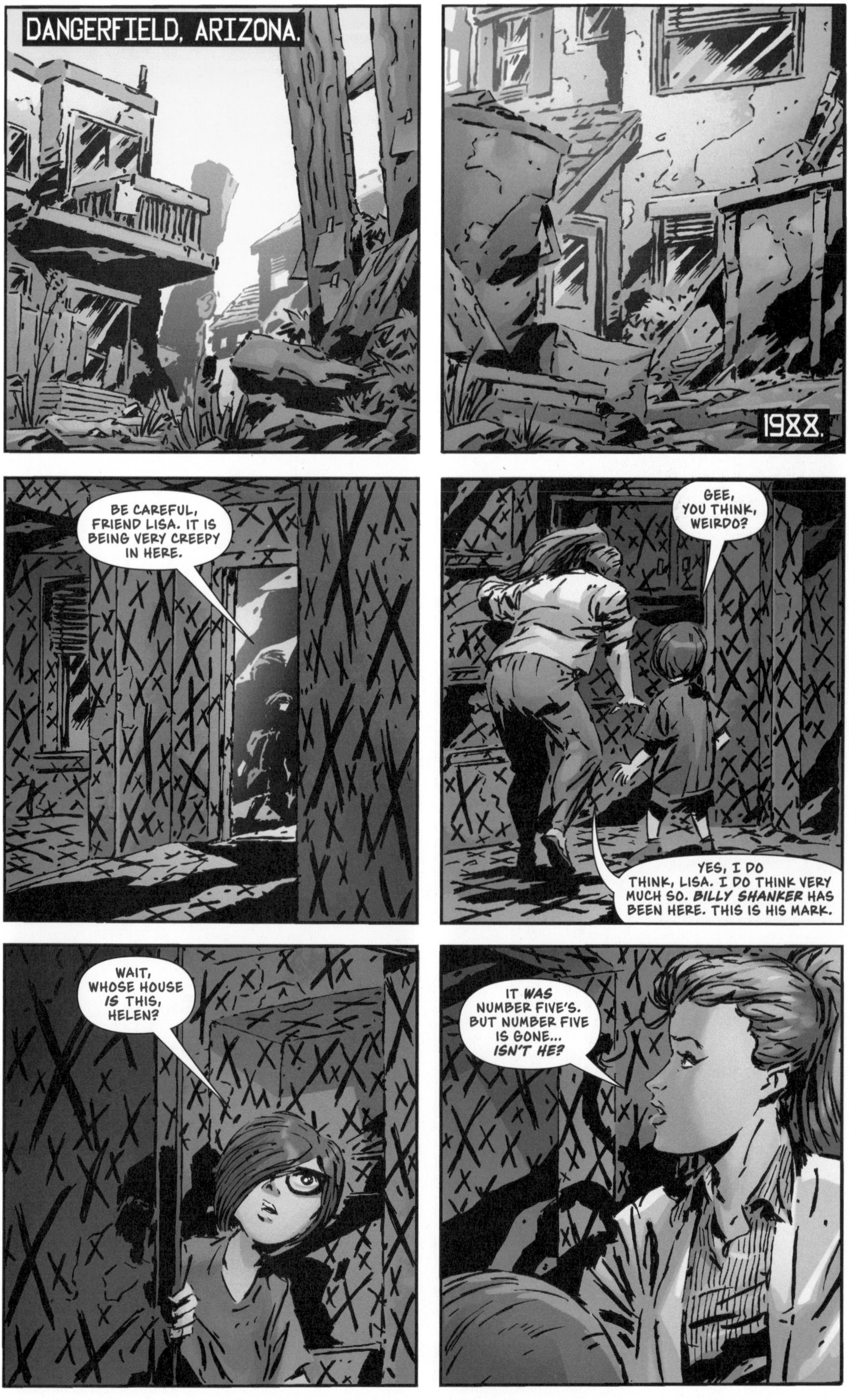
DANGERFIELD, ARIZONA.
1988.
BE CAREFUL, FRIEND LISA. IT IS BEING VERY CREEPY IN HERE.
GEE, YOU THINK, WEIRDO?
YES, I DO THINK, LISA. I DO THINK VERY MUCH SO. BILLY SHANKER HAS BEEN HERE. THIS IS HIS MARK.
WAIT, WHOSE HOUSE IS THIS, HELEN?
IT WAS NUMBER FIVE'S. BUT NUMBER FIVE IS GONE... ISN'T HE?

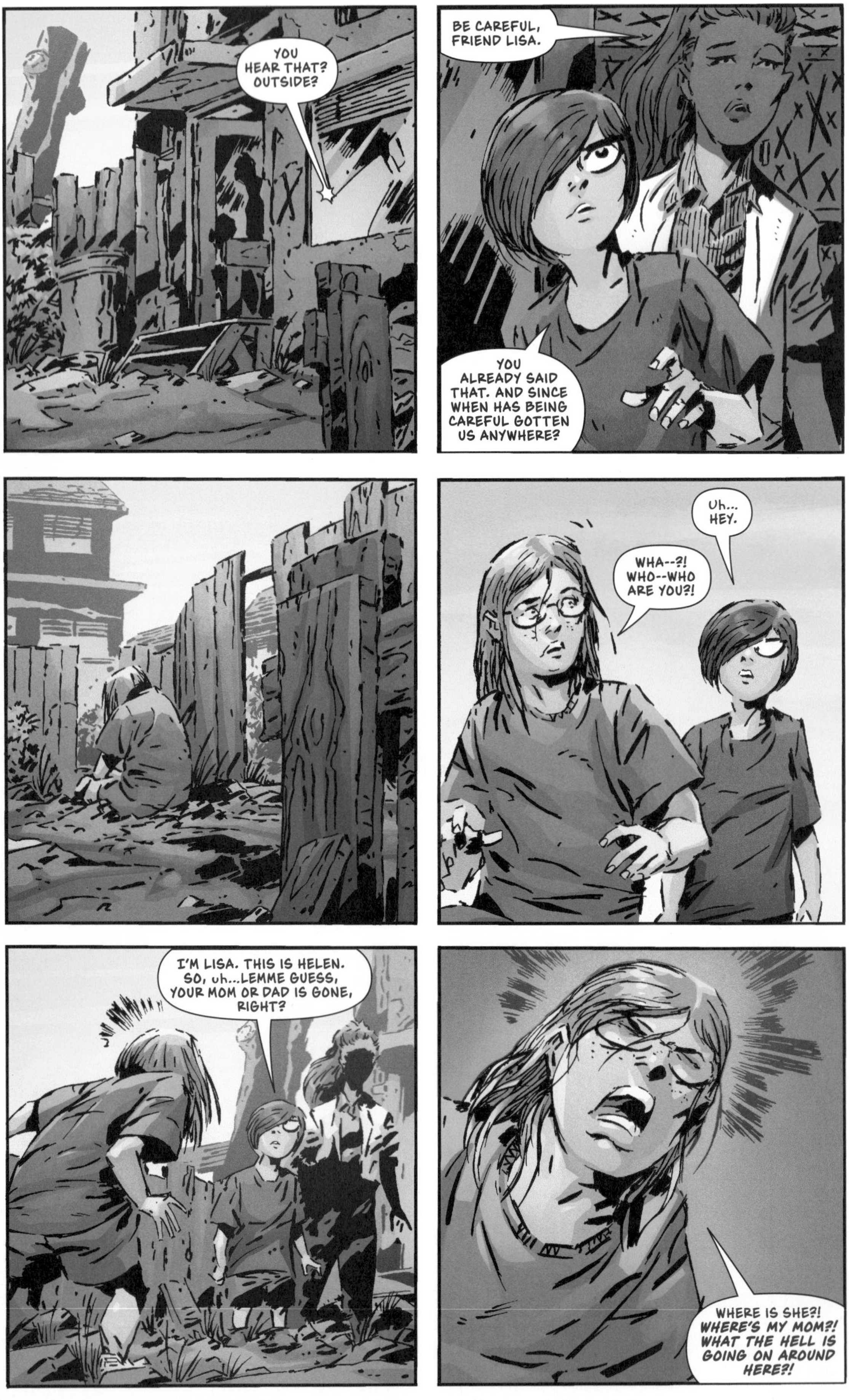
YOU HEAR THAT? OUTSIDE?
BE CAREFUL, FRIEND LISA.
YOU ALREADY SAID THAT. AND SINCE WHEN HAS BEING CAREFUL GOTTEN US ANYWHERE?
Uh... HEY.
WHA--?! WHO--WHO ARE YOU?!
I'M LISA. THIS IS HELEN. SO, uh...LEMME GUESS, YOUR MOM OR DAD IS GONE, RIGHT?
WHERE IS SHE?! WHERE'S MY MOM?! WHAT THE HELL IS GOING ON AROUND HERE?!

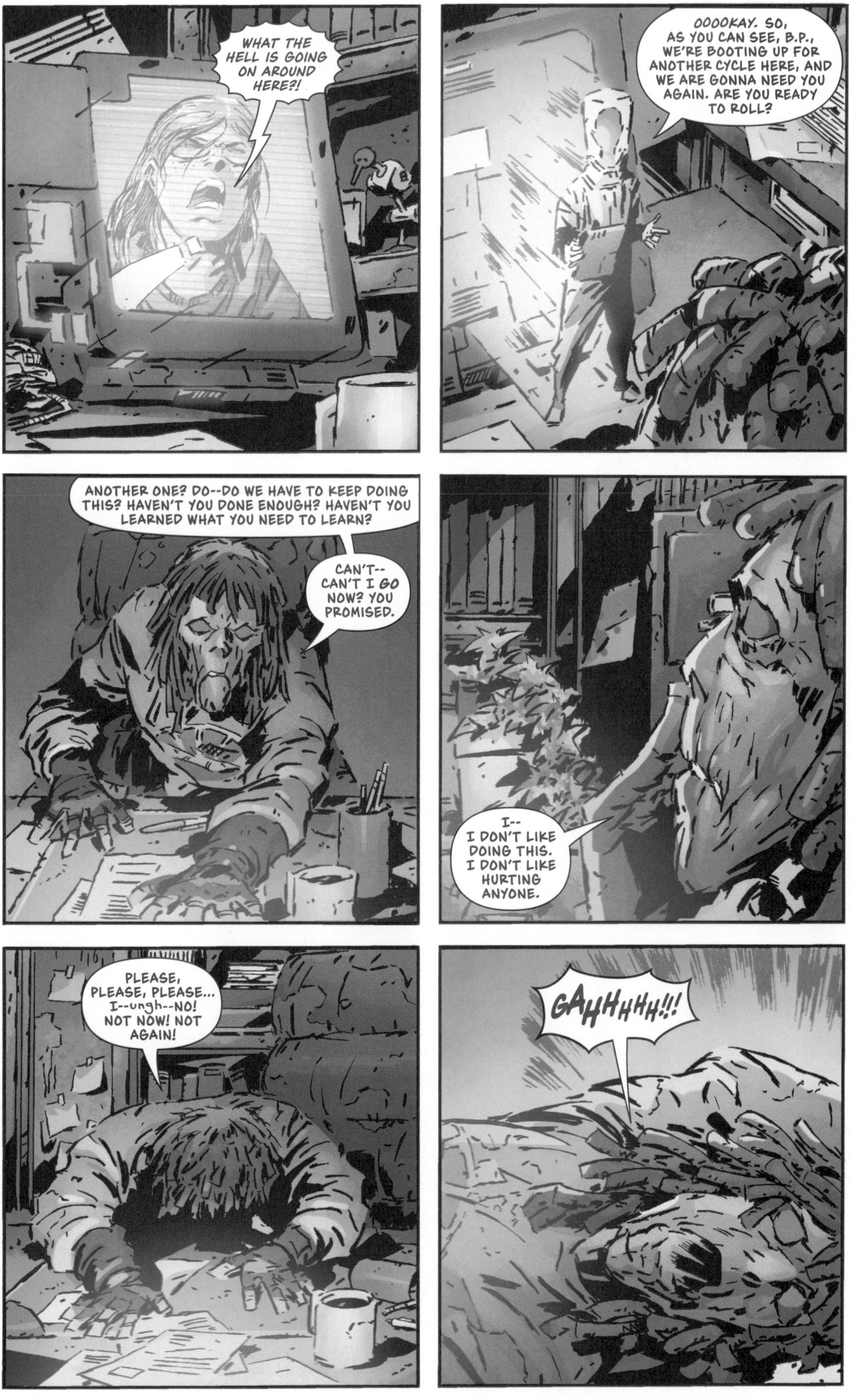
WHAT THE HELL IS GOING ON AROUND HERE?!
OOOOKAY. SO, AS YOU CAN SEE, B.P., WE'RE BOOTING UP FOR ANOTHER CYCLE HERE, AND WE ARE GONNA NEED YOU AGAIN. ARE YOU READY TO ROLL?
ANOTHER ONE? DO--DO WE HAVE TO KEEP DOING THIS? HAVEN'T YOU DONE ENOUGH? HAVEN'T YOU LEARNED WHAT YOU NEED TO LEARN?
CAN'T-- CAN'T I GO NOW? YOU PROMISED.
I-- I DON'T LIKE DOING THIS. I DON'T LIKE HURTING ANYONE.
PLEASE, PLEASE, PLEASE... I--ungh--NO! NOT NOW! NOT AGAIN!
GAHHHHH!!!

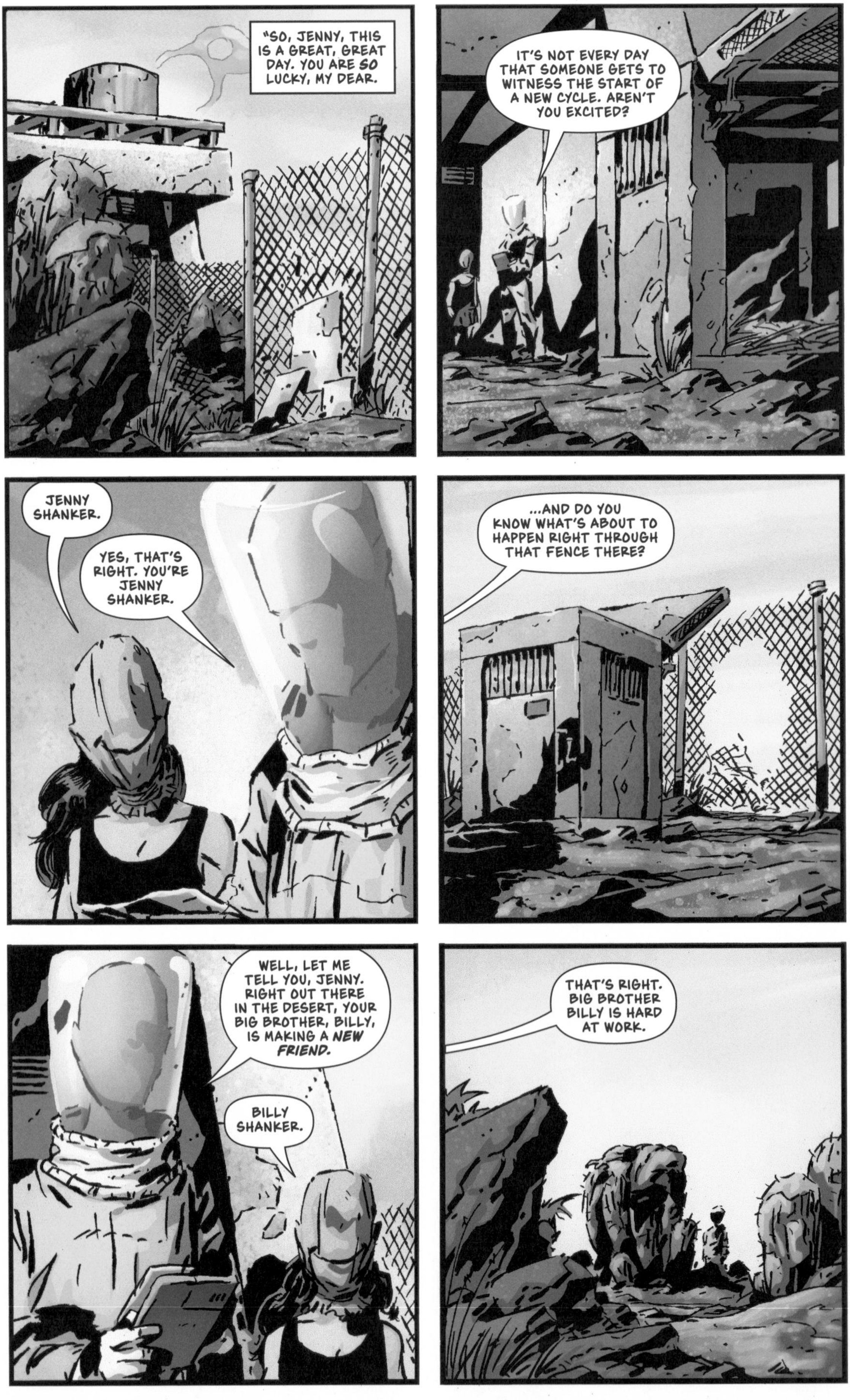
"SO, JENNY, THIS IS A GREAT, GREAT DAY. YOU ARE *SO* LUCKY, MY DEAR.
IT'S NOT EVERY DAY THAT SOMEONE GETS TO WITNESS THE START OF A NEW CYCLE. AREN'T YOU EXCITED?
JENNY SHANKER.
YES, THAT'S RIGHT. YOU'RE JENNY SHANKER.
...AND DO YOU KNOW WHAT'S ABOUT TO HAPPEN RIGHT THROUGH THAT FENCE THERE?
WELL, LET ME TELL YOU, JENNY. RIGHT OUT THERE IN THE DESERT, YOUR BIG BROTHER, BILLY, IS MAKING A ***NEW FRIEND.***
BILLY SHANKER.
THAT'S RIGHT. BIG BROTHER BILLY IS HARD AT WORK.

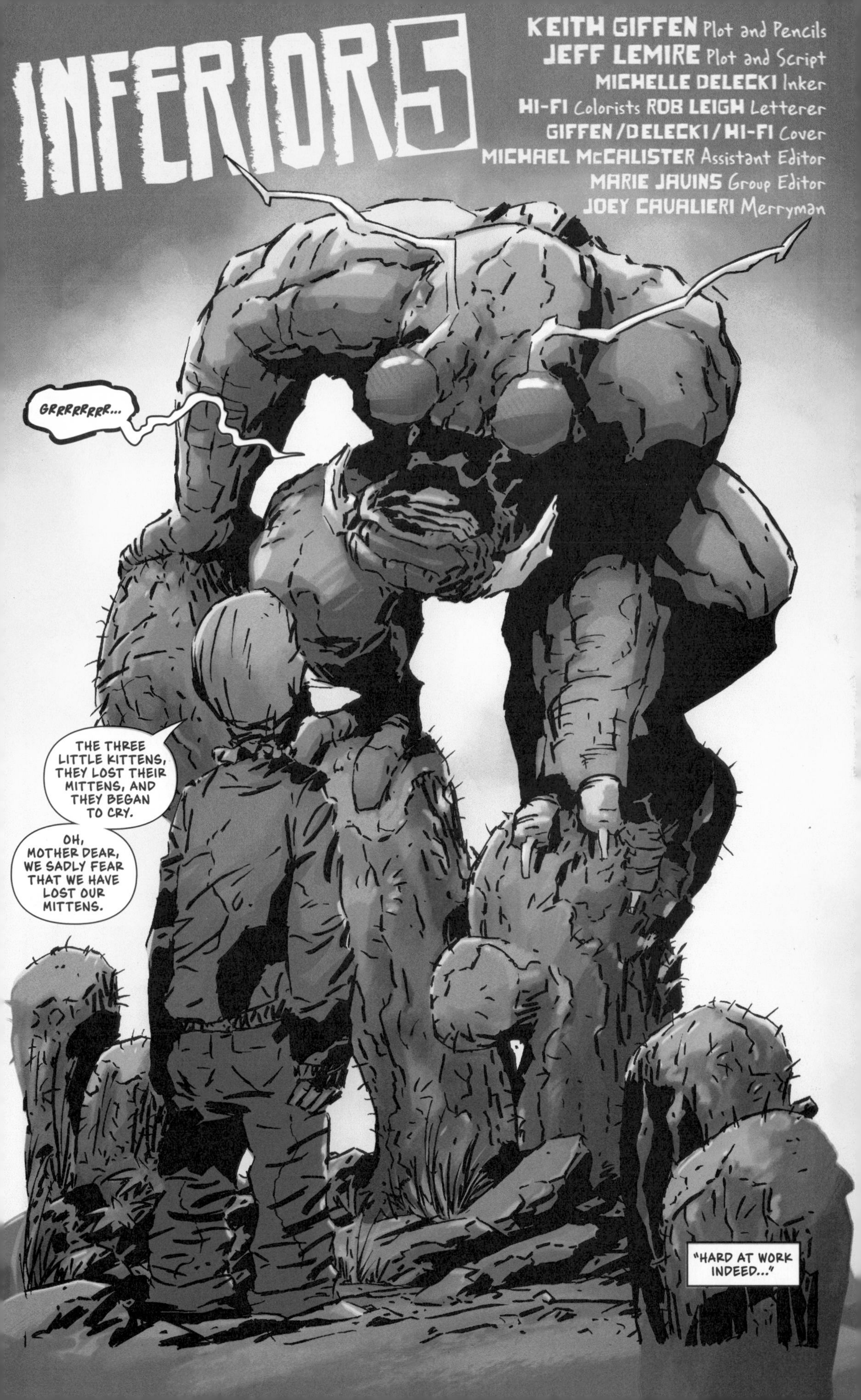

INFERIOR 5
KEITH GIFFEN Plot and Pencils
JEFF LEMIRE Plot and Script
MICHELLE DELECKI Inker
HI-FI Colorists ROB LEIGH Letterer
GIFFEN/DELECKI/HI-FI Cover
MICHAEL McCALISTER Assistant Editor
MARIE JAVINS Group Editor
JOEY CAVALIERI Merryman
GRRRRRRR...
THE THREE LITTLE KITTENS, THEY LOST THEIR MITTENS, AND THEY BEGAN TO CRY.
OH, MOTHER DEAR, WE SADLY FEAR THAT WE HAVE LOST OUR MITTENS.
"HARD AT WORK INDEED..."

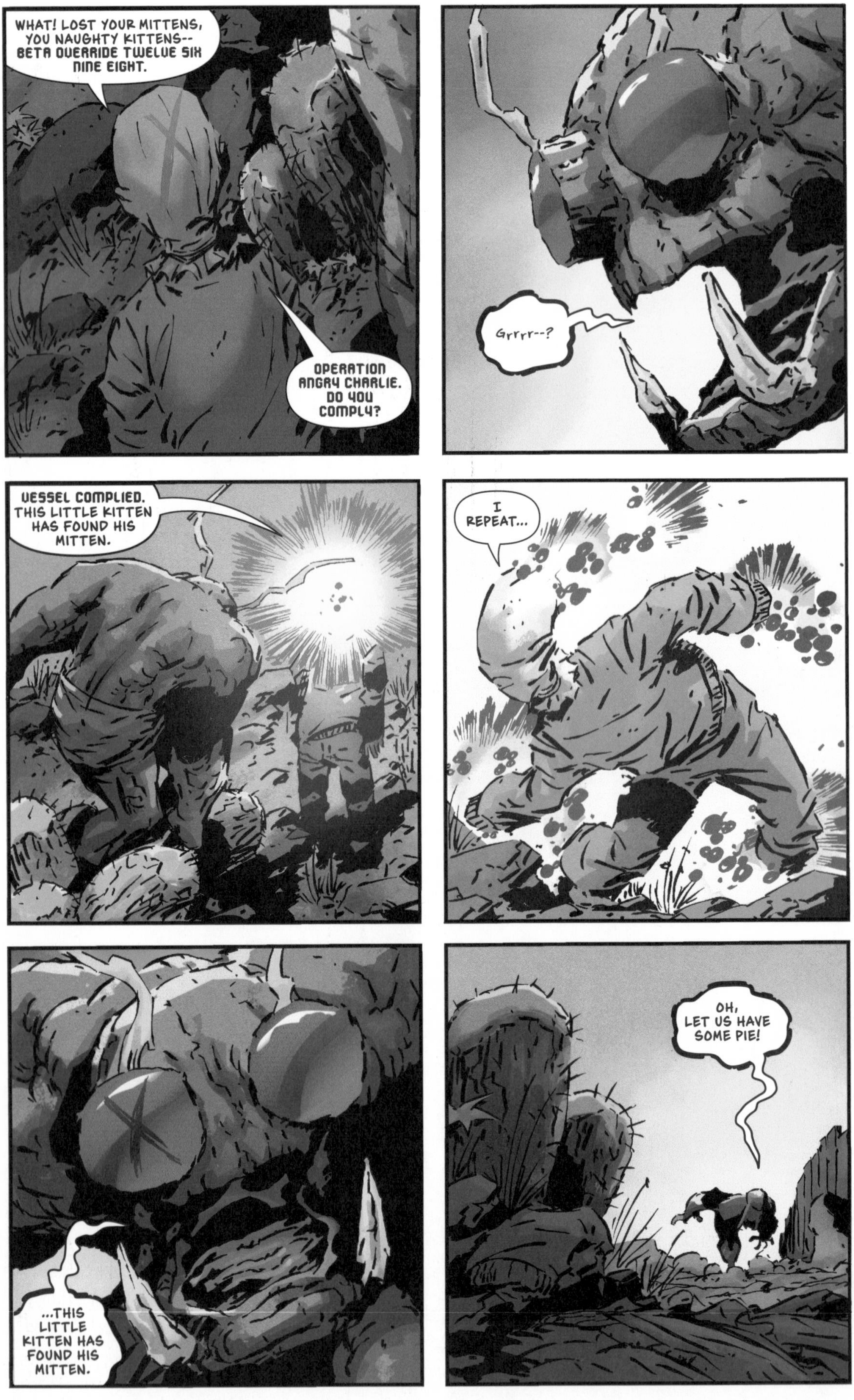
WHAT! LOST YOUR MITTENS, YOU NAUGHTY KITTENS-- BETA OVERRIDE TWELVE SIX NINE EIGHT.
OPERATION ANGRY CHARLIE. DO YOU COMPLY?
Grrrr--?
VESSEL COMPLIED. THIS LITTLE KITTEN HAS FOUND HIS MITTEN.
I REPEAT...
...THIS LITTLE KITTEN HAS FOUND HIS MITTEN.
OH, LET US HAVE SOME PIE!

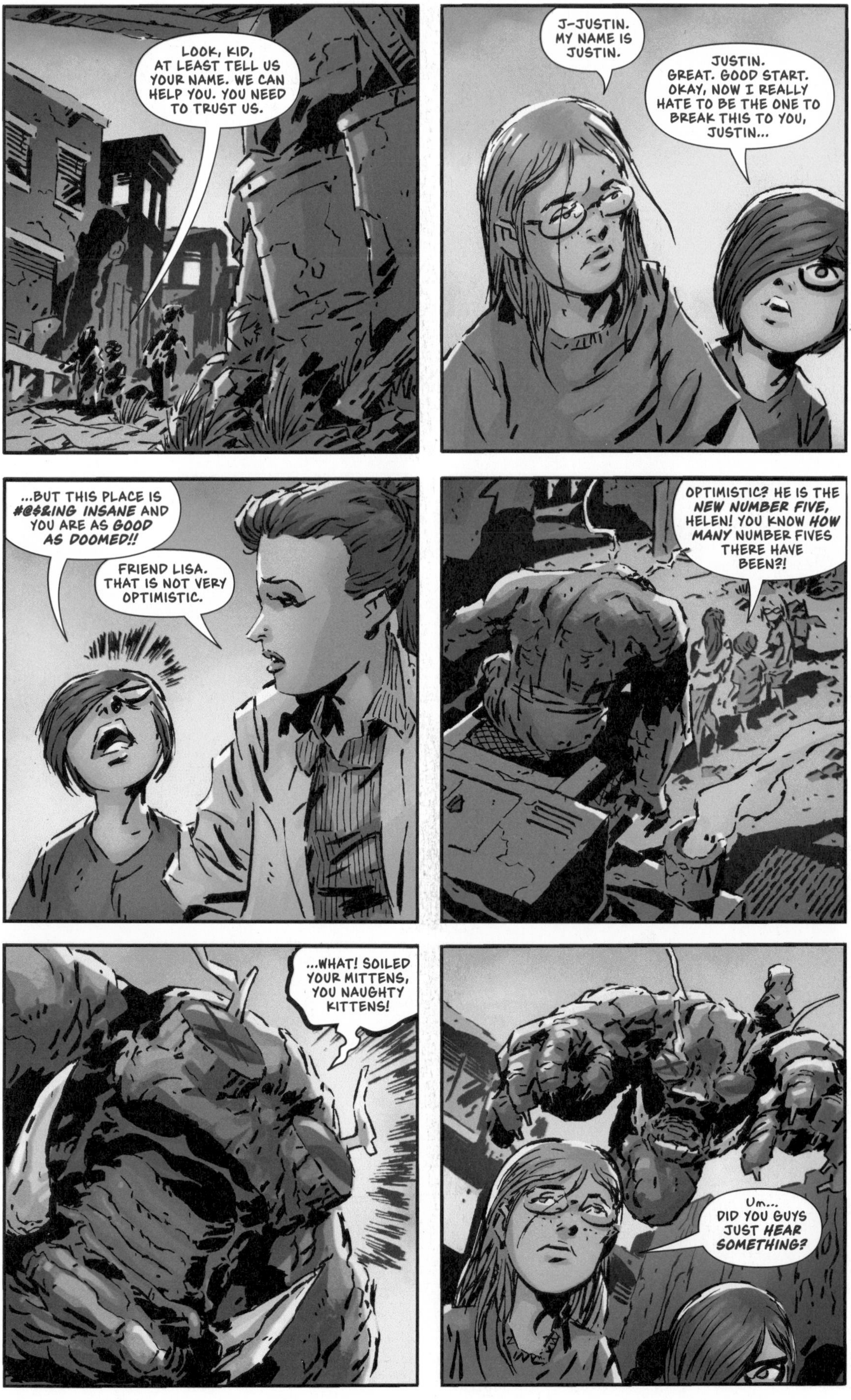
LOOK, KID, AT LEAST TELL US YOUR NAME. WE CAN HELP YOU. YOU NEED TO TRUST US.
J-JUSTIN. MY NAME IS JUSTIN.
JUSTIN. GREAT. GOOD START. OKAY, NOW I REALLY HATE TO BE THE ONE TO BREAK THIS TO YOU, JUSTIN...
...BUT THIS PLACE IS #@$&ING *INSANE* AND YOU ARE AS *GOOD AS DOOMED!!*
FRIEND LISA. THAT IS NOT VERY OPTIMISTIC.
OPTIMISTIC? HE IS THE *NEW NUMBER FIVE*, HELEN! YOU KNOW *HOW MANY* NUMBER FIVES THERE HAVE BEEN?!
...WHAT! SOILED YOUR MITTENS, YOU NAUGHTY KITTENS!
Um... DID YOU GUYS JUST *HEAR SOMETHING?*

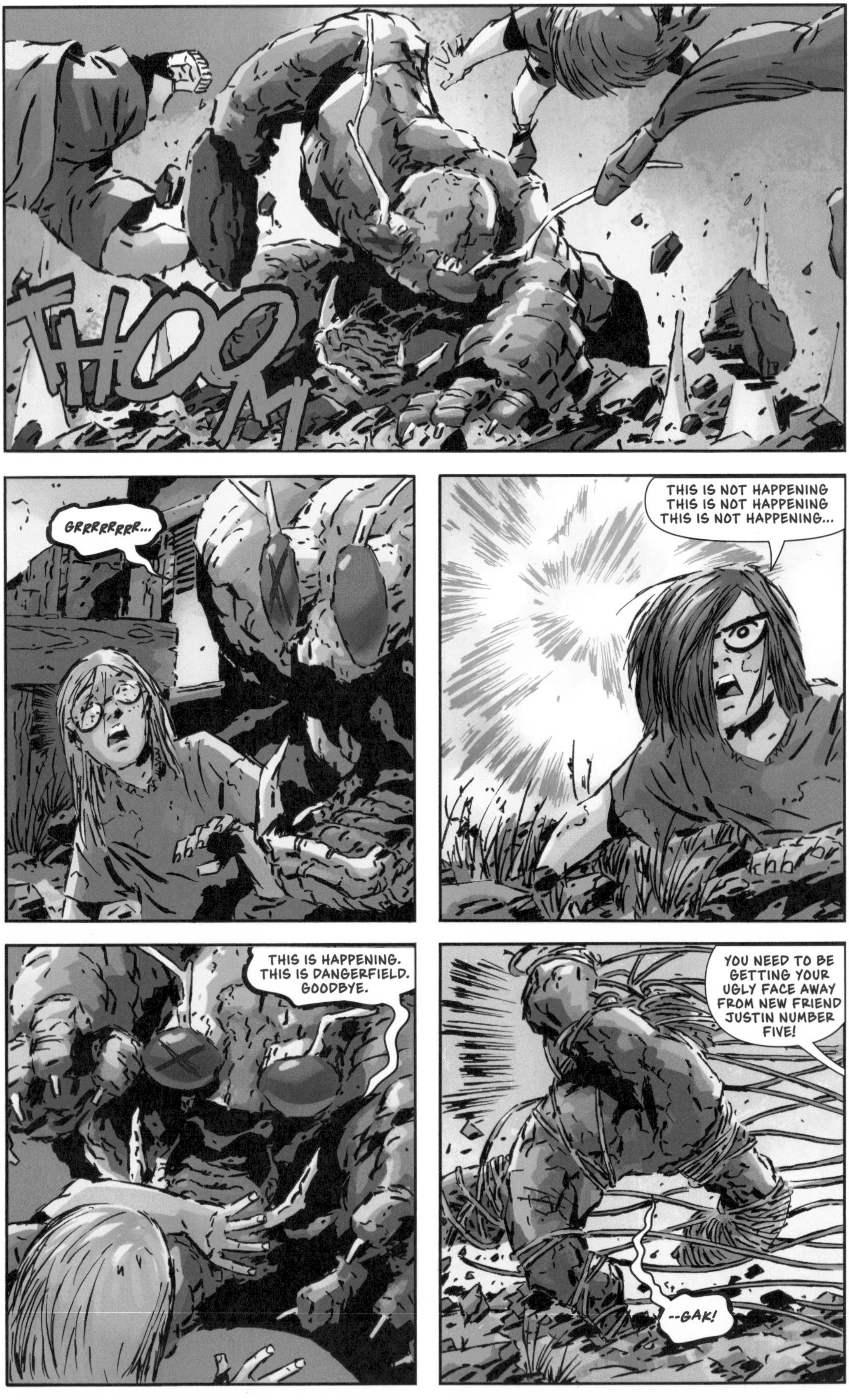
THOOM
GRRRRRRR...
THIS IS NOT HAPPENING
THIS IS NOT HAPPENING
THIS IS NOT HAPPENING...
THIS IS HAPPENING.
THIS IS DANGERFIELD.
GOODBYE.
YOU NEED TO BE GETTING YOUR UGLY FACE AWAY FROM NEW FRIEND JUSTIN NUMBER FIVE!
--GAK!

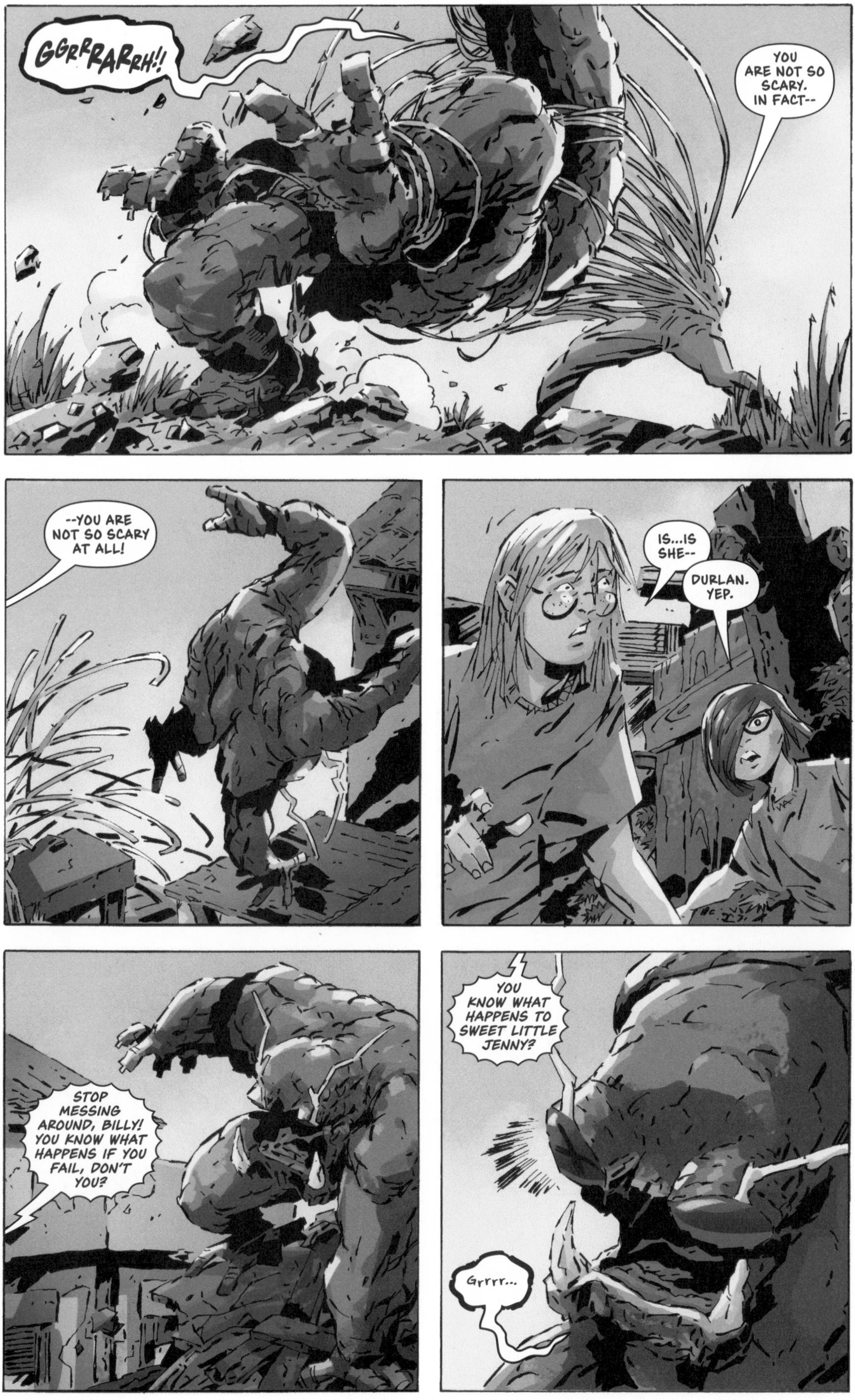
GGRRRARRRH!!
YOU ARE NOT SO SCARY. IN FACT--
--YOU ARE NOT SO SCARY AT ALL!
IS...IS SHE--
DURLAN. YEP.
STOP MESSING AROUND, BILLY! YOU KNOW WHAT HAPPENS IF YOU FAIL, DON'T YOU?
YOU KNOW WHAT HAPPENS TO SWEET LITTLE JENNY?
Grrrr...

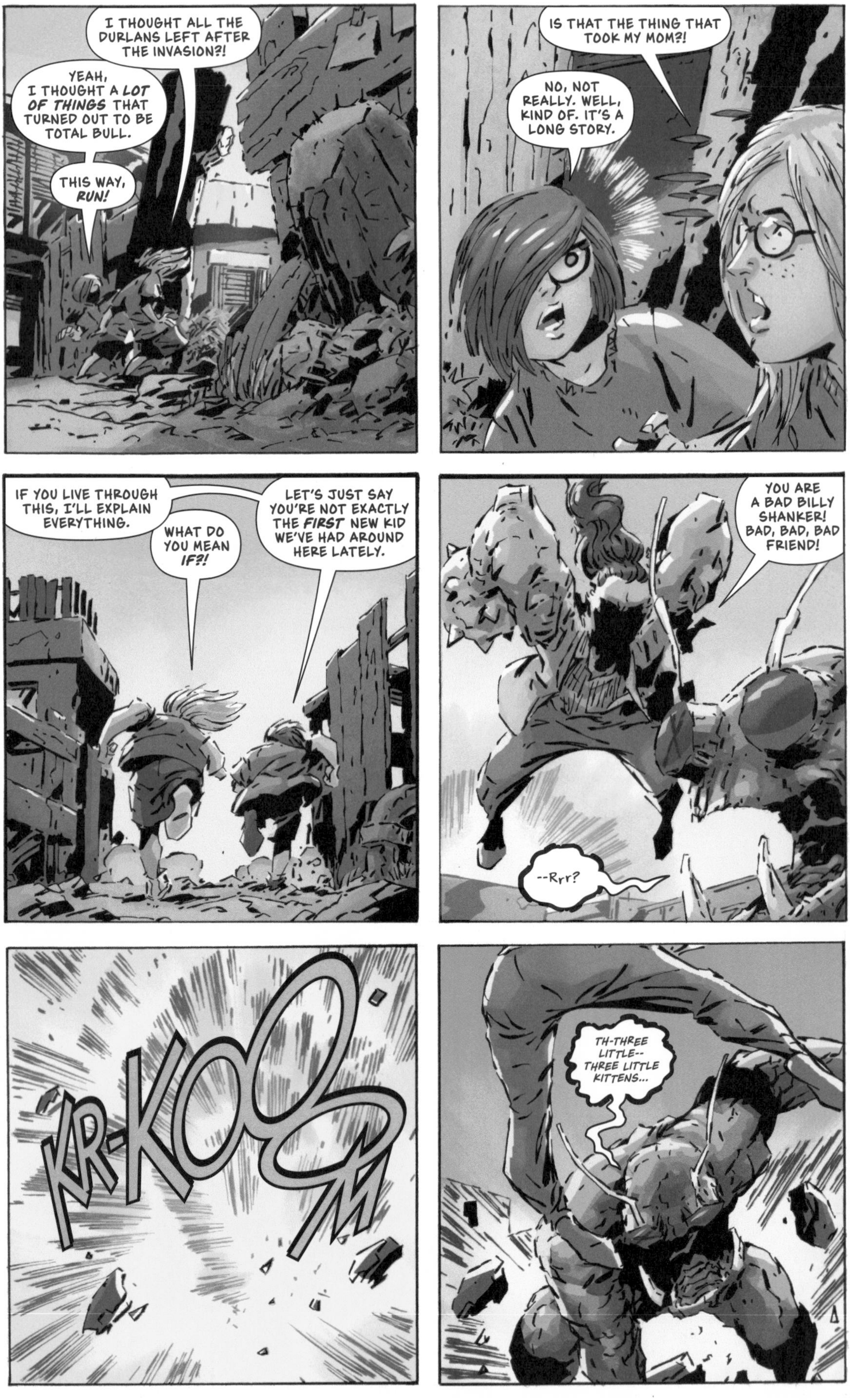
I THOUGHT ALL THE DURLANS LEFT AFTER THE INVASION?!
YEAH, I THOUGHT A *LOT OF THINGS* THAT TURNED OUT TO BE TOTAL BULL.
THIS WAY, *RUN!*
IS THAT THE THING THAT TOOK MY MOM?!
NO, NOT REALLY. WELL, KIND OF. IT'S A LONG STORY.
IF YOU LIVE THROUGH THIS, I'LL EXPLAIN EVERYTHING.
WHAT DO YOU MEAN *IF?!*
LET'S JUST SAY YOU'RE NOT EXACTLY THE *FIRST* NEW KID WE'VE HAD AROUND HERE LATELY.
YOU ARE A BAD BILLY SHANKER! BAD, BAD, BAD FRIEND!
--Rrr?
KR-KOOOM
TH-THREE LITTLE-- THREE LITTLE KITTENS...

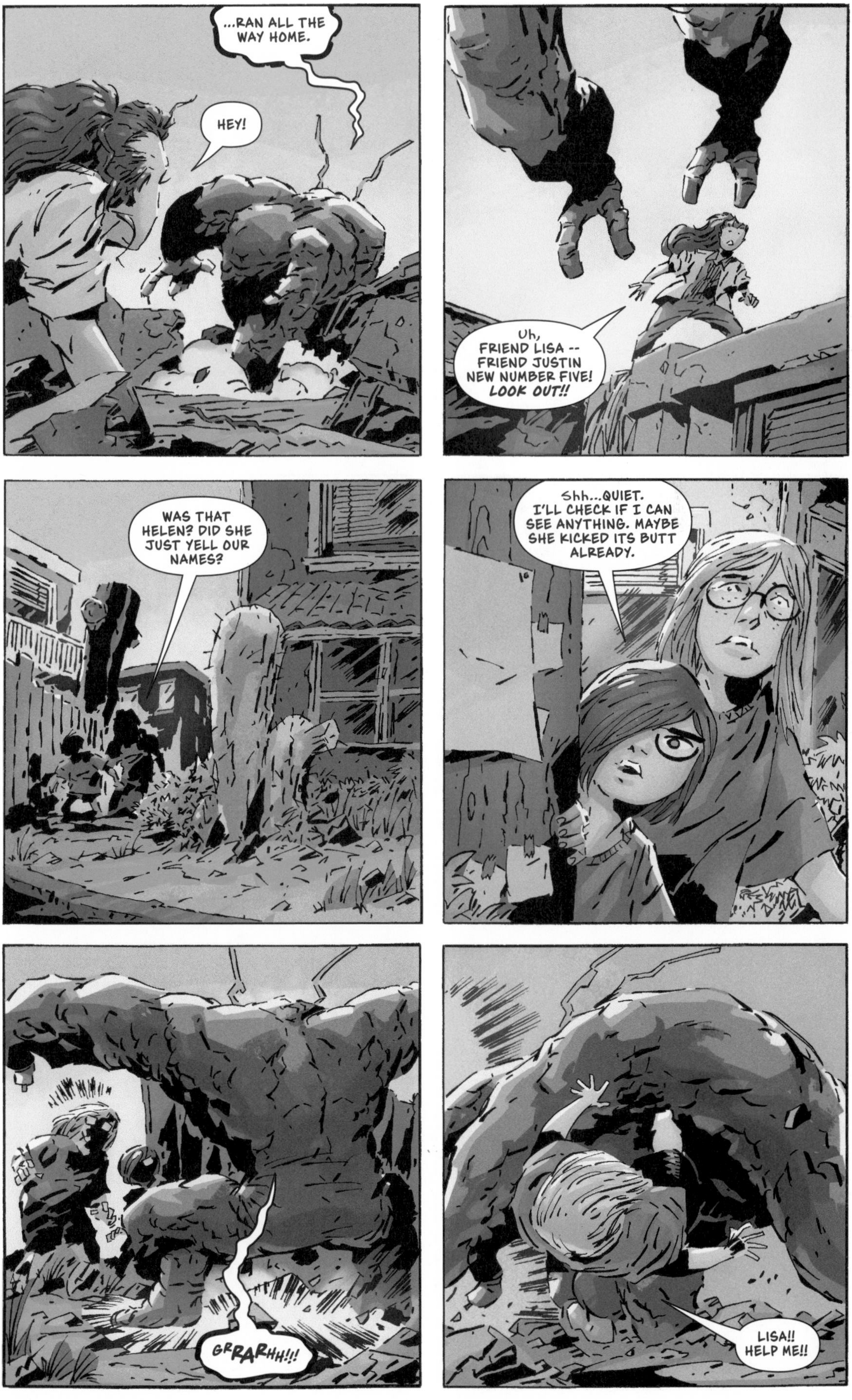
...RAN ALL THE WAY HOME.
HEY!
Uh, FRIEND LISA -- FRIEND JUSTIN NEW NUMBER FIVE! LOOK OUT!!
WAS THAT HELEN? DID SHE JUST YELL OUR NAMES?
Shh...QUIET. I'LL CHECK IF I CAN SEE ANYTHING. MAYBE SHE KICKED ITS BUTT ALREADY.
GRRARHH!!!
LISA!! HELP ME!!

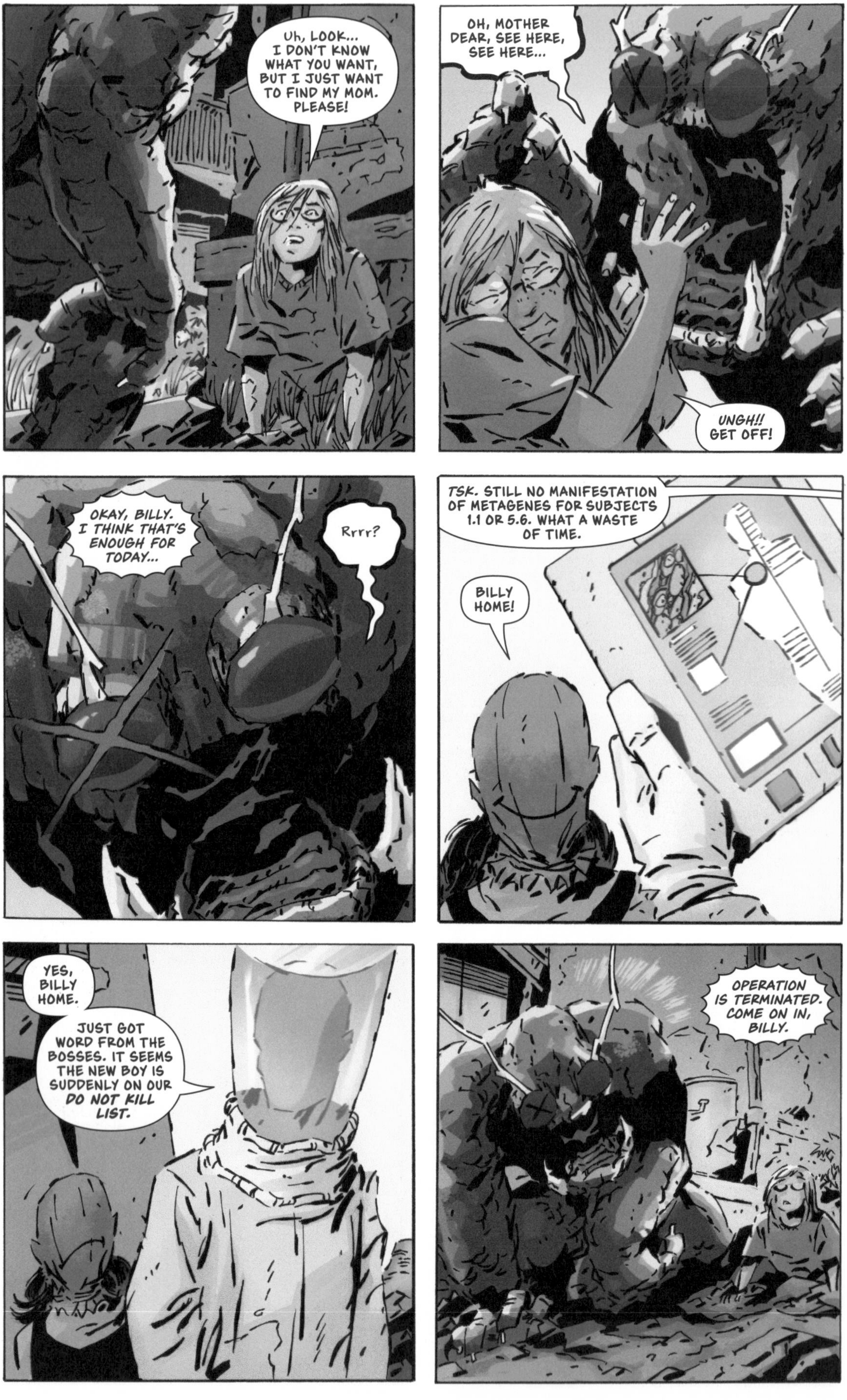
Uh, LOOK... I DON'T KNOW WHAT YOU WANT, BUT I JUST WANT TO FIND MY MOM. PLEASE!
OH, MOTHER DEAR, SEE HERE, SEE HERE...
UNGH!! GET OFF!
OKAY, BILLY. I THINK THAT'S ENOUGH FOR TODAY...
Rrrr?
TSK. STILL NO MANIFESTATION OF METAGENES FOR SUBJECTS 1.1 OR 5.6. WHAT A WASTE OF TIME.
BILLY HOME!
YES, BILLY HOME.
JUST GOT WORD FROM THE BOSSES. IT SEEMS THE NEW BOY IS SUDDENLY ON OUR DO NOT KILL LIST.
OPERATION IS TERMINATED. COME ON IN, BILLY.

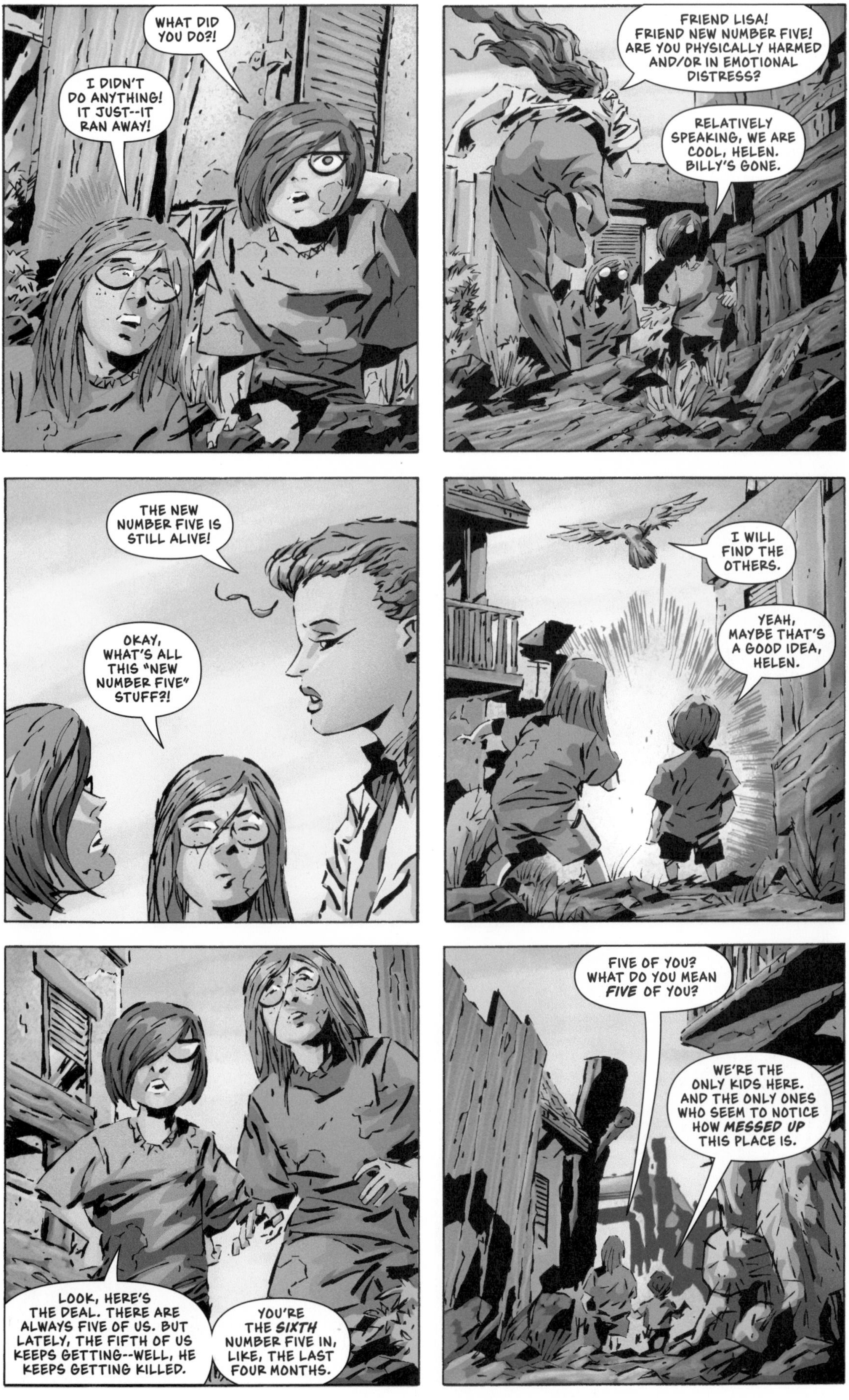
WHAT DID YOU DO?!
I DIDN'T DO ANYTHING! IT JUST--IT RAN AWAY!
FRIEND LISA! FRIEND NEW NUMBER FIVE! ARE YOU PHYSICALLY HARMED AND/OR IN EMOTIONAL DISTRESS?
RELATIVELY SPEAKING, WE ARE COOL, HELEN. BILLY'S GONE.
THE NEW NUMBER FIVE IS STILL ALIVE!
OKAY, WHAT'S ALL THIS "NEW NUMBER FIVE" STUFF?!
I WILL FIND THE OTHERS.
YEAH, MAYBE THAT'S A GOOD IDEA, HELEN.
LOOK, HERE'S THE DEAL. THERE ARE ALWAYS FIVE OF US. BUT LATELY, THE FIFTH OF US KEEPS GETTING--WELL, HE KEEPS GETTING KILLED.
YOU'RE THE *SIXTH* NUMBER FIVE IN, LIKE, THE LAST FOUR MONTHS.
FIVE OF YOU? WHAT DO YOU MEAN *FIVE* OF YOU?
WE'RE THE ONLY KIDS HERE. AND THE ONLY ONES WHO SEEM TO NOTICE HOW *MESSED UP* THIS PLACE IS.

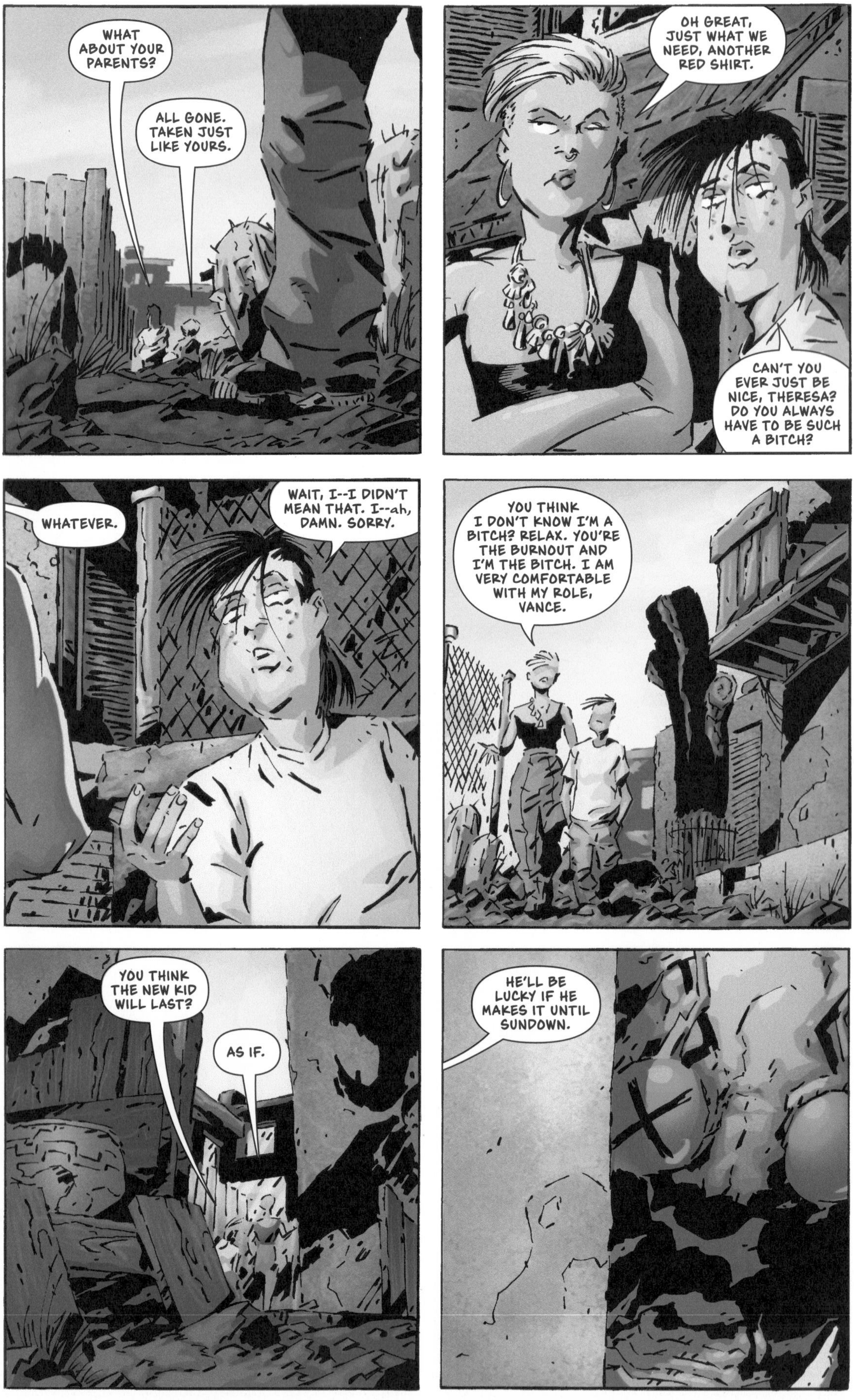
WHAT ABOUT YOUR PARENTS?
ALL GONE. TAKEN JUST LIKE YOURS.
OH GREAT, JUST WHAT WE NEED, ANOTHER RED SHIRT.
CAN'T YOU EVER JUST BE NICE, THERESA? DO YOU ALWAYS HAVE TO BE SUCH A BITCH?
WHATEVER.
WAIT, I--I DIDN'T MEAN THAT. I--ah, DAMN. SORRY.
YOU THINK I DON'T KNOW I'M A BITCH? RELAX. YOU'RE THE BURNOUT AND I'M THE BITCH. I AM VERY COMFORTABLE WITH MY ROLE, VANCE.
YOU THINK THE NEW KID WILL LAST?
AS IF.
HE'LL BE LUCKY IF HE MAKES IT UNTIL SUNDOWN.

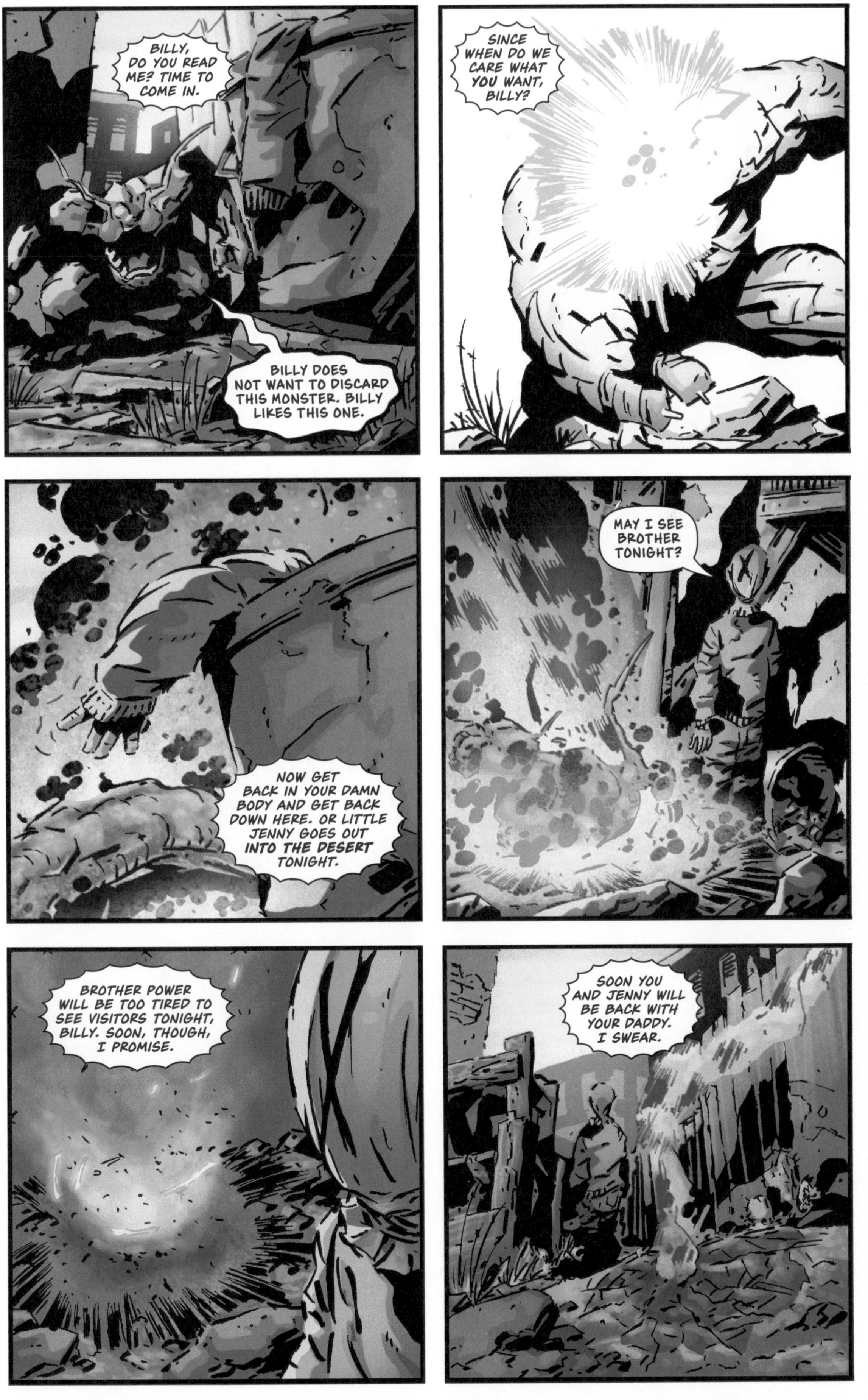
BILLY, DO YOU READ ME? TIME TO COME IN.
BILLY DOES NOT WANT TO DISCARD THIS MONSTER. BILLY LIKES THIS ONE.
SINCE WHEN DO WE CARE WHAT YOU WANT, BILLY?
NOW GET BACK IN YOUR DAMN BODY AND GET BACK DOWN HERE. OR LITTLE JENNY GOES OUT INTO THE DESERT TONIGHT.
MAY I SEE BROTHER TONIGHT?
BROTHER POWER WILL BE TOO TIRED TO SEE VISITORS TONIGHT, BILLY. SOON, THOUGH, I PROMISE.
SOON YOU AND JENNY WILL BE BACK WITH YOUR DADDY. I SWEAR.

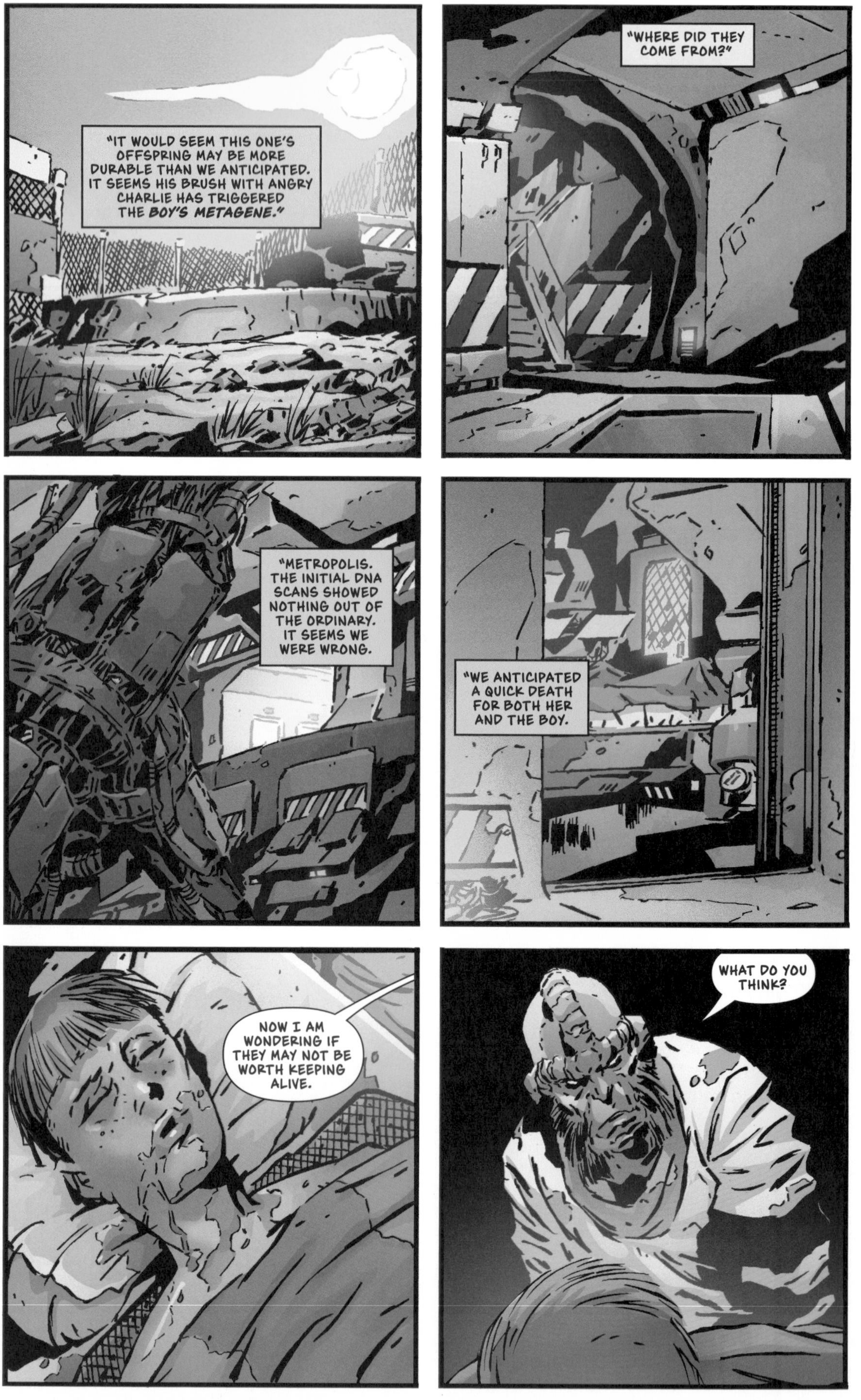
"IT WOULD SEEM THIS ONE'S OFFSPRING MAY BE MORE DURABLE THAN WE ANTICIPATED. IT SEEMS HIS BRUSH WITH ANGRY CHARLIE HAS TRIGGERED THE *BOY'S METAGENE.*"
"WHERE DID THEY COME FROM?"
"METROPOLIS. THE INITIAL DNA SCANS SHOWED NOTHING OUT OF THE ORDINARY. IT SEEMS WE WERE WRONG.
"WE ANTICIPATED A QUICK DEATH FOR BOTH HER AND THE BOY.
NOW I AM WONDERING IF THEY MAY NOT BE WORTH KEEPING ALIVE.
WHAT DO YOU THINK?

IS SHE WORTHY OF FURTHER TESTING? IS SHE WORTHY OF THE PROCEDURE?

NONE OF THESE SSSSTINKING HUMAN FLESH BAGSSSS ARE WORTHY, MY PSSSION FRIEND.

BUT ALASSSSS, I SSSSSUPPOSE SHE ISSSS AS GOOD A CANDIDATE AS ANY.

AND HER CHILD? THE BOY?

I HAVE LITTLE INTERESSSST IN THE EXPERIMENTSSSS ABOVE.

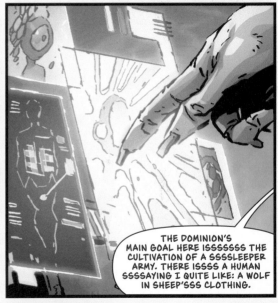

THE DOMINION'S MAIN GOAL HERE ISSSSSS THE CULTIVATION OF A SSSSLEEPER ARMY. THERE ISSSS A HUMAN SSSSAYING I QUITE LIKE: A WOLF IN SHEEP'SSS CLOTHING.

SSSO LET USSSS MAKE HER A WOLF. WHAT HAPPENS TO HER CUB ISSS OF NO INTEREST TO ME, METAGENE OR NO.

YOU SSSSEEE, THE WAR MAY BE OVER, BUT THE *REAL INVASION* HAS JUSSST BEGUN.

TO BE CONTINUED!

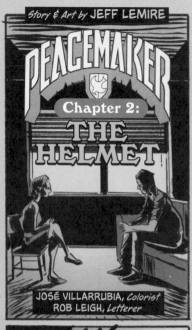

Story & Art by JEFF LEMIRE

PEACEMAKER
Chapter 2:
THE HELMET

JOSÉ VILLARRUBIA, Colorist
ROB LEIGH, Letterer

--YOU DO KNOW WHY YOU'RE HERE, DON'T YOU, CHRISTOPHER?

CHRISTOPHER?

SORRY?

I ASKED IF YOU KNEW WHY YOU'RE HERE. WHY YOU NEEDED TO START SEEING ME.

I'M HERE BECAUSE DIRECTOR WALLER ORDERED ME TO BE HERE.

WELL, THAT'S TRUE. BUT THIS ISN'T A MISSION, CHRISTOPHER. THIS ISN'T ABOUT FOLLOWING ORDERS. AMANDA IS WORRIED ABOUT YOU.

Heh. YEAH. SURE, SHE IS. AMANDA WALLER IS A REAL BLEEDING HEART, ALL RIGHT.

DON'T B.S. ME, DOC. I'M HERE BECAUSE SHE NEEDS ME BACK OUT IN THE FIELD, BUT I'VE TURNED INTO A BASKET CASE.

IS THAT WHAT YOU FEEL LIKE, CHRIS? A BASKET CASE?

I FEEL LIKE SOMEONE ELSE HAS TAKEN CONTROL OF MY BRAIN. I FEEL LIKE A DAMN INVALID.

I WANT TO GET BACK TO WORK. I WANT TO BE THE PEACEMAKER. BUT WHENEVER I THINK OF GOING BACK OUT, I JUST--WELL, I CAN'T.

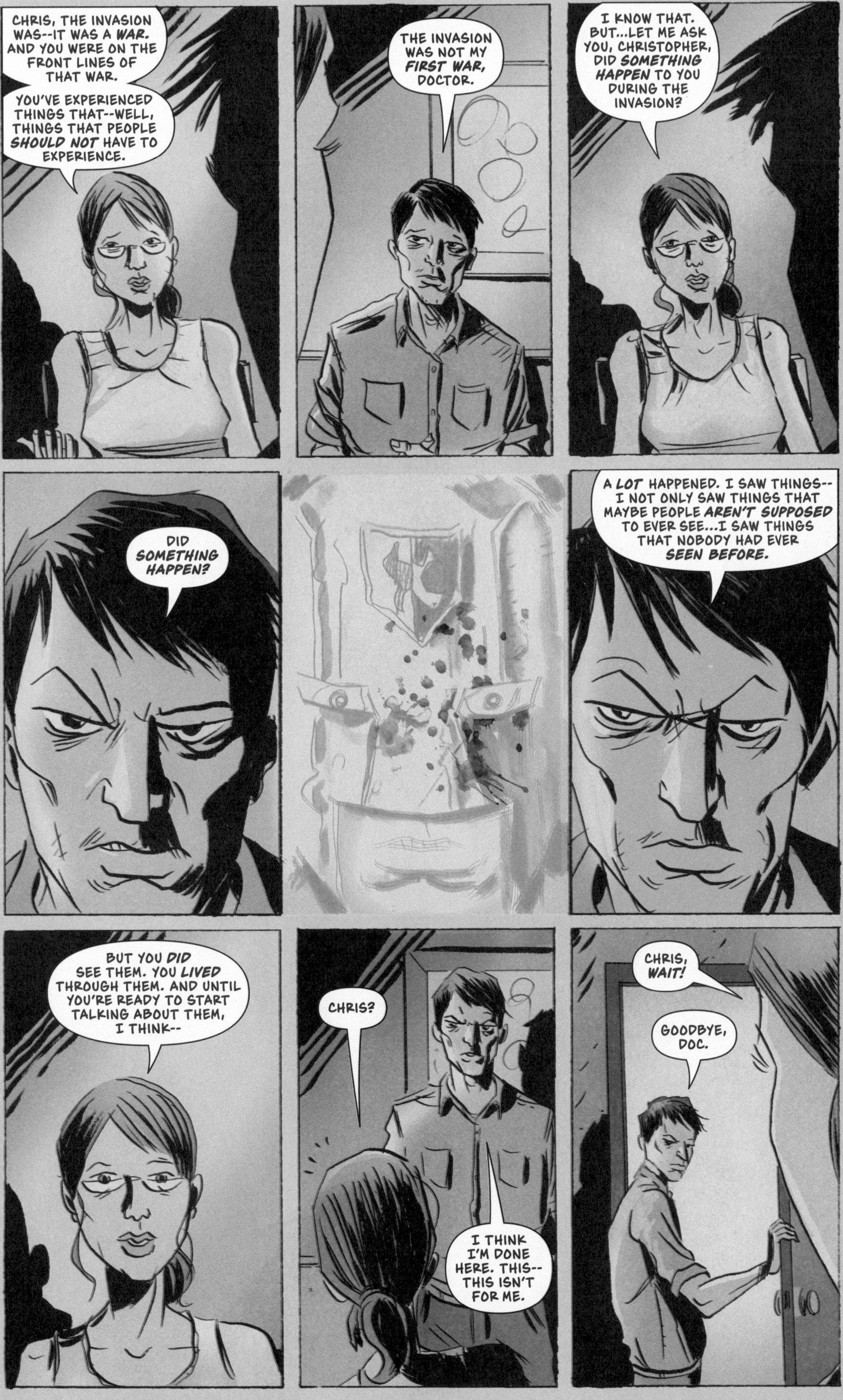
CHRIS, THE INVASION WAS--IT WAS A WAR. AND YOU WERE ON THE FRONT LINES OF THAT WAR.
YOU'VE EXPERIENCED THINGS THAT--WELL, THINGS THAT PEOPLE SHOULD NOT HAVE TO EXPERIENCE.
THE INVASION WAS NOT MY FIRST WAR, DOCTOR.
I KNOW THAT. BUT...LET ME ASK YOU, CHRISTOPHER, DID SOMETHING HAPPEN TO YOU DURING THE INVASION?
DID SOMETHING HAPPEN?
A LOT HAPPENED. I SAW THINGS-- I NOT ONLY SAW THINGS THAT MAYBE PEOPLE AREN'T SUPPOSED TO EVER SEE...I SAW THINGS THAT NOBODY HAD EVER SEEN BEFORE.
BUT YOU DID SEE THEM. YOU LIVED THROUGH THEM. AND UNTIL YOU'RE READY TO START TALKING ABOUT THEM, I THINK--
CHRIS?
I THINK I'M DONE HERE. THIS-- THIS ISN'T FOR ME.
CHRIS, WAIT!
GOODBYE, DOC.

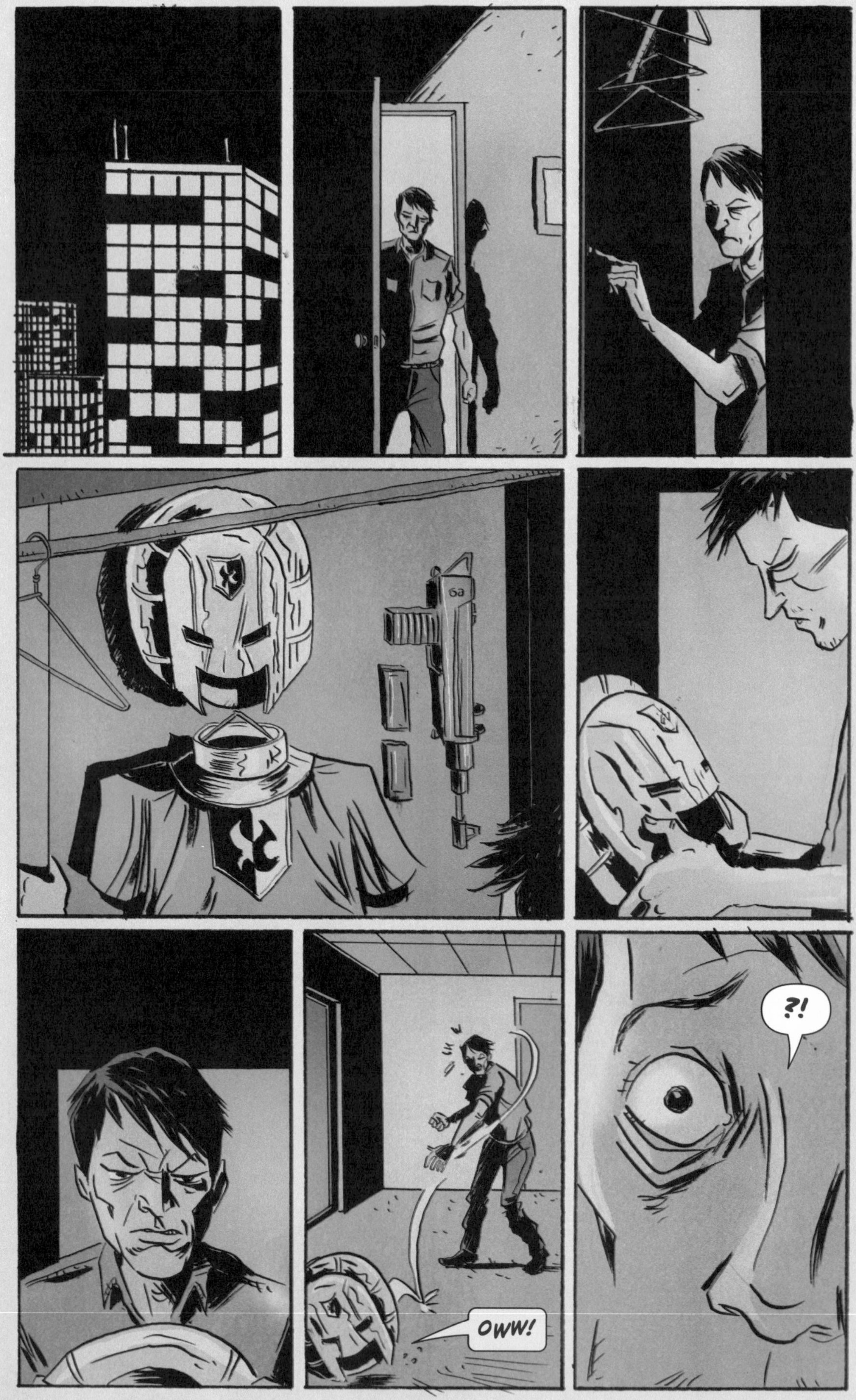
OWW!
?!

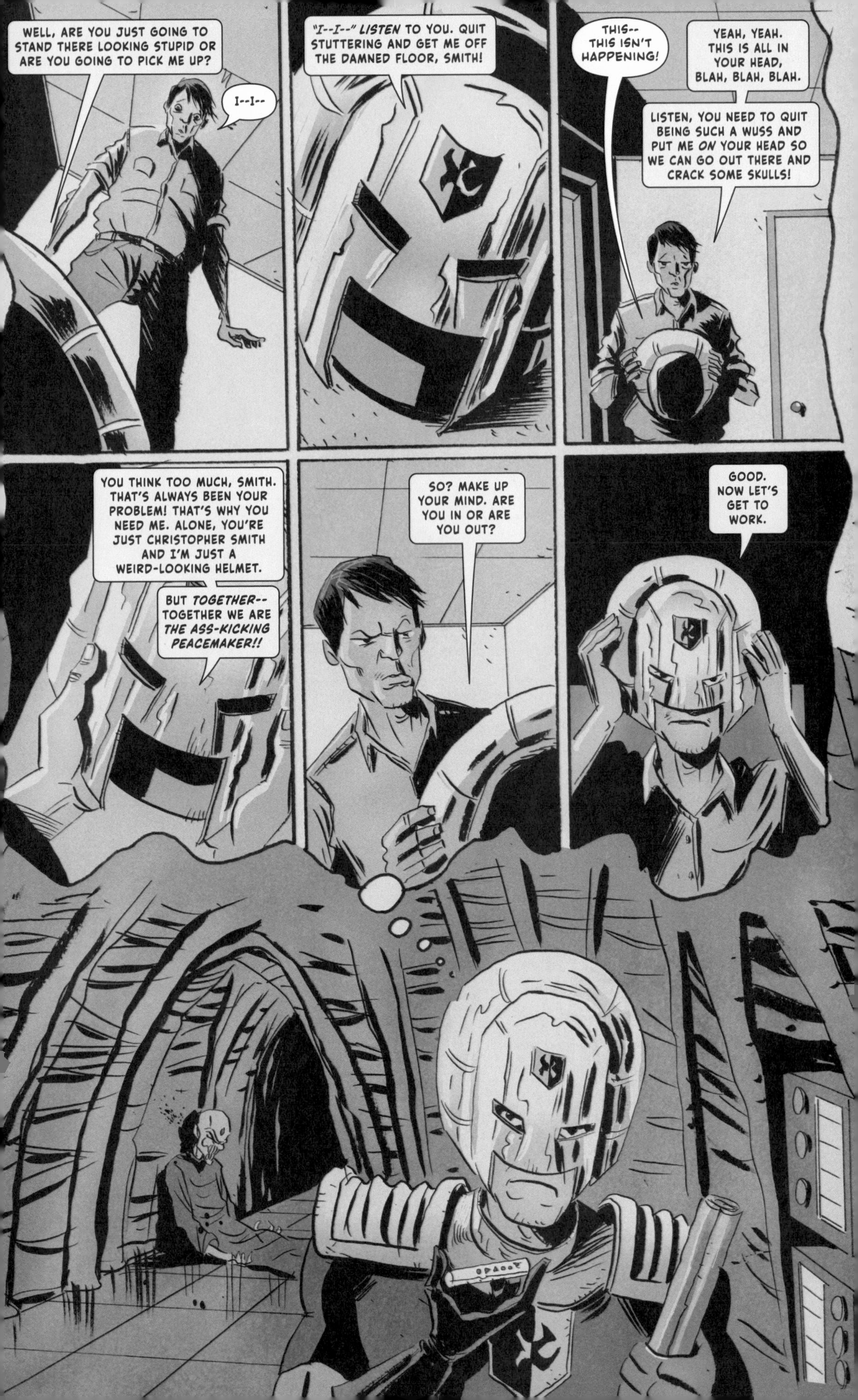
WELL, ARE YOU JUST GOING TO STAND THERE LOOKING STUPID OR ARE YOU GOING TO PICK ME UP?
I--I--
"I--I--" LISTEN TO YOU. QUIT STUTTERING AND GET ME OFF THE DAMNED FLOOR, SMITH!
THIS-- THIS ISN'T HAPPENING!
YEAH, YEAH. THIS IS ALL IN YOUR HEAD, BLAH, BLAH, BLAH.
LISTEN, YOU NEED TO QUIT BEING SUCH A WUSS AND PUT ME ON YOUR HEAD SO WE CAN GO OUT THERE AND CRACK SOME SKULLS!
YOU THINK TOO MUCH, SMITH. THAT'S ALWAYS BEEN YOUR PROBLEM! THAT'S WHY YOU NEED ME. ALONE, YOU'RE JUST CHRISTOPHER SMITH AND I'M JUST A WEIRD-LOOKING HELMET.
BUT TOGETHER-- TOGETHER WE ARE THE ASS-KICKING PEACEMAKER!!
SO? MAKE UP YOUR MIND. ARE YOU IN OR ARE YOU OUT?
GOOD. NOW LET'S GET TO WORK.

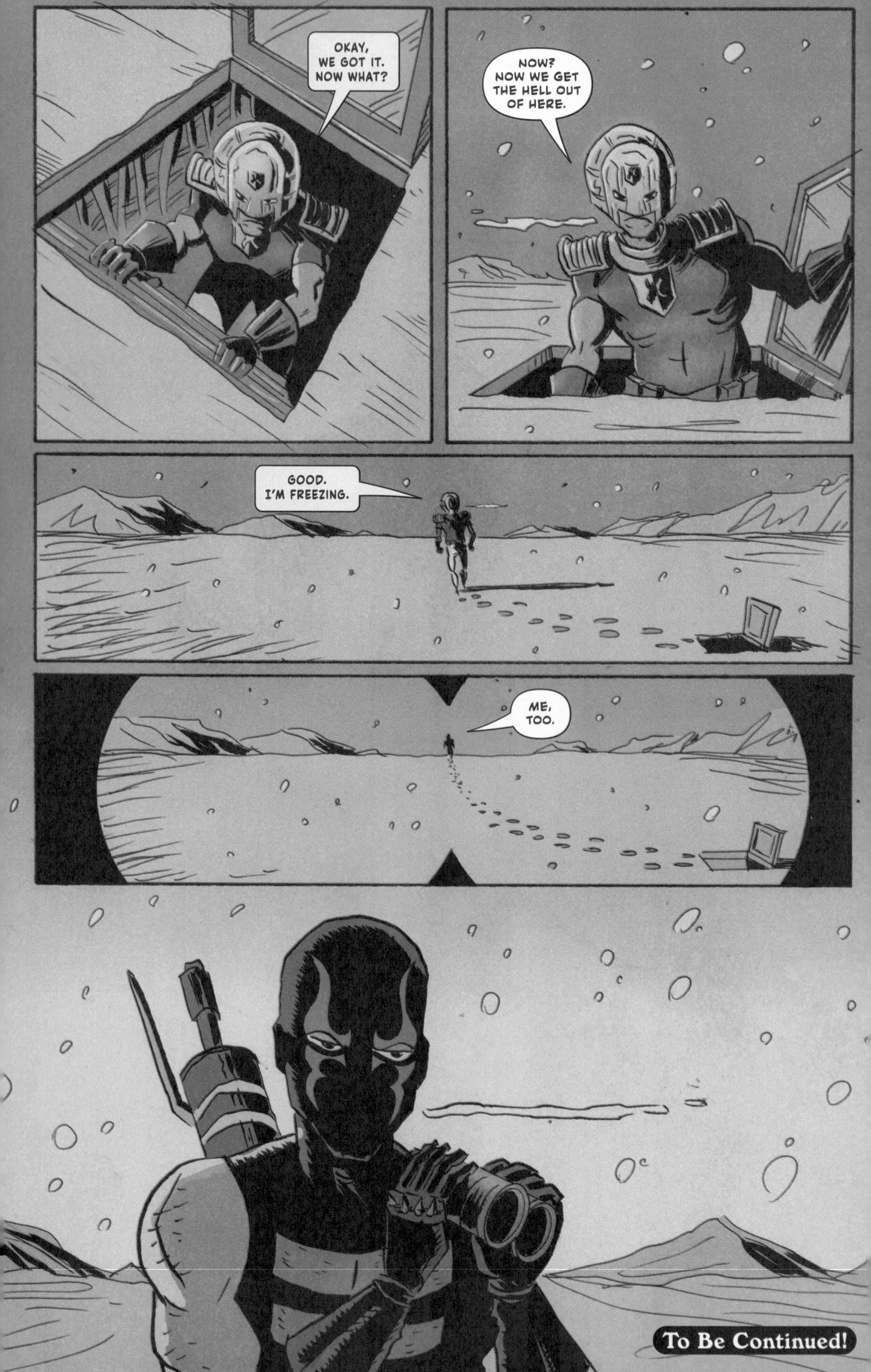
OKAY, WE GOT IT. NOW WHAT?
NOW? NOW WE GET THE HELL OUT OF HERE.
GOOD. I'M FREEZING.
ME, TOO.
To Be Continued!

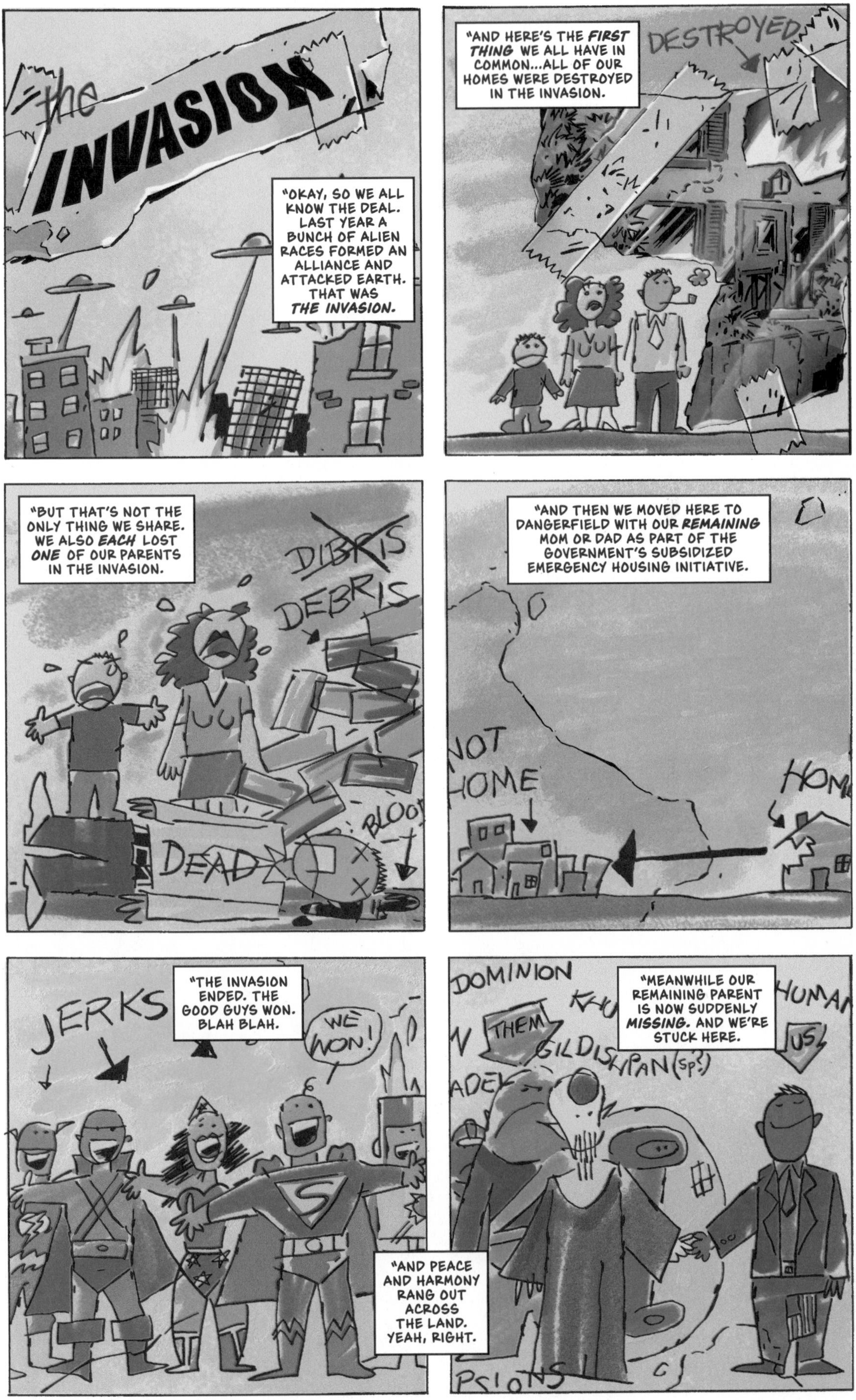
the INVASION
"OKAY, SO WE ALL KNOW THE DEAL. LAST YEAR A BUNCH OF ALIEN RACES FORMED AN ALLIANCE AND ATTACKED EARTH. THAT WAS *THE INVASION.*
"AND HERE'S THE *FIRST THING* WE ALL HAVE IN COMMON...ALL OF OUR HOMES WERE DESTROYED IN THE INVASION.
DESTROYED
"BUT THAT'S NOT THE ONLY THING WE SHARE. WE ALSO *EACH* LOST *ONE* OF OUR PARENTS IN THE INVASION.
DIBRIS
DEBRIS
DEAD
BLOOD
"AND THEN WE MOVED HERE TO DANGERFIELD WITH OUR *REMAINING* MOM OR DAD AS PART OF THE GOVERNMENT'S SUBSIDIZED EMERGENCY HOUSING INITIATIVE.
NOT HOME
HOME
JERKS
"THE INVASION ENDED. THE GOOD GUYS WON. BLAH BLAH.
WE WON!
"AND PEACE AND HARMONY RANG OUT ACROSS THE LAND. YEAH, RIGHT.
DOMINION
THEM
GILDISHPAN (sp?)
"MEANWHILE OUR REMAINING PARENT IS NOW SUDDENLY *MISSING.* AND WE'RE STUCK HERE.
US
PSIONS

INFERIOR5

KEITH GIFFEN Plot and Pencils
JEFF LEMIRE Plot and Script
MICHELLE DELECKI Inker
HI-FI Colorists **ROB LEIGH** Letterer
GIFFEN/DELECKI/HI-FI Cover
MICHAEL McCALISTER Assistant Editor
MARIE JAVINS Group Editor
JOEY CAVALIERI Awkwardman

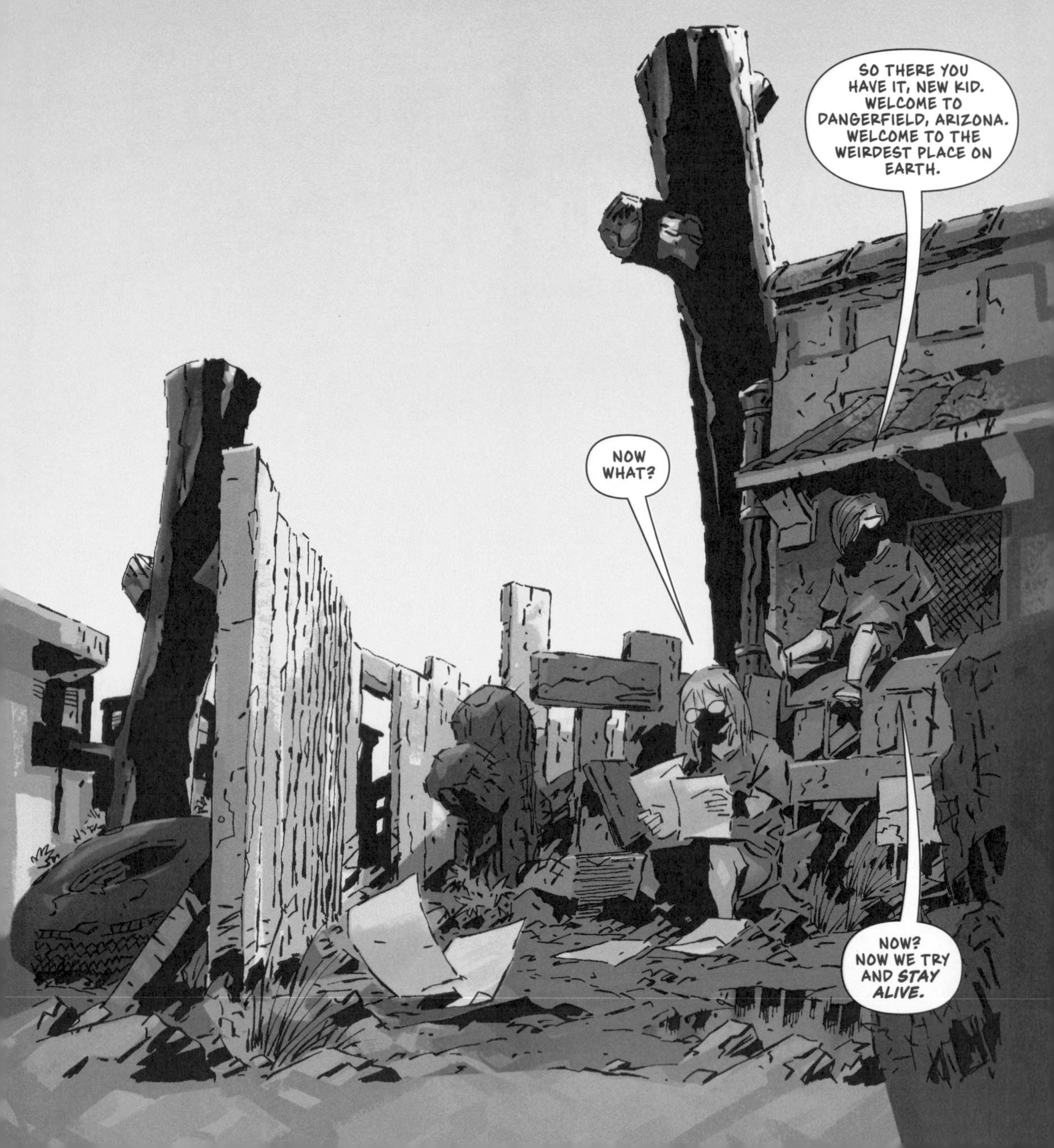
SO THERE YOU HAVE IT, NEW KID. WELCOME TO DANGERFIELD, ARIZONA. WELCOME TO THE WEIRDEST PLACE ON EARTH.
NOW WHAT?
NOW? NOW WE TRY AND STAY ALIVE.

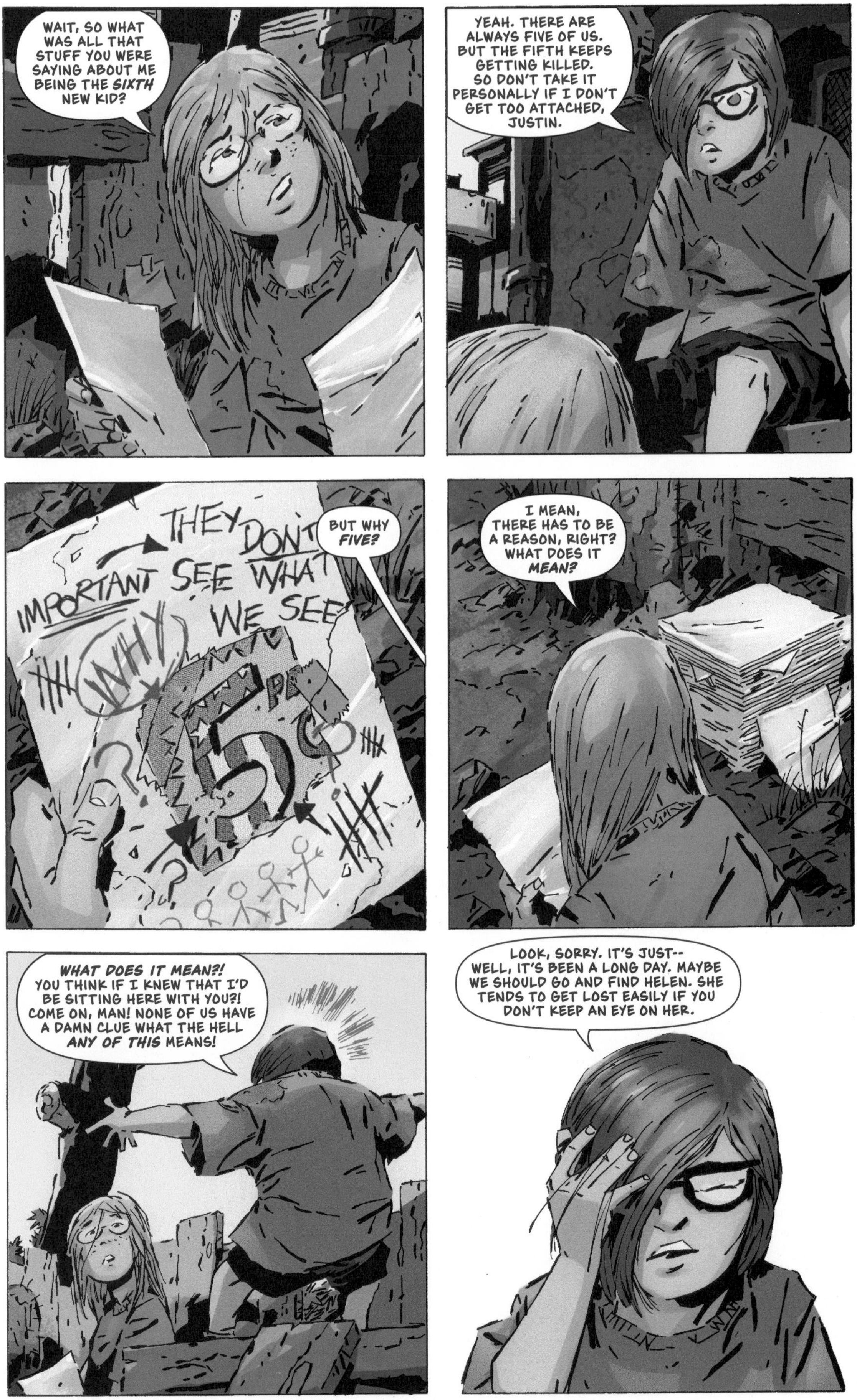
WAIT, SO WHAT WAS ALL THAT STUFF YOU WERE SAYING ABOUT ME BEING THE *SIXTH* NEW KID?
YEAH. THERE ARE ALWAYS FIVE OF US. BUT THE FIFTH KEEPS GETTING KILLED. SO DON'T TAKE IT PERSONALLY IF I DON'T GET TOO ATTACHED, JUSTIN.
THEY DON'T
IMPORTANT SEE WHAT
WE SEE
WHY
5
BUT WHY *FIVE?*
I MEAN, THERE HAS TO BE A REASON, RIGHT? WHAT DOES IT *MEAN?*
WHAT DOES IT MEAN?! YOU THINK IF I KNEW THAT I'D BE SITTING HERE WITH YOU?! COME ON, MAN! NONE OF US HAVE A DAMN CLUE WHAT THE HELL *ANY OF THIS* MEANS!
LOOK, SORRY. IT'S JUST-- WELL, IT'S BEEN A LONG DAY. MAYBE WE SHOULD GO AND FIND HELEN. SHE TENDS TO GET LOST EASILY IF YOU DON'T KEEP AN EYE ON HER.

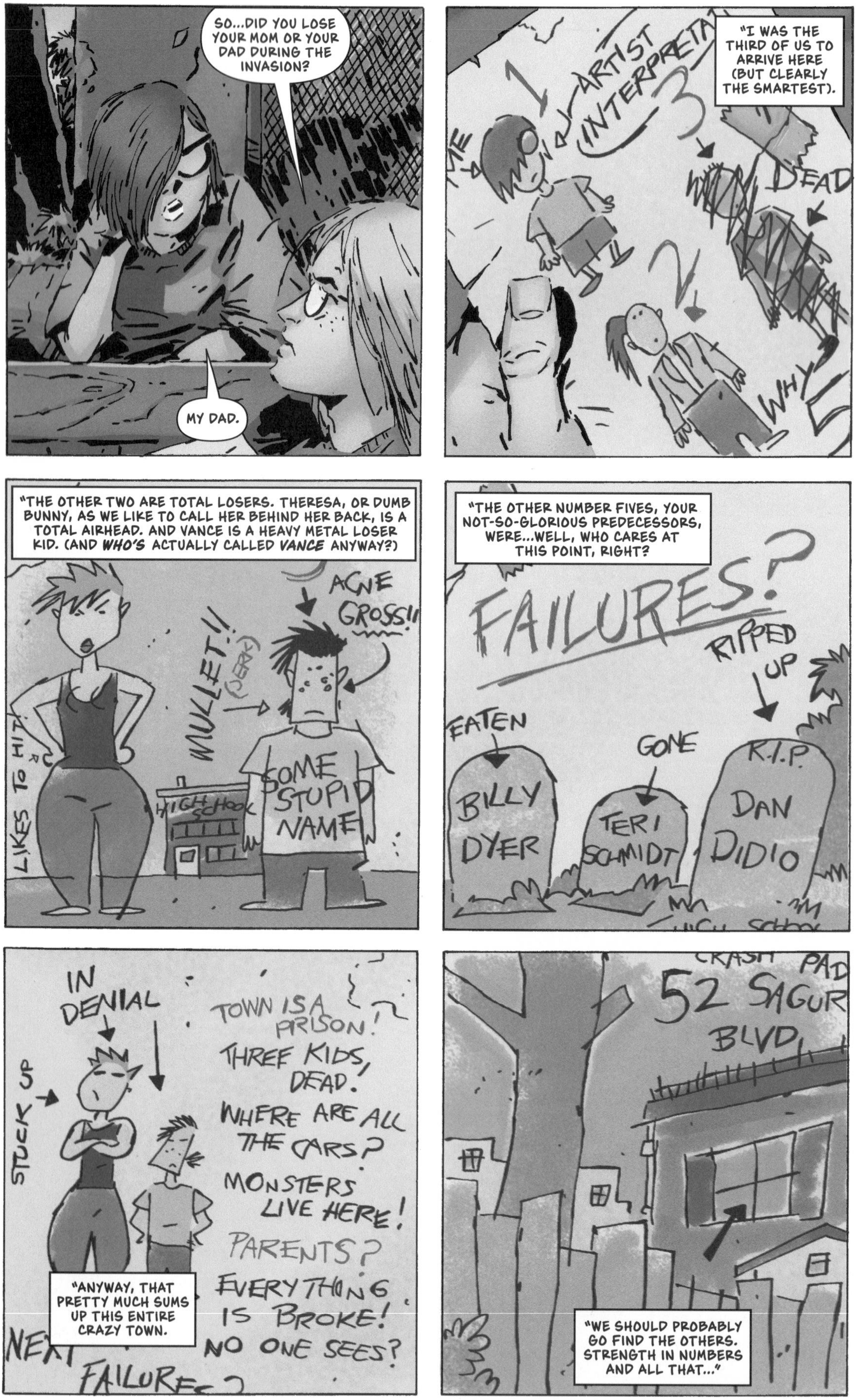
SO...DID YOU LOSE YOUR MOM OR YOUR DAD DURING THE INVASION?
MY DAD.
"I WAS THE THIRD OF US TO ARRIVE HERE (BUT CLEARLY THE SMARTEST).
ARTIST INTERPRETAT
ME
1
3
2
DEAD
WHY
"THE OTHER TWO ARE TOTAL LOSERS. THERESA, OR DUMB BUNNY, AS WE LIKE TO CALL HER BEHIND HER BACK, IS A TOTAL AIRHEAD. AND VANCE IS A HEAVY METAL LOSER KID. (AND *WHO'S* ACTUALLY CALLED *VANCE* ANYWAY?)
ACNE GROSS!!
MULLET!!
LIKES TO HIT
HIGH SCHOOL
SOME STUPID NAME
"THE OTHER NUMBER FIVES, YOUR NOT-SO-GLORIOUS PREDECESSORS, WERE...WELL, WHO CARES AT THIS POINT, RIGHT?
FAILURES?
RIPPED UP
EATEN
GONE
R.I.P.
BILLY DYER
TERI SCHMIDT
DAN DIDIO
IN DENIAL
STUCK UP
TOWN IS A PRISON!
THREE KIDS, DEAD.
WHERE ARE ALL THE CARS?
MONSTERS LIVE HERE!
PARENTS?
EVERYTHING IS BROKE!
NO ONE SEES?
"ANYWAY, THAT PRETTY MUCH SUMS UP THIS ENTIRE CRAZY TOWN.
52 SAGUR BLVD
"WE SHOULD PROBABLY GO FIND THE OTHERS. STRENGTH IN NUMBERS AND ALL THAT..."

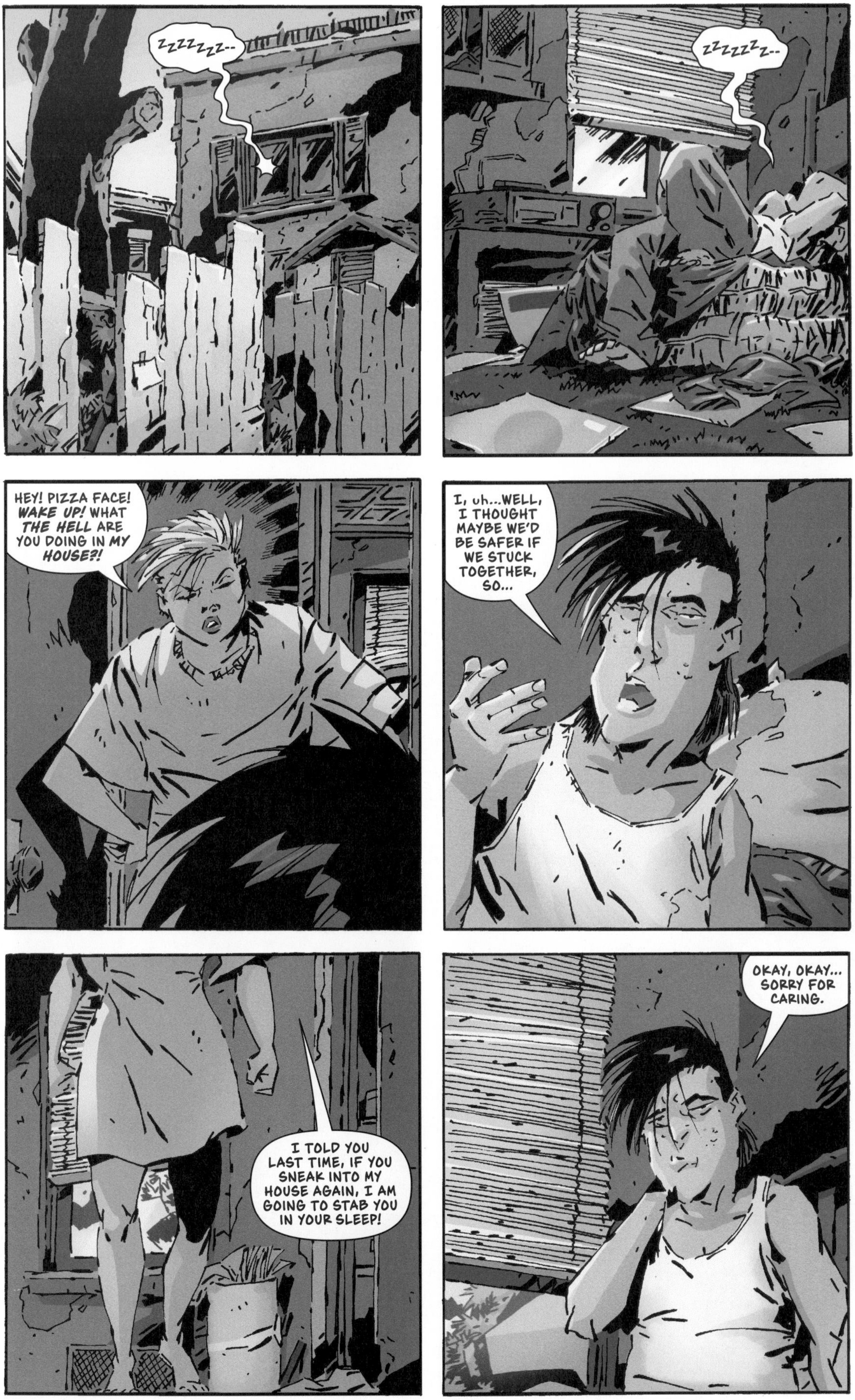
ZZZZZZZ--
ZZZZZZZ--
HEY! PIZZA FACE! WAKE UP! WHAT THE HELL ARE YOU DOING IN MY HOUSE?!
I, uh...WELL, I THOUGHT MAYBE WE'D BE SAFER IF WE STUCK TOGETHER, SO...
I TOLD YOU LAST TIME, IF YOU SNEAK INTO MY HOUSE AGAIN, I AM GOING TO STAB YOU IN YOUR SLEEP!
OKAY, OKAY... SORRY FOR CARING.

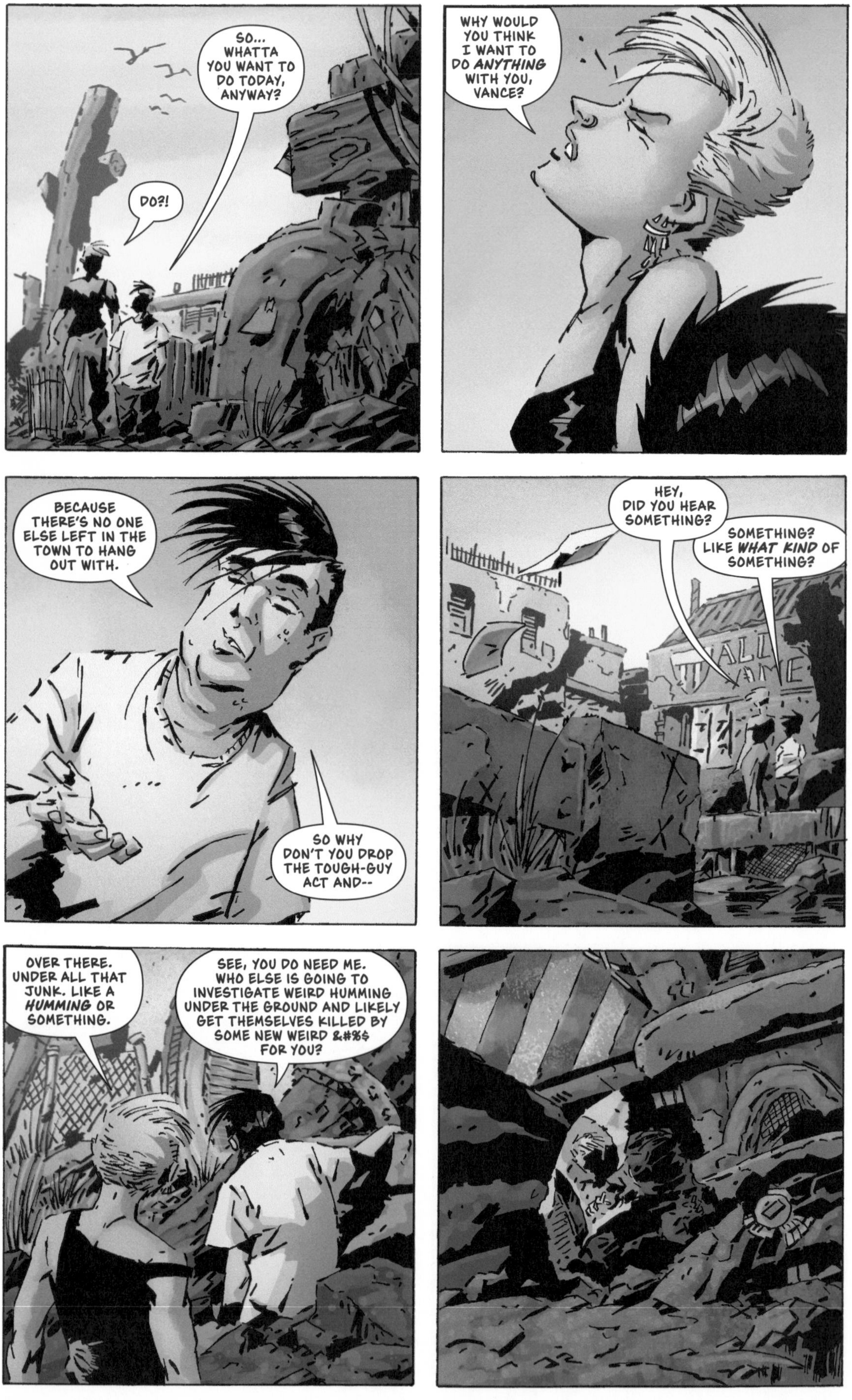
SO... WHATTA YOU WANT TO DO TODAY, ANYWAY?
DO?!
WHY WOULD YOU THINK I WANT TO DO *ANYTHING* WITH YOU, VANCE?
BECAUSE THERE'S NO ONE ELSE LEFT IN THE TOWN TO HANG OUT WITH.
SO WHY DON'T YOU DROP THE TOUGH-GUY ACT AND--
HEY, DID YOU HEAR SOMETHING?
SOMETHING? LIKE *WHAT KIND* OF SOMETHING?
OVER THERE. UNDER ALL THAT JUNK. LIKE A *HUMMING* OR SOMETHING.
SEE, YOU DO NEED ME. WHO ELSE IS GOING TO INVESTIGATE WEIRD HUMMING UNDER THE GROUND AND LIKELY GET THEMSELVES KILLED BY SOME NEW WEIRD &#%$ FOR YOU?

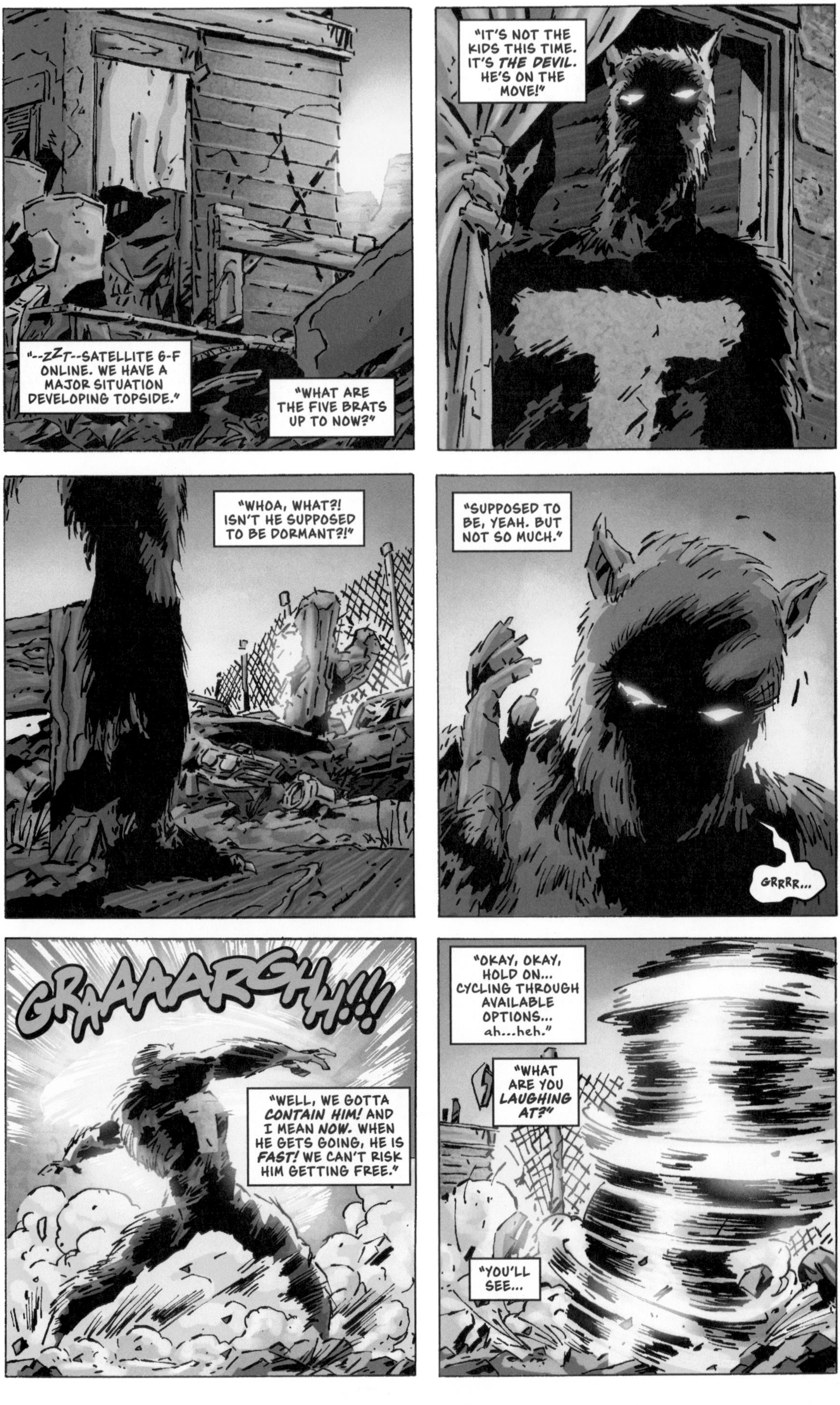
"--ZZT--SATELLITE 6-F ONLINE. WE HAVE A MAJOR SITUATION DEVELOPING TOPSIDE."
"WHAT ARE THE FIVE BRATS UP TO NOW?"
"IT'S NOT THE KIDS THIS TIME. IT'S THE DEVIL. HE'S ON THE MOVE!"
"WHOA, WHAT?! ISN'T HE SUPPOSED TO BE DORMANT?!"
"SUPPOSED TO BE, YEAH. BUT NOT SO MUCH."
GRRRR...
GRAAAARGHH!!!
"WELL, WE GOTTA CONTAIN HIM! AND I MEAN NOW. WHEN HE GETS GOING, HE IS FAST! WE CAN'T RISK HIM GETTING FREE."
"OKAY, OKAY, HOLD ON... CYCLING THROUGH AVAILABLE OPTIONS... ah...heh."
"WHAT ARE YOU LAUGHING AT?"
"YOU'LL SEE...

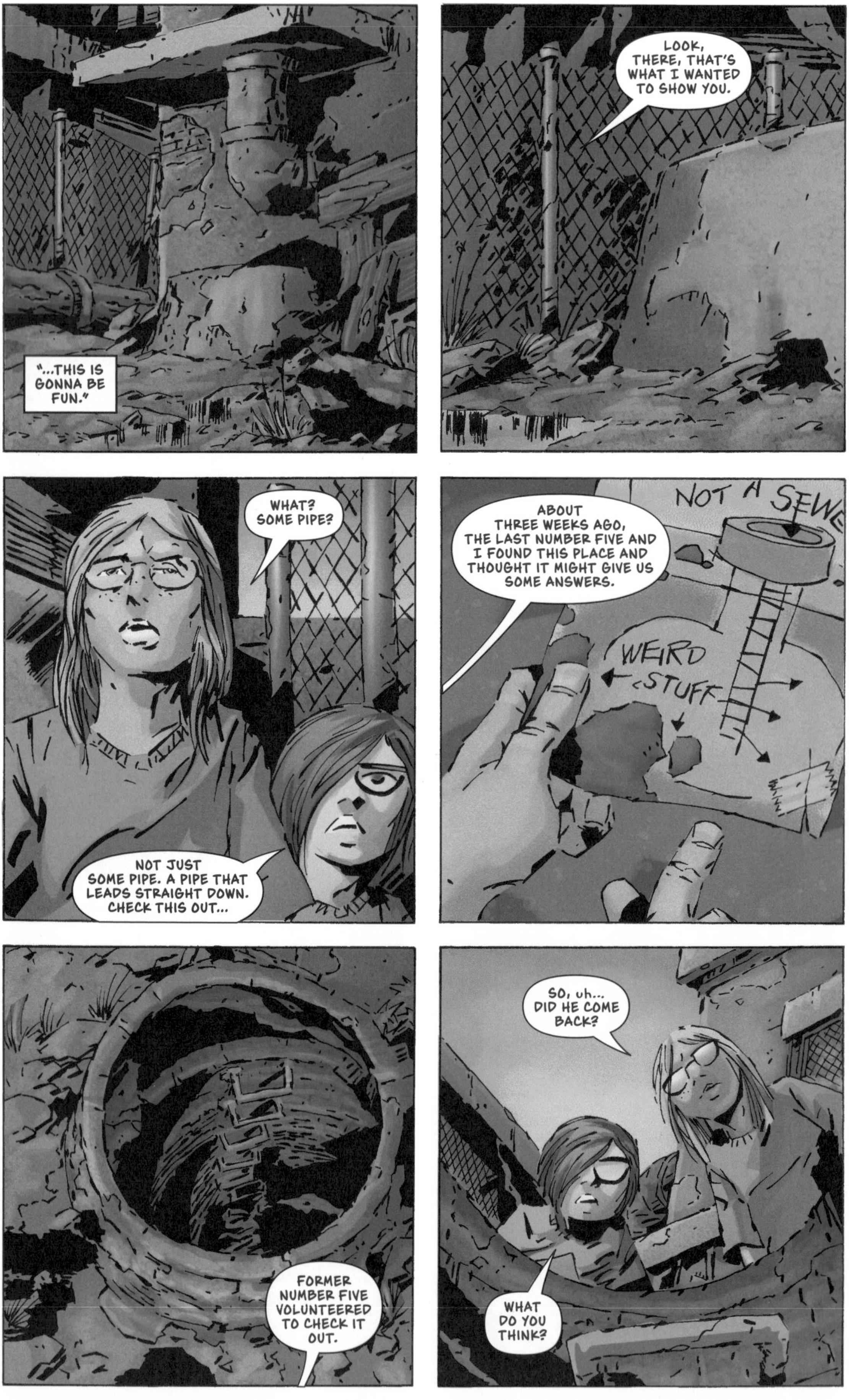
"...THIS IS GONNA BE FUN."
LOOK, THERE, THAT'S WHAT I WANTED TO SHOW YOU.
WHAT? SOME PIPE?
NOT JUST SOME PIPE. A PIPE THAT LEADS STRAIGHT DOWN. CHECK THIS OUT...
ABOUT THREE WEEKS AGO, THE LAST NUMBER FIVE AND I FOUND THIS PLACE AND THOUGHT IT MIGHT GIVE US SOME ANSWERS.
NOT A SEWE
WEIRD STUFF
FORMER NUMBER FIVE VOLUNTEERED TO CHECK IT OUT.
SO, uh... DID HE COME BACK?
WHAT DO YOU THINK?

HOLD ON... YEAH, HERE THEY ARE.

I LEAVE MY JOURNALS CACHED ALL OVER THE PLACE. FIGURE IF SOMETHING HAPPENS TO ME, AT LEAST THERE WILL BE SOME RECORD OF IT LEFT BEHIND FOR THE NEXT KIDS.

SO, THE LAST VERSION OF ME... WHAT *WAS* HIS NAME?

DEREK.

HE CAME HERE WITH HIS DAD. THEY WERE FROM *TASMANIA*, IF YOU CAN BELIEVE THAT.

ANYWAY. HIS DAD WENT MISSING JUST LIKE OUR PARENTS, AND MR. TASMANIA GOT ALL BRAVE...

DUMB!

NOT A SEWER

DELUSION OF GRANDER

DUMB! DUMB! DUMB!

I MEAN, WE DON'T REALLY KNOW WHAT HAPPENED TO HIM DOWN THERE. JUST HEARD HIM SCREAMING.

ARTIST INTERPITATION

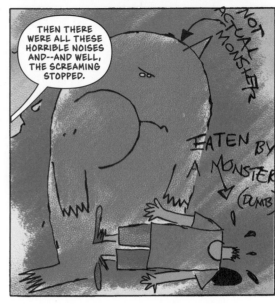

THEN THERE WERE ALL THESE HORRIBLE NOISES AND--AND WELL, THE SCREAMING STOPPED.

NOT ACTUAL MONSTER

EATEN BY A MONSTER (DUMB)

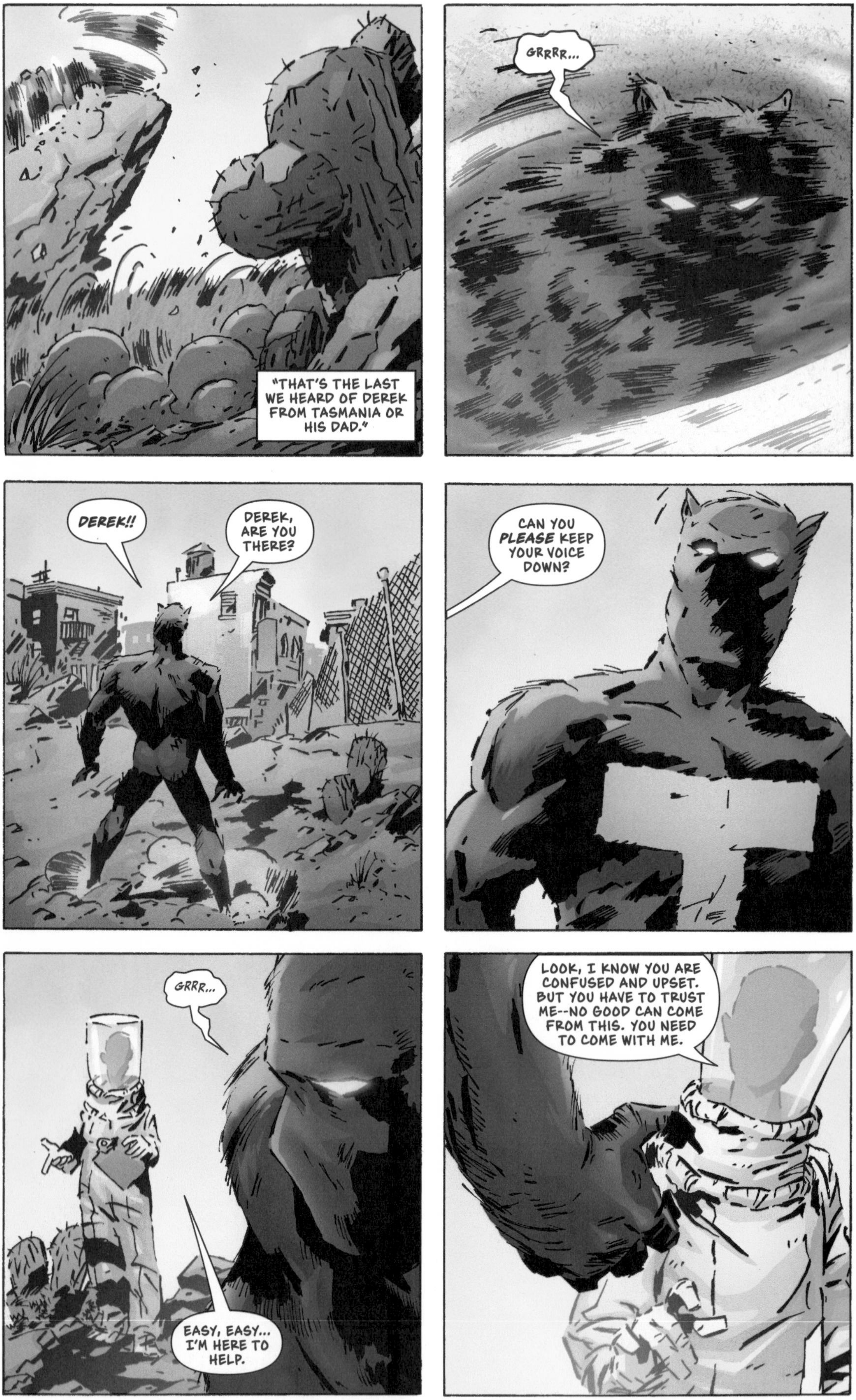
"THAT'S THE LAST WE HEARD OF DEREK FROM TASMANIA OR HIS DAD."
GRRRR...
DEREK!!
DEREK, ARE YOU THERE?
CAN YOU PLEASE KEEP YOUR VOICE DOWN?
GRRR...
EASY, EASY... I'M HERE TO HELP.
LOOK, I KNOW YOU ARE CONFUSED AND UPSET. BUT YOU HAVE TO TRUST ME--NO GOOD CAN COME FROM THIS. YOU NEED TO COME WITH ME.

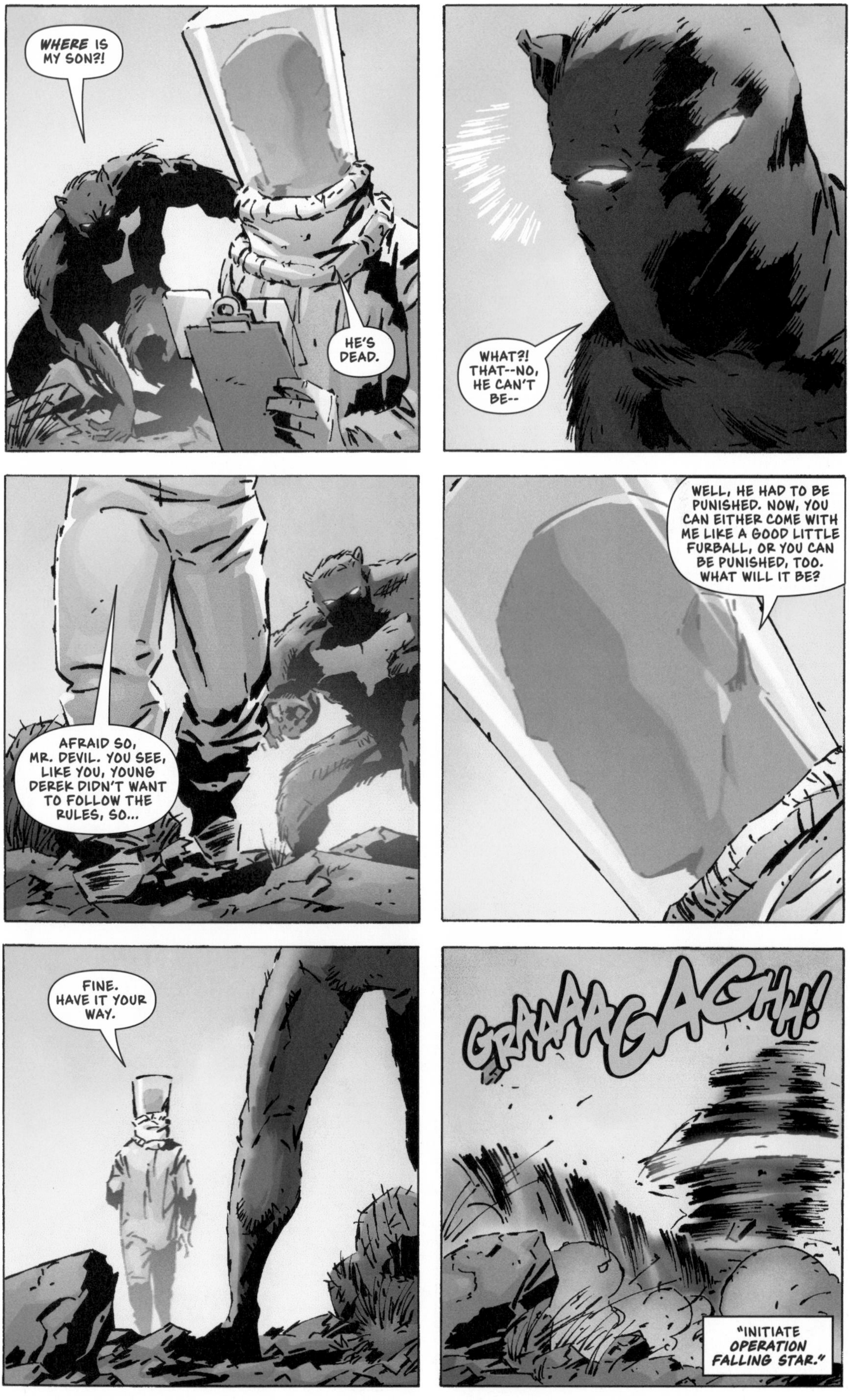
WHERE IS MY SON?!
HE'S DEAD.
WHAT?! THAT--NO, HE CAN'T BE--
AFRAID SO, MR. DEVIL. YOU SEE, LIKE YOU, YOUNG DEREK DIDN'T WANT TO FOLLOW THE RULES, SO...
WELL, HE HAD TO BE PUNISHED. NOW, YOU CAN EITHER COME WITH ME LIKE A GOOD LITTLE FURBALL, OR YOU CAN BE PUNISHED, TOO. WHAT WILL IT BE?
FINE. HAVE IT YOUR WAY.
GRAAAAGAGHH!
"INITIATE OPERATION FALLING STAR."

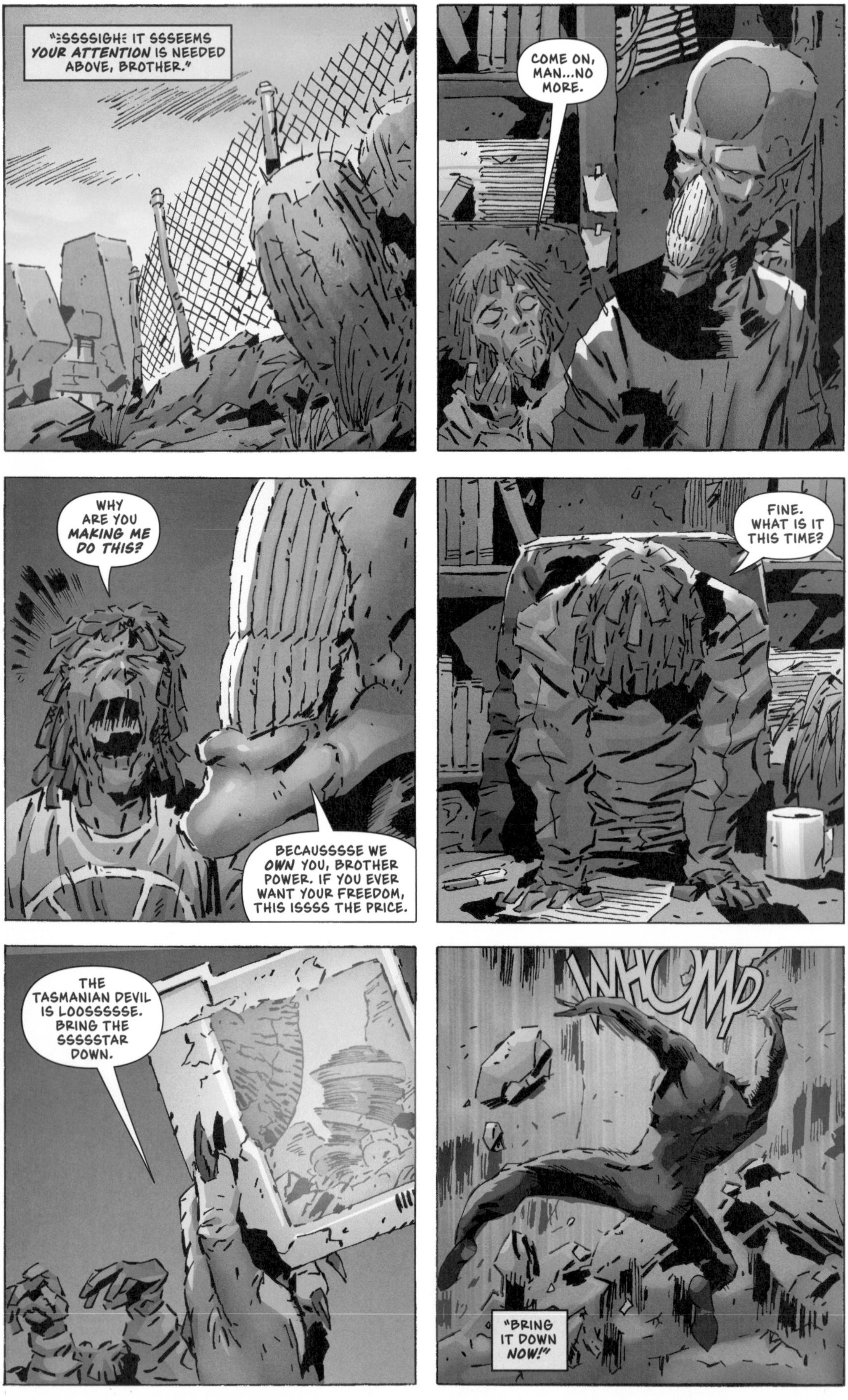
"SSSSIGH: IT SSSEEMS YOUR ATTENTION IS NEEDED ABOVE, BROTHER."
COME ON, MAN...NO MORE.
WHY ARE YOU MAKING ME DO THIS?
BECAUSSSSE WE OWN YOU, BROTHER POWER. IF YOU EVER WANT YOUR FREEDOM, THIS ISSSS THE PRICE.
FINE. WHAT IS IT THIS TIME?
THE TASMANIAN DEVIL IS LOOSSSSSE. BRING THE SSSSSTAR DOWN.
WHOMP
"BRING IT DOWN NOW!"

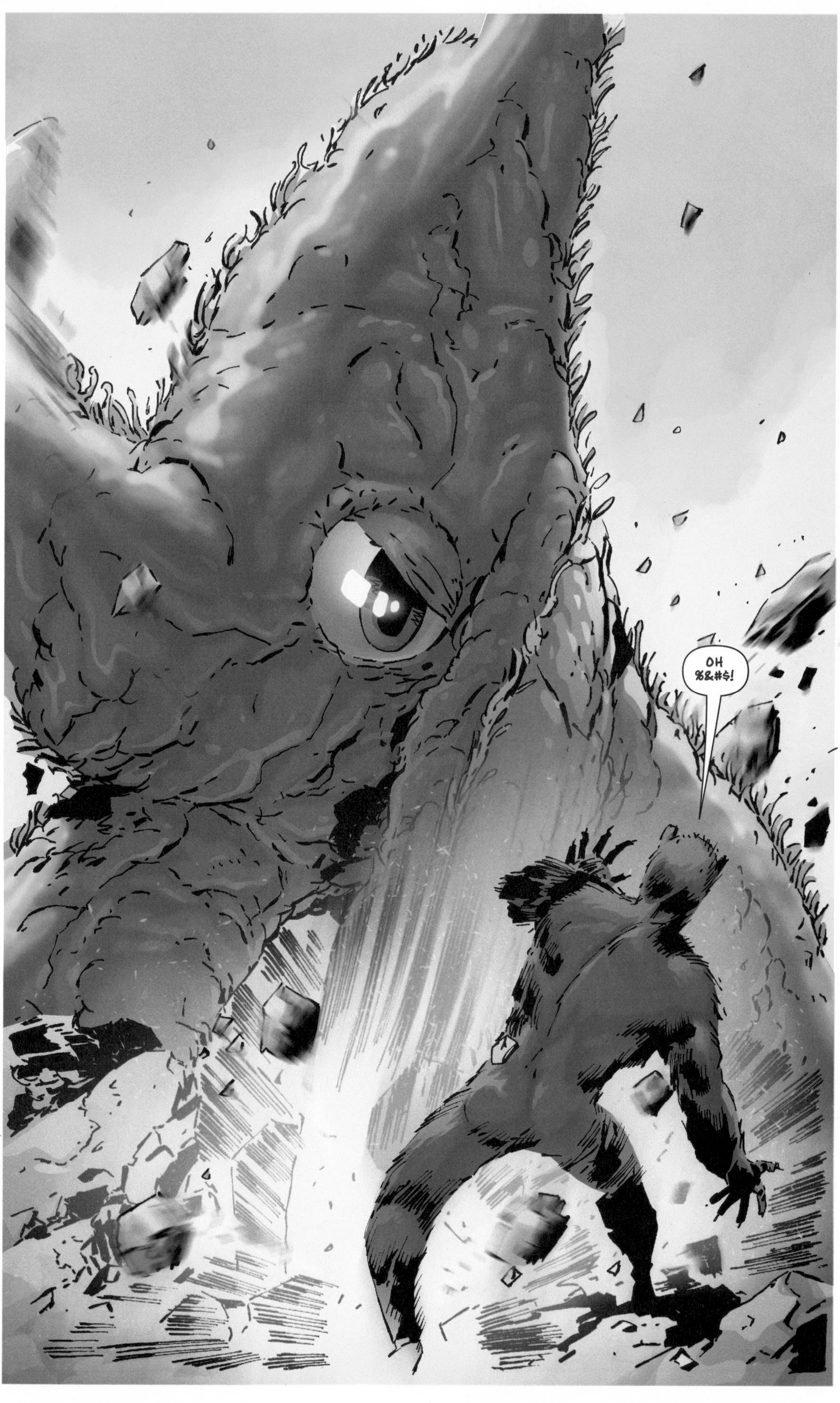
OH %&#$!

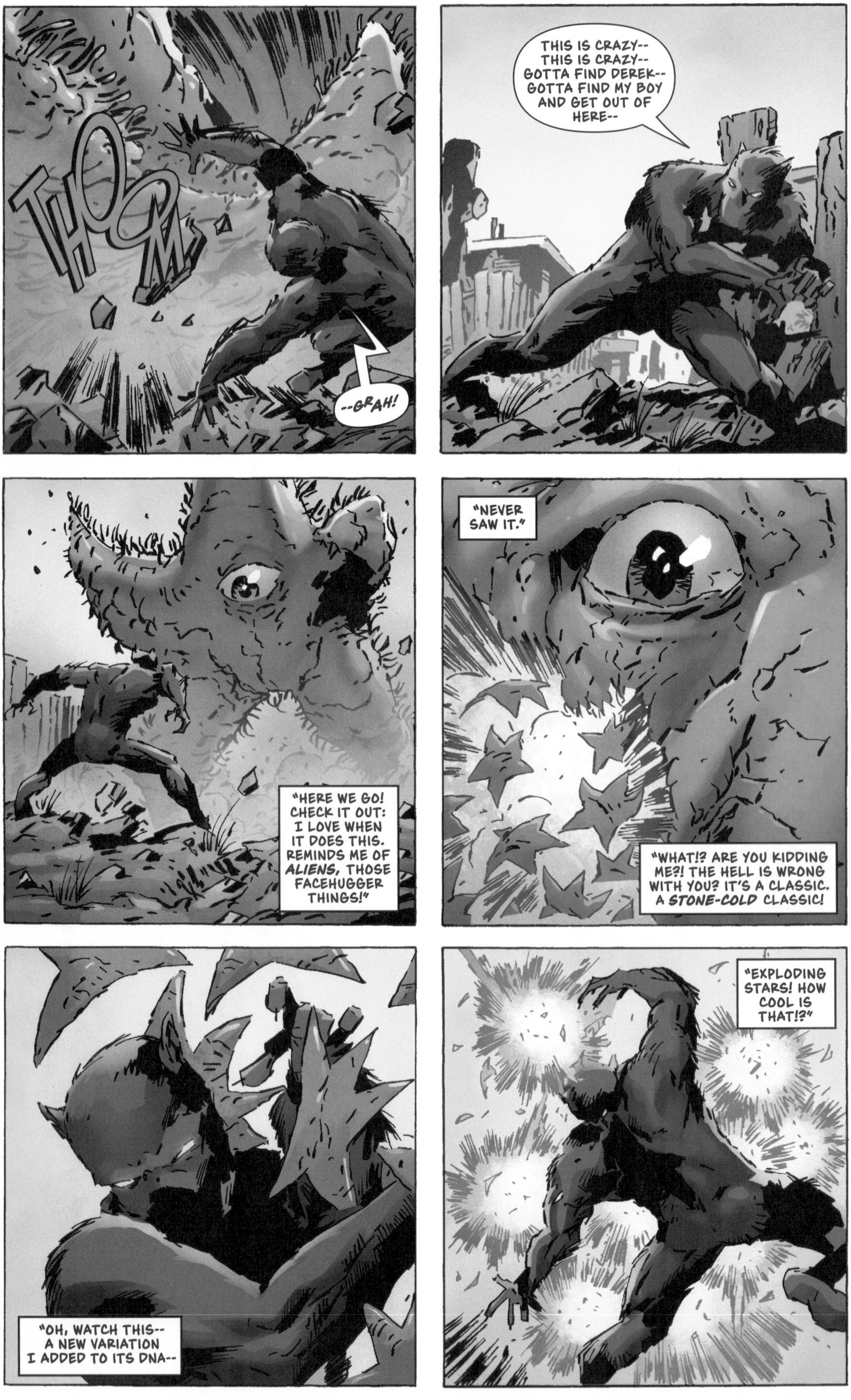
THOOM
--GRAH!
THIS IS CRAZY-- THIS IS CRAZY-- GOTTA FIND DEREK-- GOTTA FIND MY BOY AND GET OUT OF HERE--
"HERE WE GO! CHECK IT OUT: I LOVE WHEN IT DOES THIS. REMINDS ME OF *ALIENS*, THOSE FACEHUGGER THINGS!"
"NEVER SAW IT."
"WHAT!? ARE YOU KIDDING ME?! THE HELL IS WRONG WITH YOU? IT'S A CLASSIC. A *STONE-COLD* CLASSIC!
"OH, WATCH THIS-- A NEW VARIATION I ADDED TO ITS DNA--
"EXPLODING STARS! HOW COOL IS THAT!?"

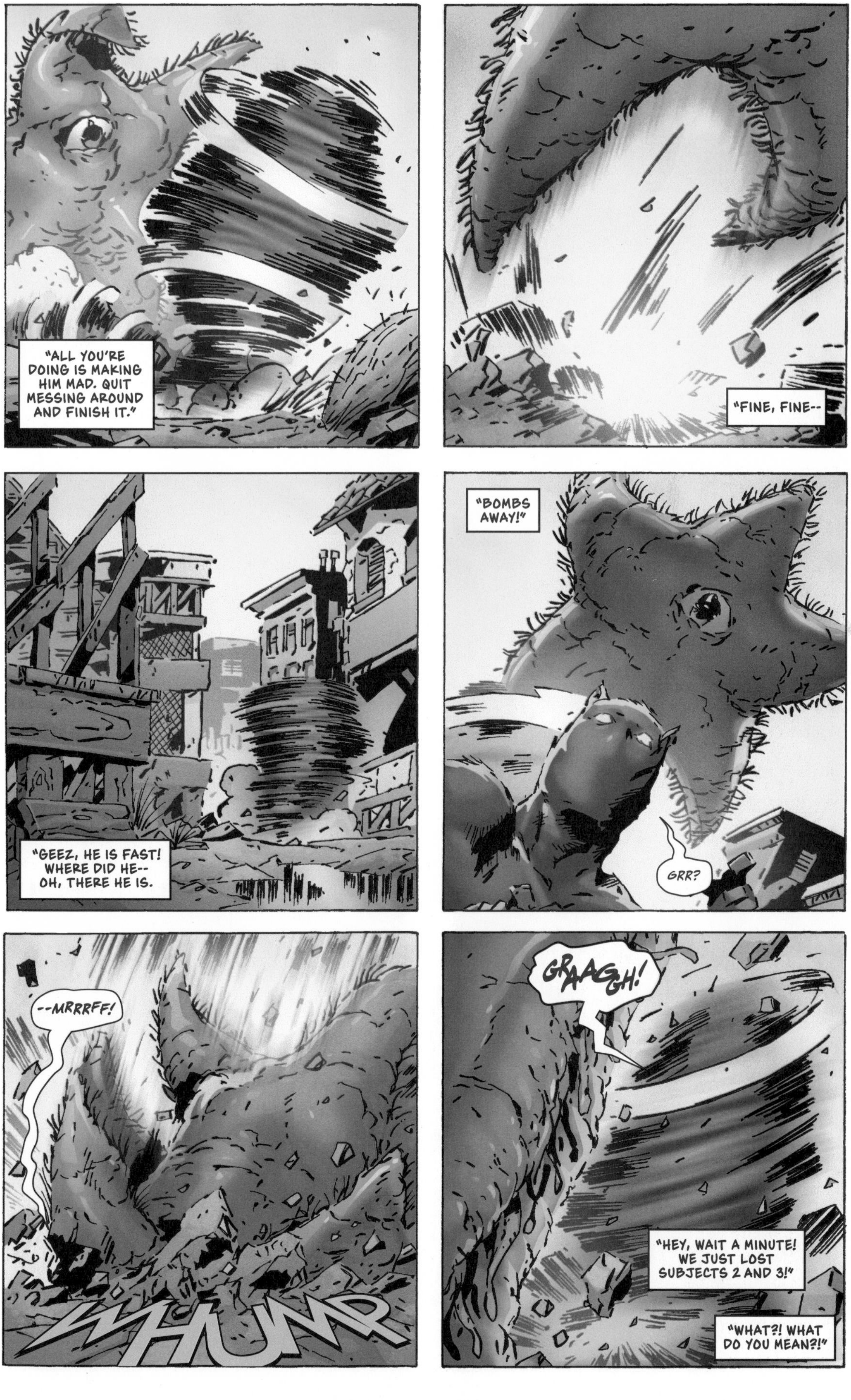
"ALL YOU'RE DOING IS MAKING HIM MAD. QUIT MESSING AROUND AND FINISH IT."
"FINE, FINE--
"GEEZ, HE IS FAST! WHERE DID HE-- OH, THERE HE IS.
"BOMBS AWAY!"
GRR?
--MRRRFF!
WHUMP
GRAAGGH!
"HEY, WAIT A MINUTE! WE JUST LOST SUBJECTS 2 AND 3!"
"WHAT?! WHAT DO YOU MEAN?!"

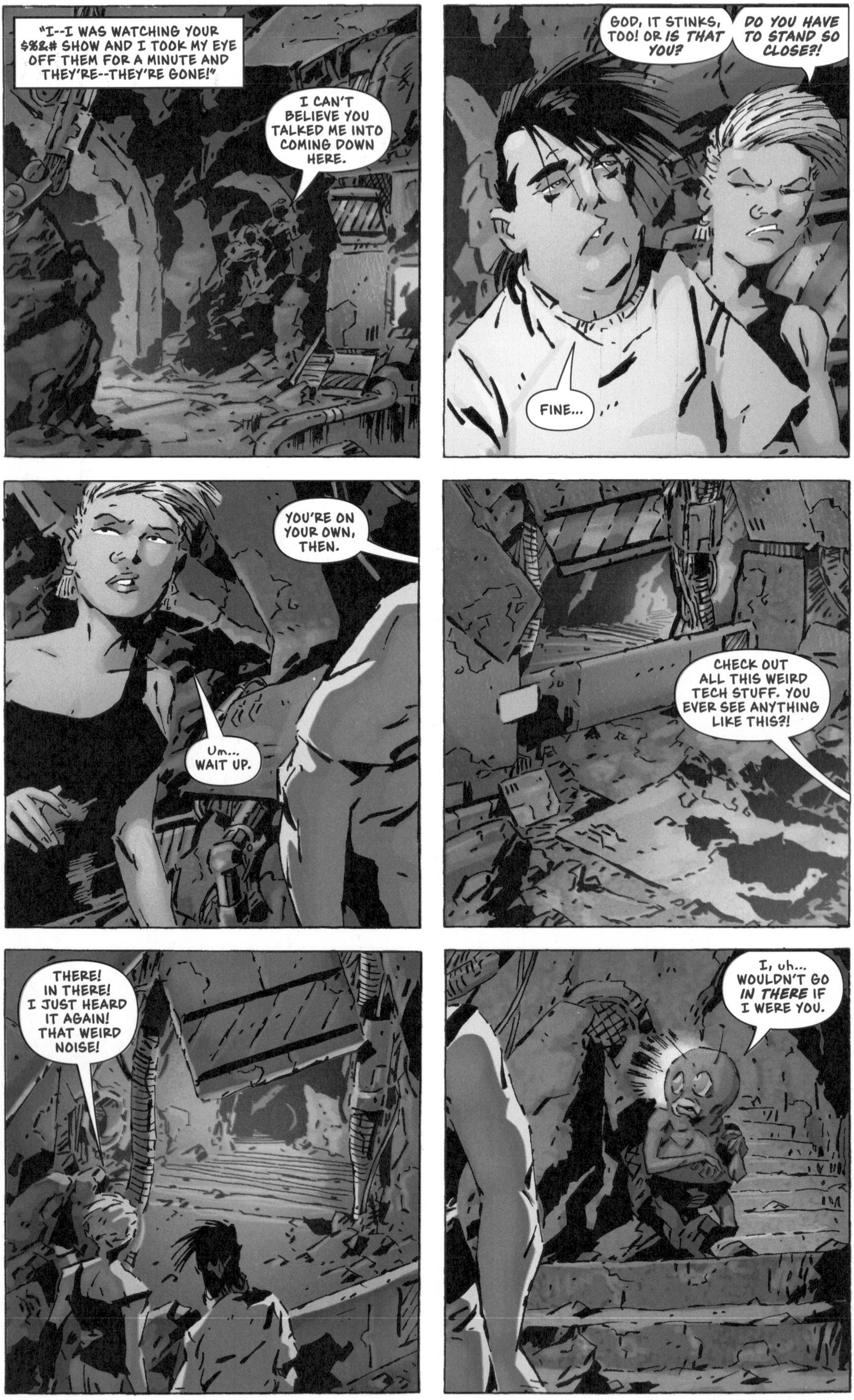
"I--I WAS WATCHING YOUR $%&# SHOW AND I TOOK MY EYE OFF THEM FOR A MINUTE AND THEY'RE--THEY'RE GONE!"
I CAN'T BELIEVE YOU TALKED ME INTO COMING DOWN HERE.
GOD, IT STINKS, TOO! OR IS THAT YOU?
DO YOU HAVE TO STAND SO CLOSE?!
FINE...
YOU'RE ON YOUR OWN, THEN.
UM... WAIT UP.
CHECK OUT ALL THIS WEIRD TECH STUFF. YOU EVER SEE ANYTHING LIKE THIS?!
THERE! IN THERE! I JUST HEARD IT AGAIN! THAT WEIRD NOISE!
I, UH... WOULDN'T GO IN THERE IF I WERE YOU.

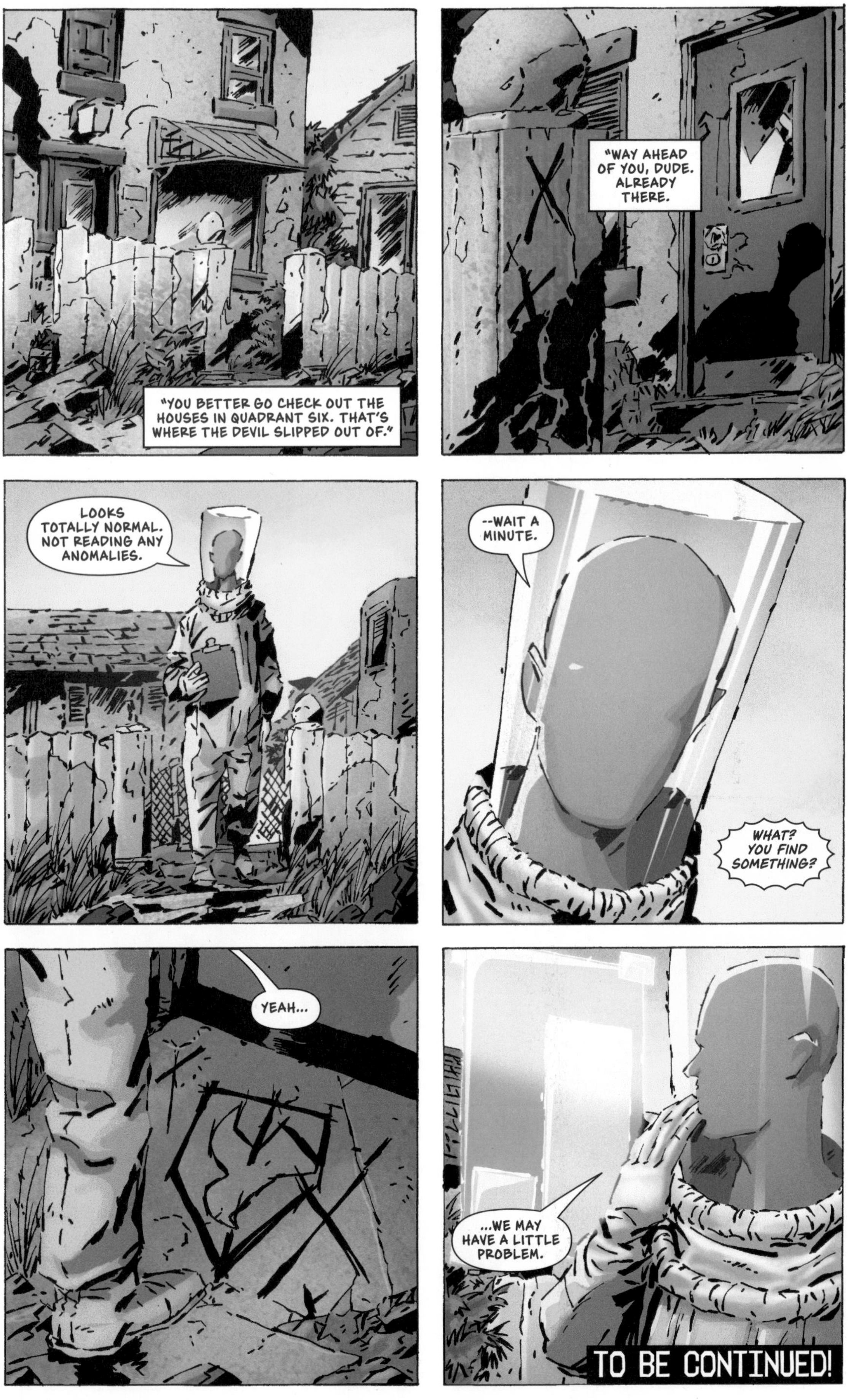
"YOU BETTER GO CHECK OUT THE HOUSES IN QUADRANT SIX. THAT'S WHERE THE DEVIL SLIPPED OUT OF."
"WAY AHEAD OF YOU, DUDE. ALREADY THERE.
LOOKS TOTALLY NORMAL. NOT READING ANY ANOMALIES.
--WAIT A MINUTE.
WHAT? YOU FIND SOMETHING?
YEAH...
...WE MAY HAVE A LITTLE PROBLEM.
TO BE CONTINUED!

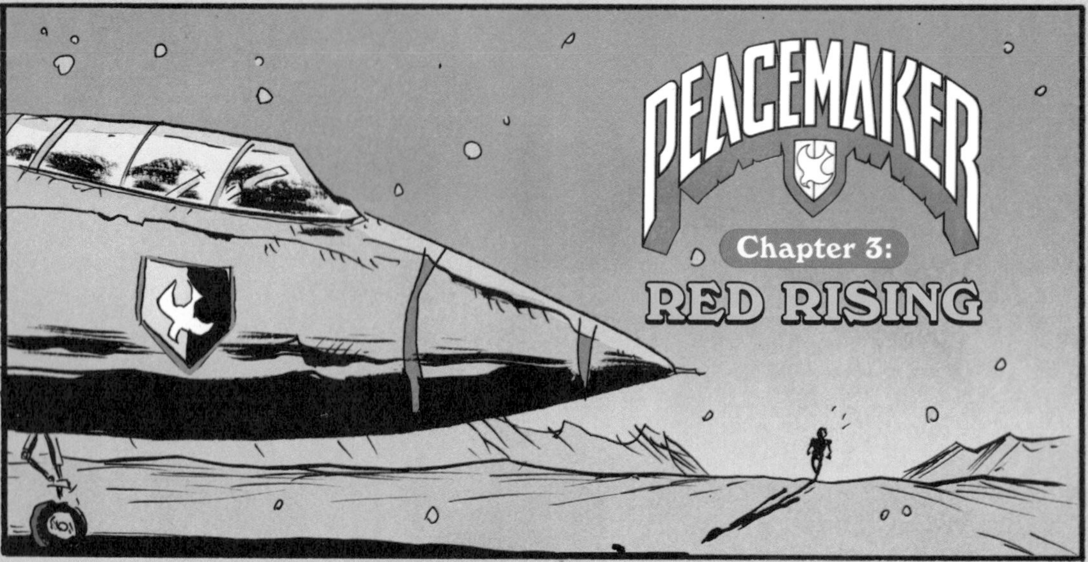
PEACEMAKER
Chapter 3:
RED RISING

Story & Art by JEFF LEMIRE • JOSÉ VILLARRUBIA, *Colorist* • ROB LEIGH, *Letterer*

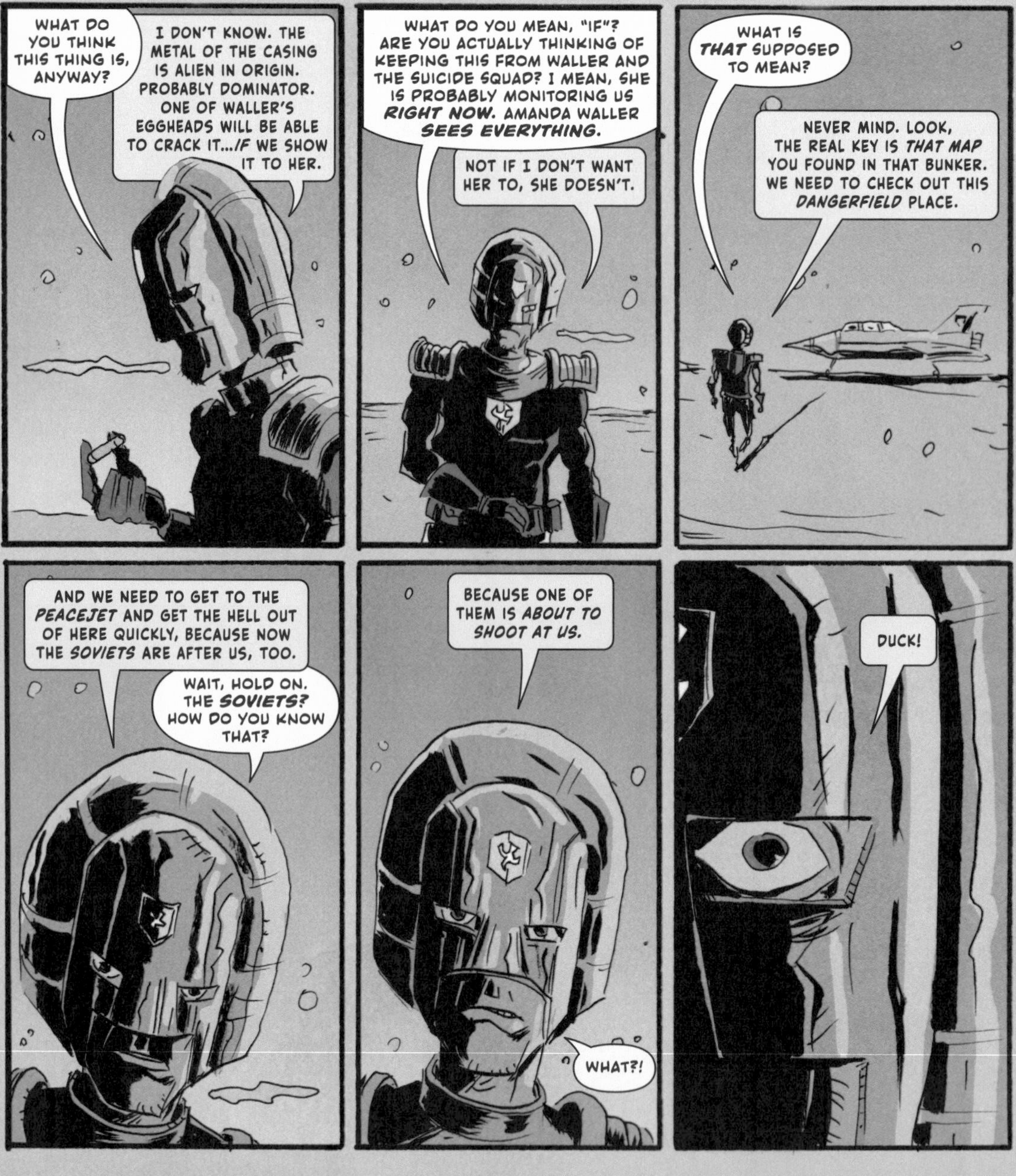
WHAT DO YOU THINK THIS THING IS, ANYWAY?
I DON'T KNOW. THE METAL OF THE CASING IS ALIEN IN ORIGIN. PROBABLY DOMINATOR. ONE OF WALLER'S EGGHEADS WILL BE ABLE TO CRACK IT...*IF* WE SHOW IT TO HER.
WHAT DO YOU MEAN, "IF"? ARE YOU ACTUALLY THINKING OF KEEPING THIS FROM WALLER AND THE SUICIDE SQUAD? I MEAN, SHE IS PROBABLY MONITORING US ***RIGHT NOW.*** AMANDA WALLER ***SEES EVERYTHING.***
NOT IF I DON'T WANT HER TO, SHE DOESN'T.
WHAT IS ***THAT*** SUPPOSED TO MEAN?
NEVER MIND. LOOK, THE REAL KEY IS *THAT MAP* YOU FOUND IN THAT BUNKER. WE NEED TO CHECK OUT THIS *DANGERFIELD* PLACE.
AND WE NEED TO GET TO THE *PEACEJET* AND GET THE HELL OUT OF HERE QUICKLY, BECAUSE NOW THE *SOVIETS* ARE AFTER US, TOO.
WAIT, HOLD ON. THE ***SOVIETS?*** HOW DO YOU KNOW THAT?
BECAUSE ONE OF THEM IS *ABOUT TO SHOOT AT US.*
WHAT?!
DUCK!

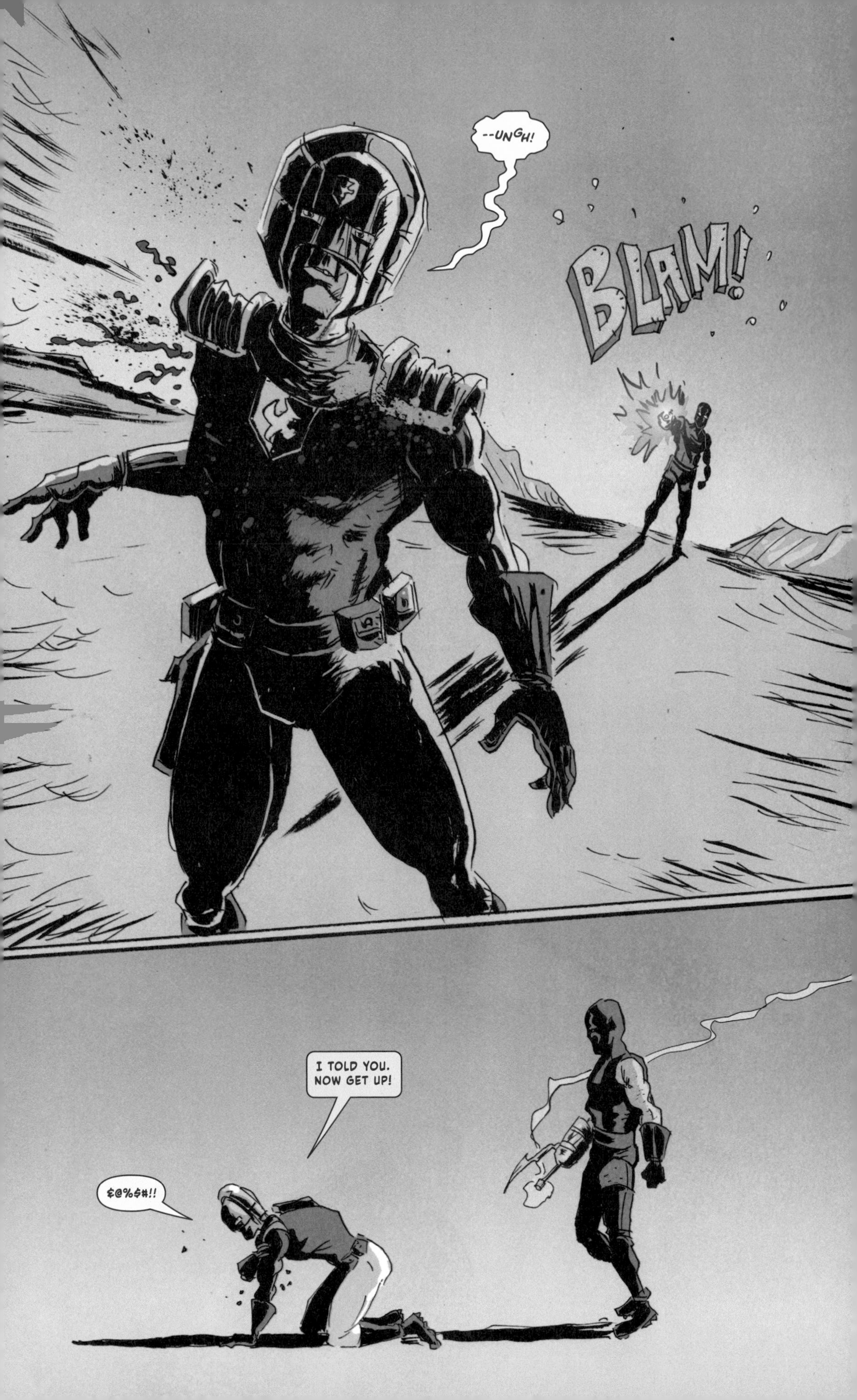
--UNGH!
BLAM!
I TOLD YOU. NOW GET UP!
$@%$#!!

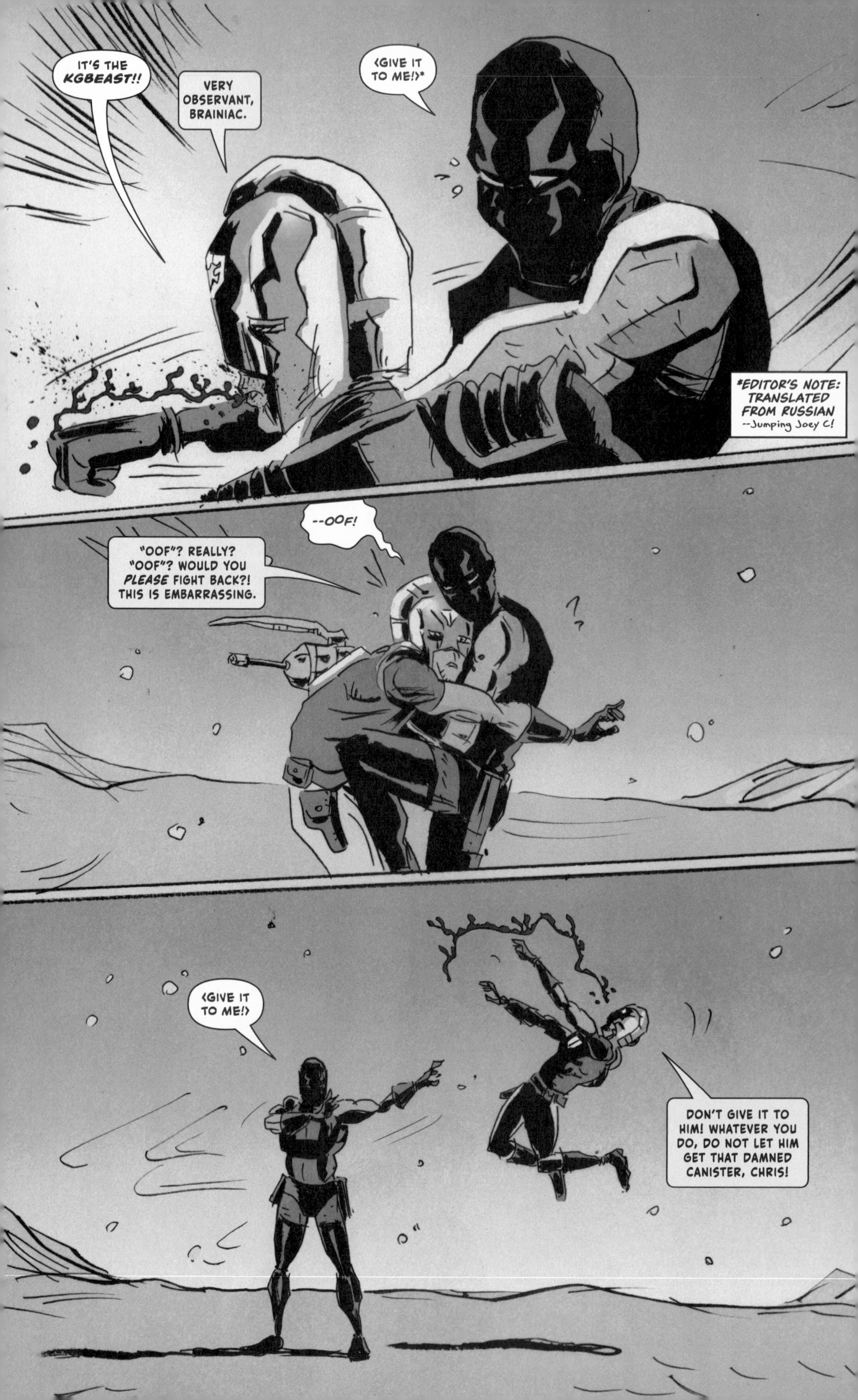
IT'S THE *KGBEAST!!*
VERY OBSERVANT, BRAINIAC.
‹GIVE IT TO ME!›*
*EDITOR'S NOTE: TRANSLATED FROM RUSSIAN --Jumping Joey C!
--OOF!
"OOF"? REALLY? "OOF"? WOULD YOU *PLEASE* FIGHT BACK?! THIS IS EMBARRASSING.
‹GIVE IT TO ME!›
DON'T GIVE IT TO HIM! WHATEVER YOU DO, DO NOT LET HIM GET THAT DAMNED CANISTER, CHRIS!

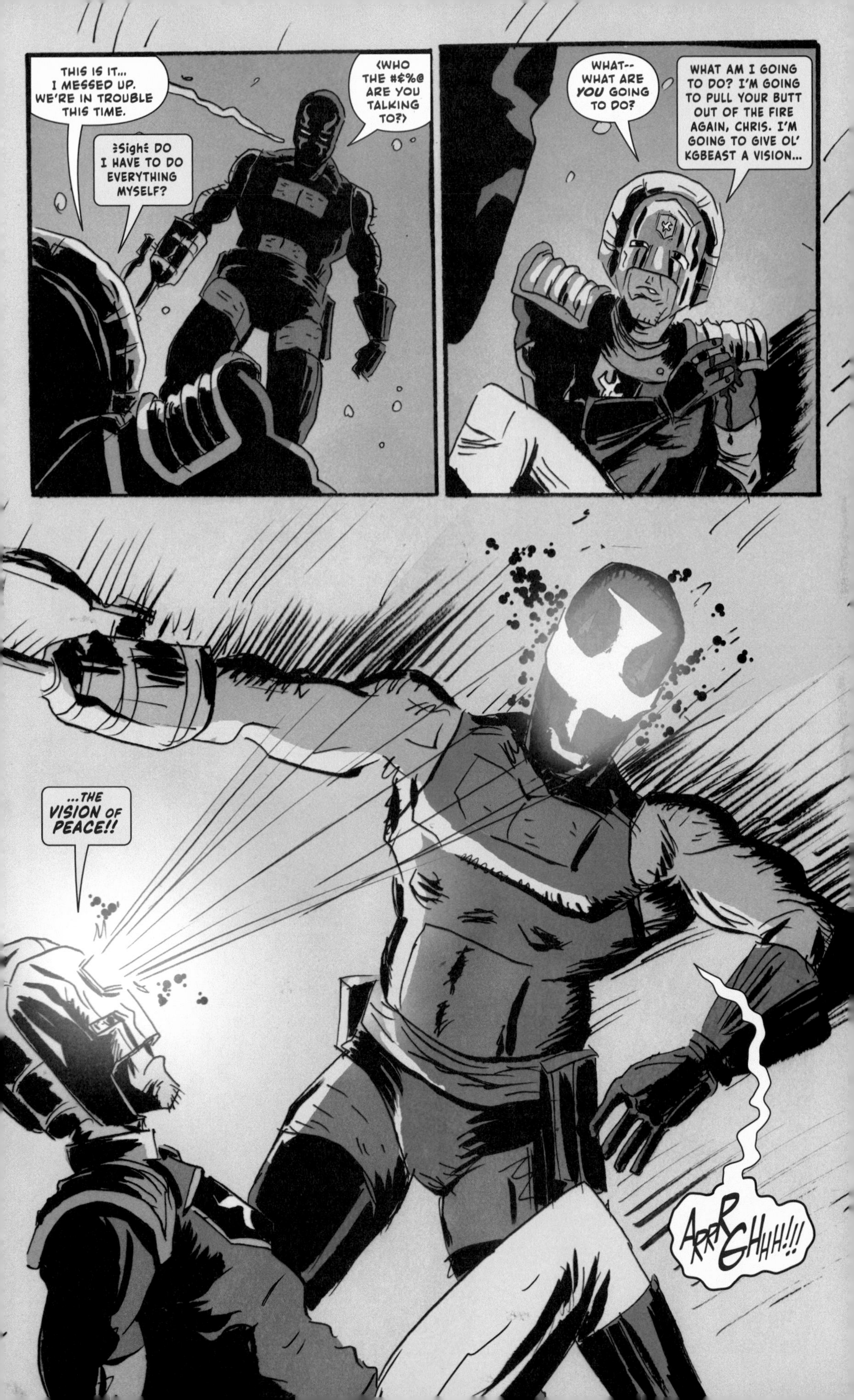
THIS IS IT... I MESSED UP. WE'RE IN TROUBLE THIS TIME.
⁝Sigh⁝ DO I HAVE TO DO EVERYTHING MYSELF?
‹WHO THE #$%@ ARE YOU TALKING TO?›
WHAT-- WHAT ARE YOU GOING TO DO?
WHAT AM I GOING TO DO? I'M GOING TO PULL YOUR BUTT OUT OF THE FIRE AGAIN, CHRIS. I'M GOING TO GIVE OL' KGBEAST A VISION...
...THE VISION OF PEACE!!
ARRRGHHH!!!

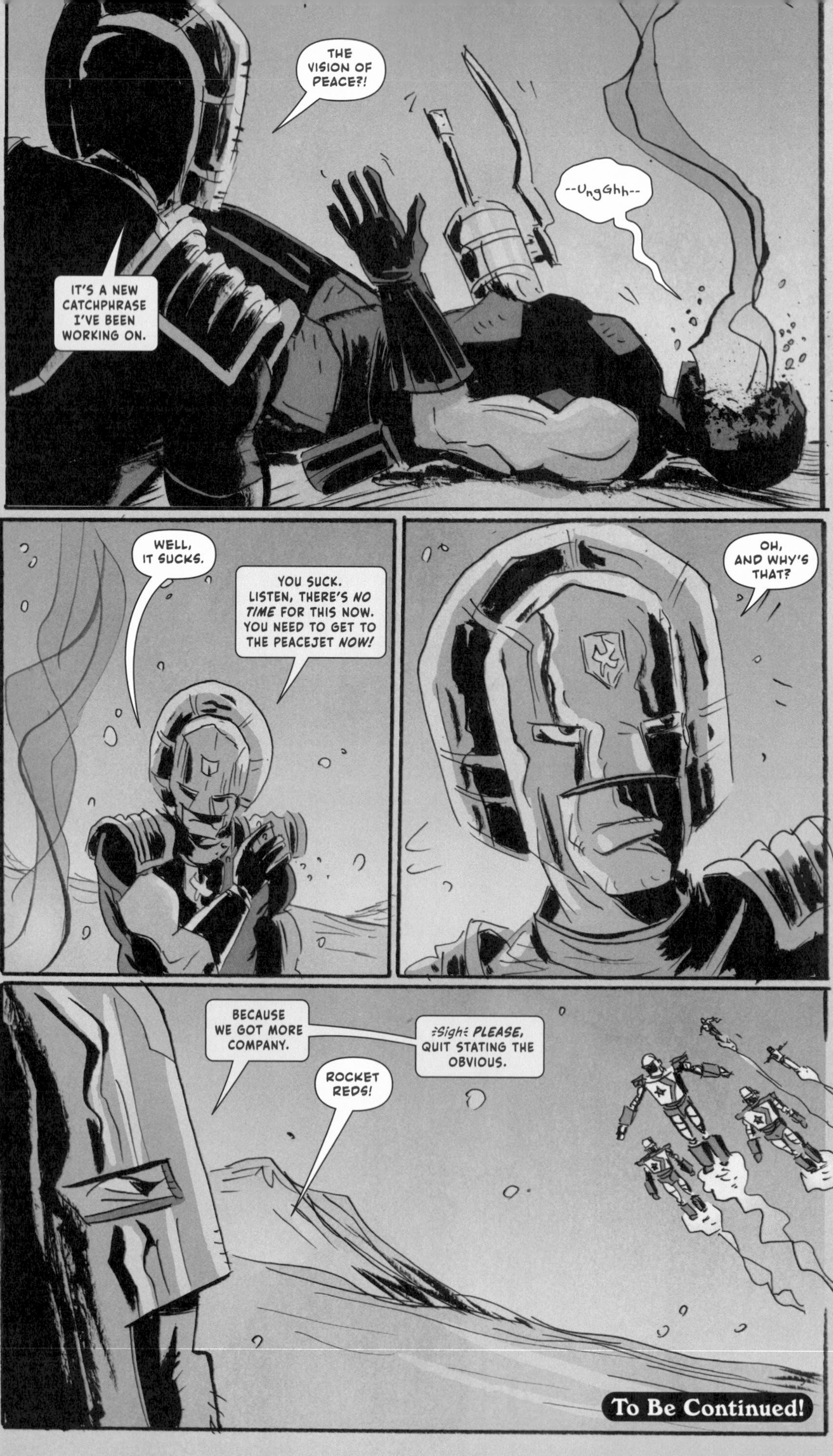
THE VISION OF PEACE?!
IT'S A NEW CATCHPHRASE I'VE BEEN WORKING ON.
--UngGhh--
WELL, IT SUCKS.
YOU SUCK. LISTEN, THERE'S *NO TIME* FOR THIS NOW. YOU NEED TO GET TO THE PEACEJET *NOW!*
OH, AND WHY'S THAT?
BECAUSE WE GOT MORE COMPANY.
ROCKET REDS!
Sigh *PLEASE,* QUIT STATING THE OBVIOUS.
To Be Continued!

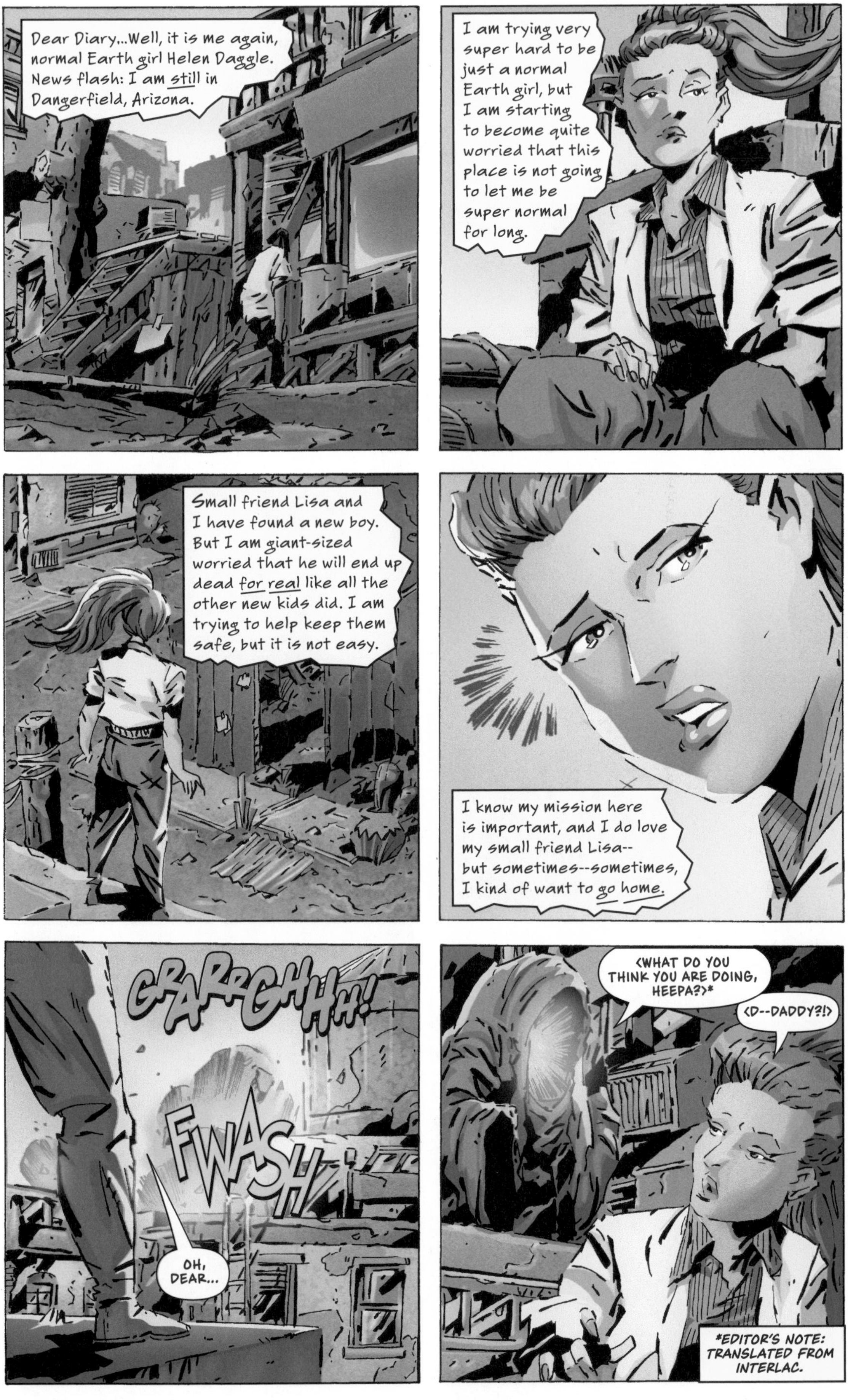
Dear Diary...Well, it is me again, normal Earth girl Helen Daggle. News flash: I am still in Dangerfield, Arizona.
I am trying very super hard to be just a normal Earth girl, but I am starting to become quite worried that this place is not going to let me be super normal for long.
Small friend Lisa and I have found a new boy. But I am giant-sized worried that he will end up dead for real like all the other new kids did. I am trying to help keep them safe, but it is not easy.
I know my mission here is important, and I do love my small friend Lisa-- but sometimes--sometimes, I kind of want to go home.
GRARRGHHH!
FWASH
OH, DEAR...
<WHAT DO YOU THINK YOU ARE DOING, HEEPA?>*
<D--DADDY?!>
*EDITOR'S NOTE: TRANSLATED FROM INTERLAC.

<What are you doing here?!>

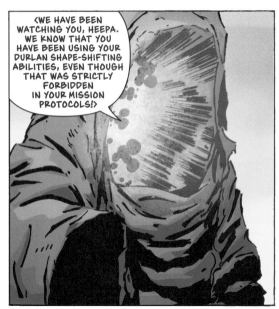

<We have been watching you, Heepa. We know that you have been using your Durlan shape-shifting abilities, even though that was strictly forbidden in your mission protocols!>

<You were to blend in. If *the Dominators* catch you using your Durlan abilities, there will be repercussions for the *entire homeworld!*>

<And I *don't care* about this mission! I didn't ask for it!>

<How dare you speak to me like that, child!>

<This was your last warning. Blend in. Follow the mission. Or you will *never see Durla* again!>

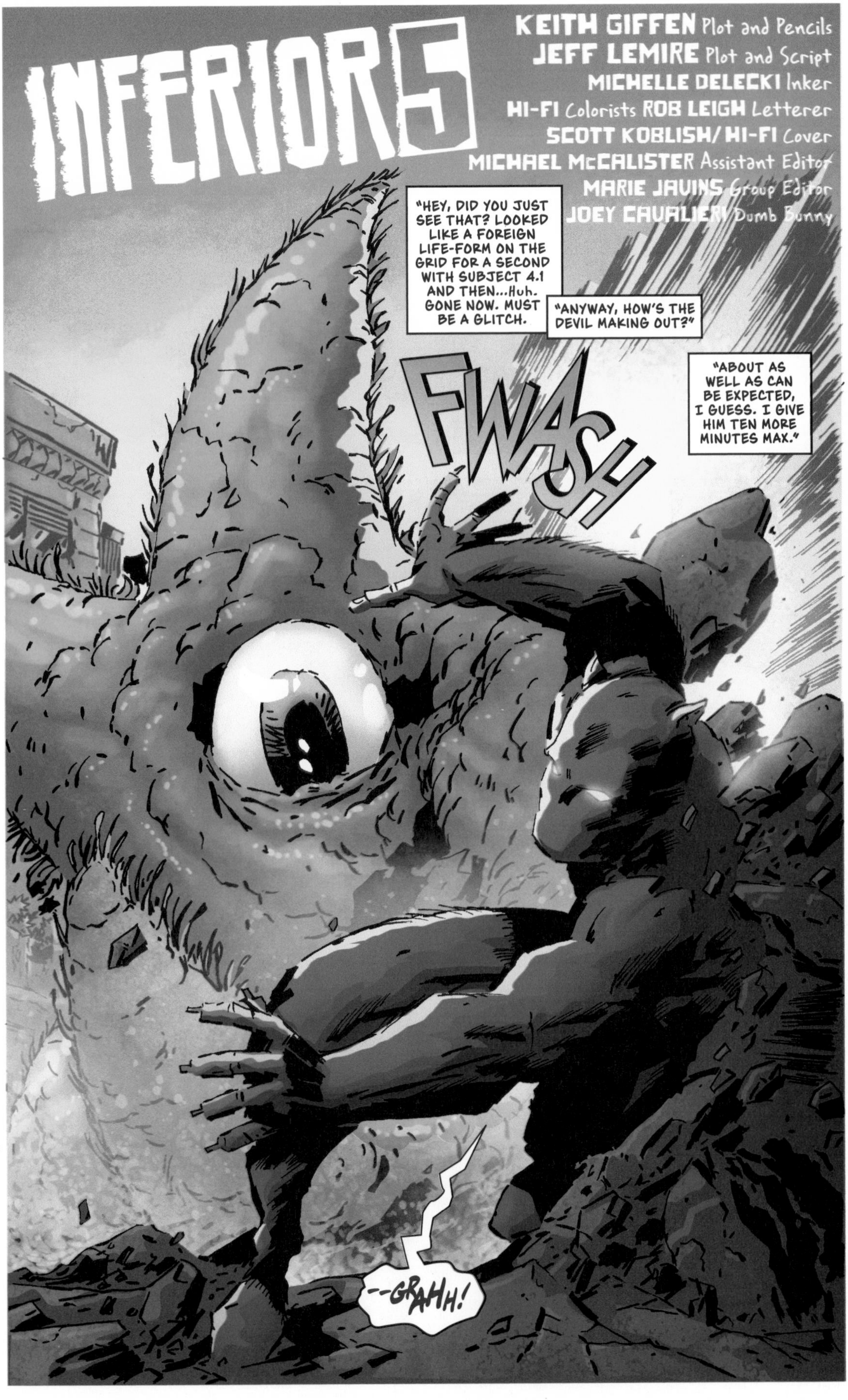
INFERIOR 5
KEITH GIFFEN Plot and Pencils
JEFF LEMIRE Plot and Script
MICHELLE DELECKI Inker
HI-FI Colorists ROB LEIGH Letterer
SCOTT KOBLISH/ HI-FI Cover
MICHAEL McCALISTER Assistant Editor
MARIE JAVINS Group Editor
JOEY CAVALIERI Dumb Bunny
"HEY, DID YOU JUST SEE THAT? LOOKED LIKE A FOREIGN LIFE-FORM ON THE GRID FOR A SECOND WITH SUBJECT 4.1 AND THEN...Huh. GONE NOW. MUST BE A GLITCH.
"ANYWAY, HOW'S THE DEVIL MAKING OUT?"
"ABOUT AS WELL AS CAN BE EXPECTED, I GUESS. I GIVE HIM TEN MORE MINUTES MAX."
FWASH
--GRAHH!

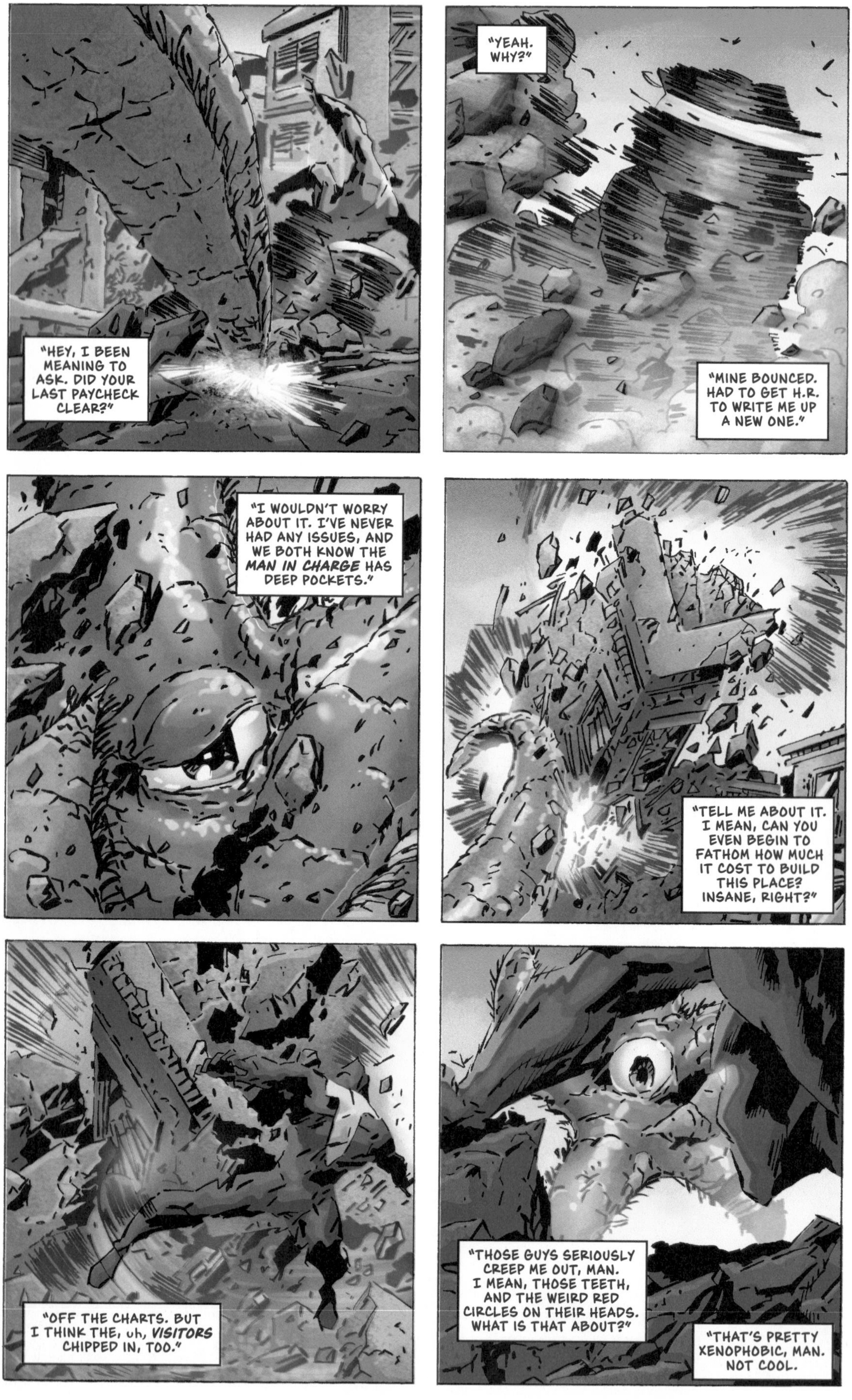
"HEY, I BEEN MEANING TO ASK. DID YOUR LAST PAYCHECK CLEAR?"
"YEAH. WHY?"
"MINE BOUNCED. HAD TO GET H.R. TO WRITE ME UP A NEW ONE."
"I WOULDN'T WORRY ABOUT IT. I'VE NEVER HAD ANY ISSUES, AND WE BOTH KNOW THE MAN IN CHARGE HAS DEEP POCKETS."
"TELL ME ABOUT IT. I MEAN, CAN YOU EVEN BEGIN TO FATHOM HOW MUCH IT COST TO BUILD THIS PLACE? INSANE, RIGHT?"
"OFF THE CHARTS. BUT I THINK THE, uh, VISITORS CHIPPED IN, TOO."
"THOSE GUYS SERIOUSLY CREEP ME OUT, MAN. I MEAN, THOSE TEETH, AND THE WEIRD RED CIRCLES ON THEIR HEADS. WHAT IS THAT ABOUT?"
"THAT'S PRETTY XENOPHOBIC, MAN. NOT COOL.

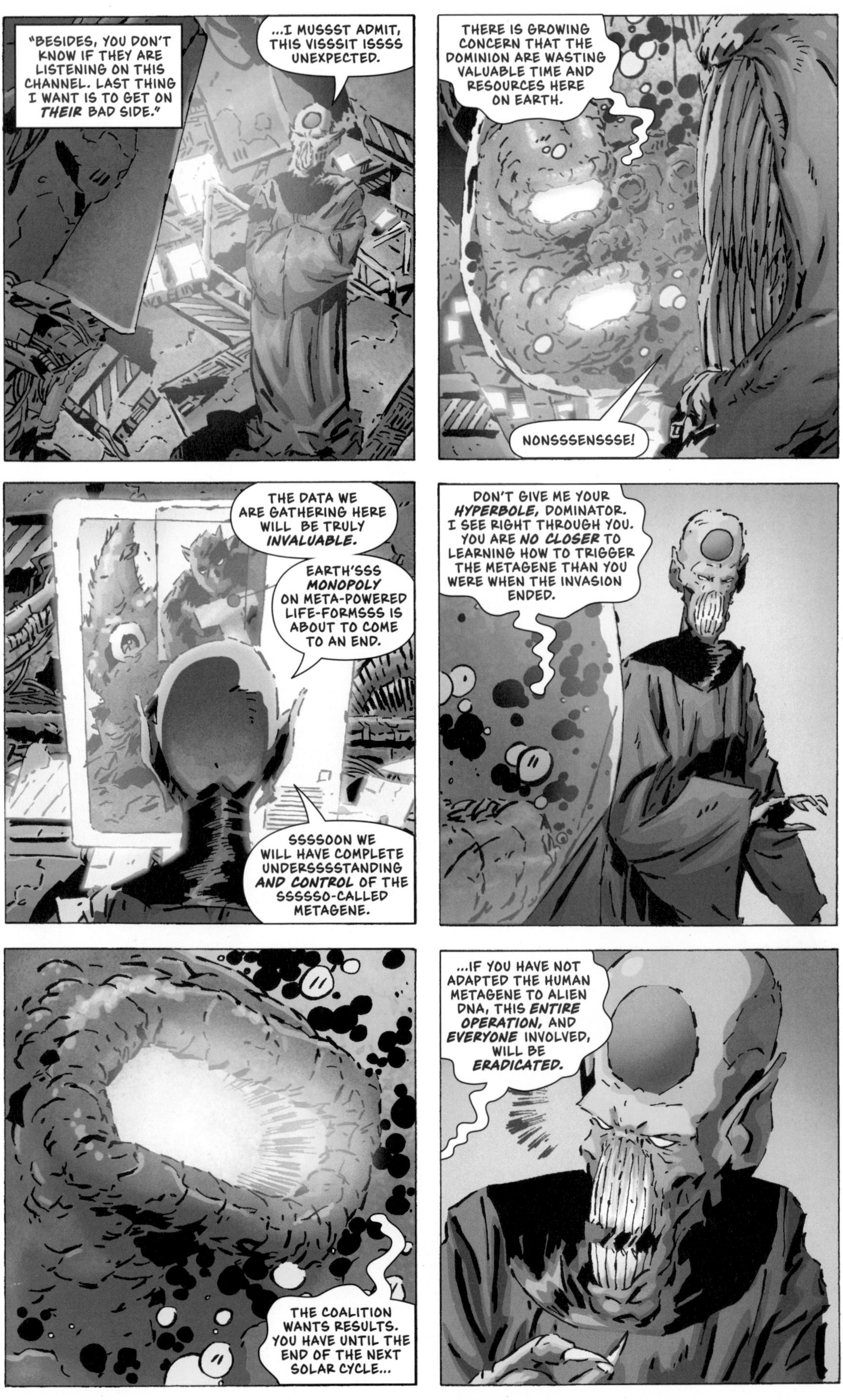
"BESIDES, YOU DON'T KNOW IF THEY ARE LISTENING ON THIS CHANNEL. LAST THING I WANT IS TO GET ON *THEIR* BAD SIDE."
...I MUSSST ADMIT, THIS VISSSIT ISSSS UNEXPECTED.
THERE IS GROWING CONCERN THAT THE DOMINION ARE WASTING VALUABLE TIME AND RESOURCES HERE ON EARTH.
NONSSSENSSSE!
THE DATA WE ARE GATHERING HERE WILL BE TRULY *INVALUABLE.*
EARTH'SSS *MONOPOLY* ON META-POWERED LIFE-FORMSSS IS ABOUT TO COME TO AN END.
SSSSOON WE WILL HAVE COMPLETE UNDERSSSSTANDING *AND CONTROL* OF THE SSSSSO-CALLED METAGENE.
DON'T GIVE ME YOUR *HYPERBOLE,* DOMINATOR. I SEE RIGHT THROUGH YOU. YOU ARE *NO CLOSER* TO LEARNING HOW TO TRIGGER THE METAGENE THAN YOU WERE WHEN THE INVASION ENDED.
THE COALITION WANTS RESULTS. YOU HAVE UNTIL THE END OF THE NEXT SOLAR CYCLE...
...IF YOU HAVE NOT ADAPTED THE HUMAN METAGENE TO ALIEN DNA, THIS *ENTIRE OPERATION,* AND *EVERYONE* INVOLVED, WILL BE *ERADICATED.*

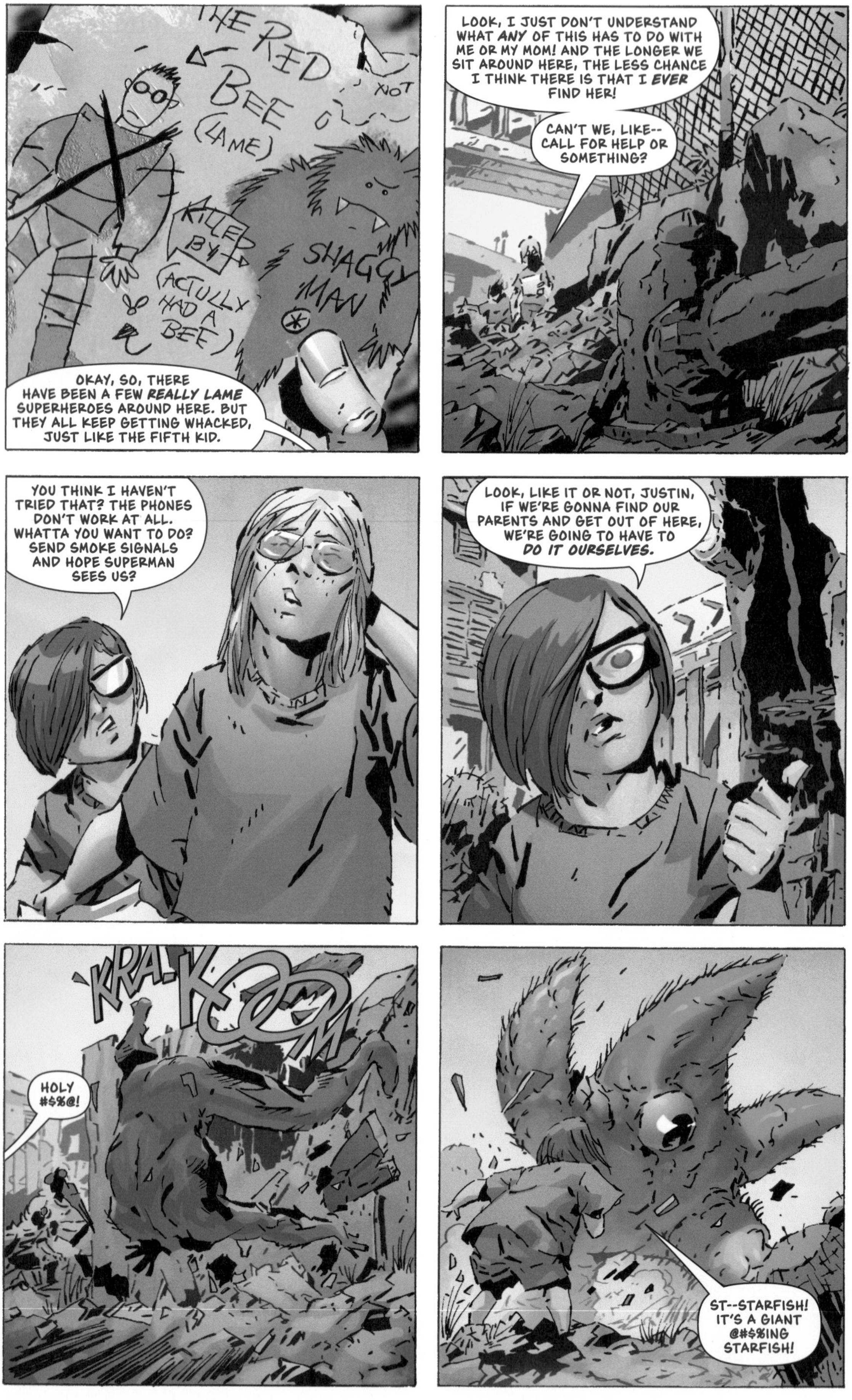
THE RED BEE
(LAME)
NOT
KILLED BY
SHAGGY MAN
(ACTULLY HAD A BEE)
OKAY, SO, THERE HAVE BEEN A FEW REALLY LAME SUPERHEROES AROUND HERE. BUT THEY ALL KEEP GETTING WHACKED, JUST LIKE THE FIFTH KID.
LOOK, I JUST DON'T UNDERSTAND WHAT ANY OF THIS HAS TO DO WITH ME OR MY MOM! AND THE LONGER WE SIT AROUND HERE, THE LESS CHANCE I THINK THERE IS THAT I EVER FIND HER!
CAN'T WE, LIKE-- CALL FOR HELP OR SOMETHING?
YOU THINK I HAVEN'T TRIED THAT? THE PHONES DON'T WORK AT ALL. WHATTA YOU WANT TO DO? SEND SMOKE SIGNALS AND HOPE SUPERMAN SEES US?
LOOK, LIKE IT OR NOT, JUSTIN, IF WE'RE GONNA FIND OUR PARENTS AND GET OUT OF HERE, WE'RE GOING TO HAVE TO DO IT OURSELVES.
KRA-KOOM
HOLY #$%@!
ST--STARFISH! IT'S A GIANT @#$%ING STARFISH!

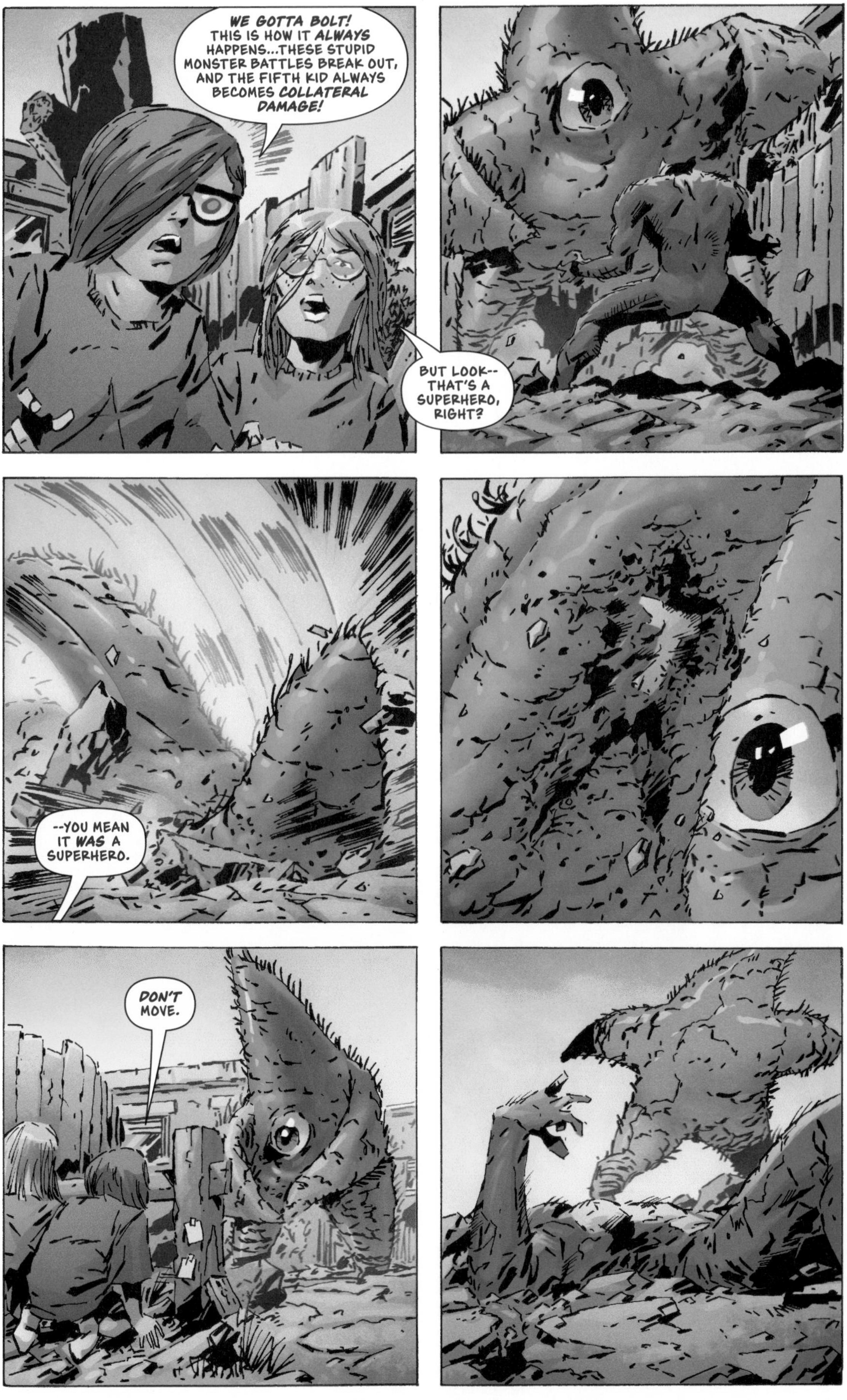
WE GOTTA BOLT! THIS IS HOW IT ALWAYS HAPPENS...THESE STUPID MONSTER BATTLES BREAK OUT, AND THE FIFTH KID ALWAYS BECOMES COLLATERAL DAMAGE!
BUT LOOK-- THAT'S A SUPERHERO, RIGHT?
--YOU MEAN IT WAS A SUPERHERO.
DON'T MOVE.

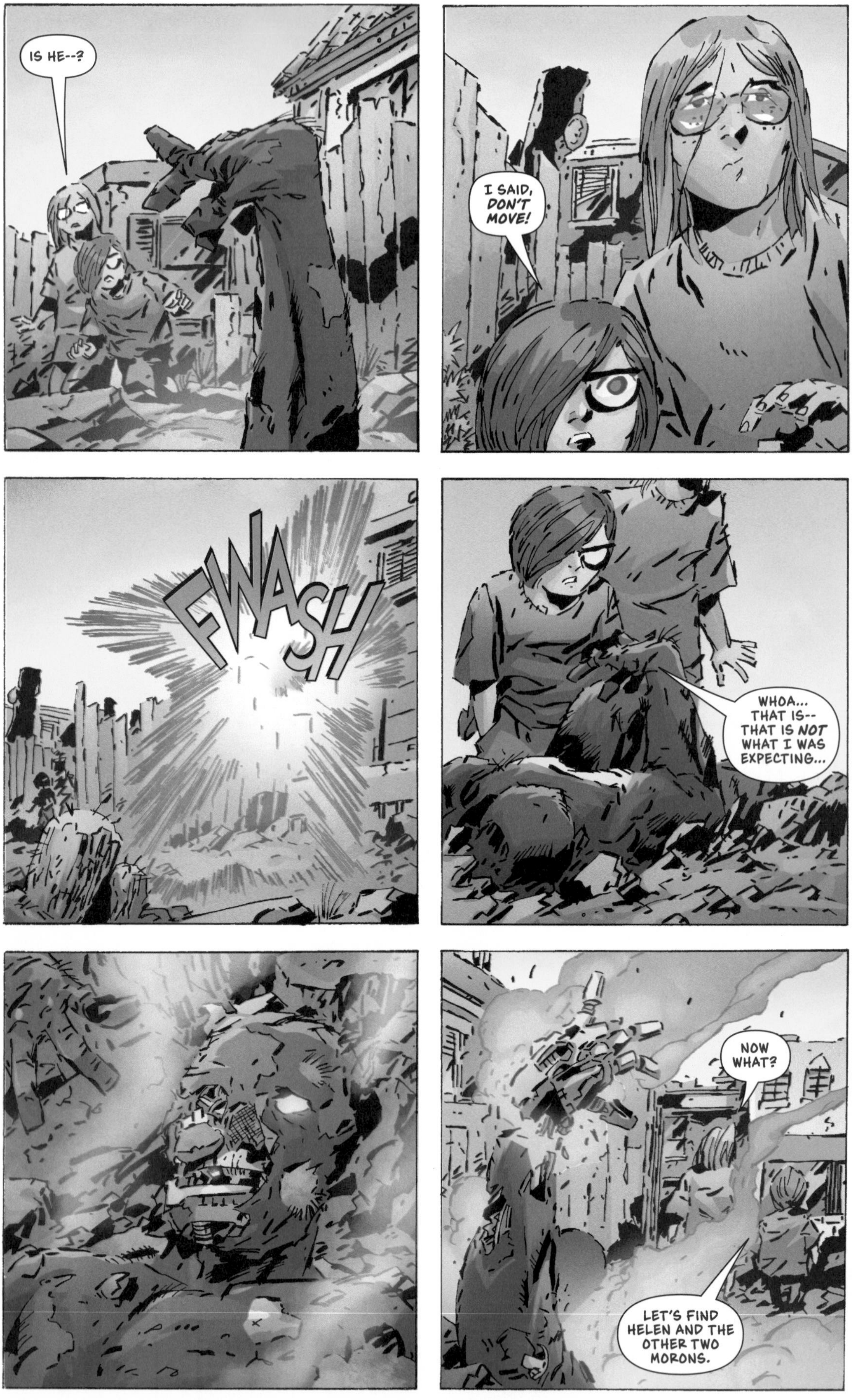
IS HE--?
I SAID, DON'T MOVE!
FWASH
WHOA... THAT IS-- THAT IS NOT WHAT I WAS EXPECTING...
NOW WHAT?
LET'S FIND HELEN AND THE OTHER TWO MORONS.

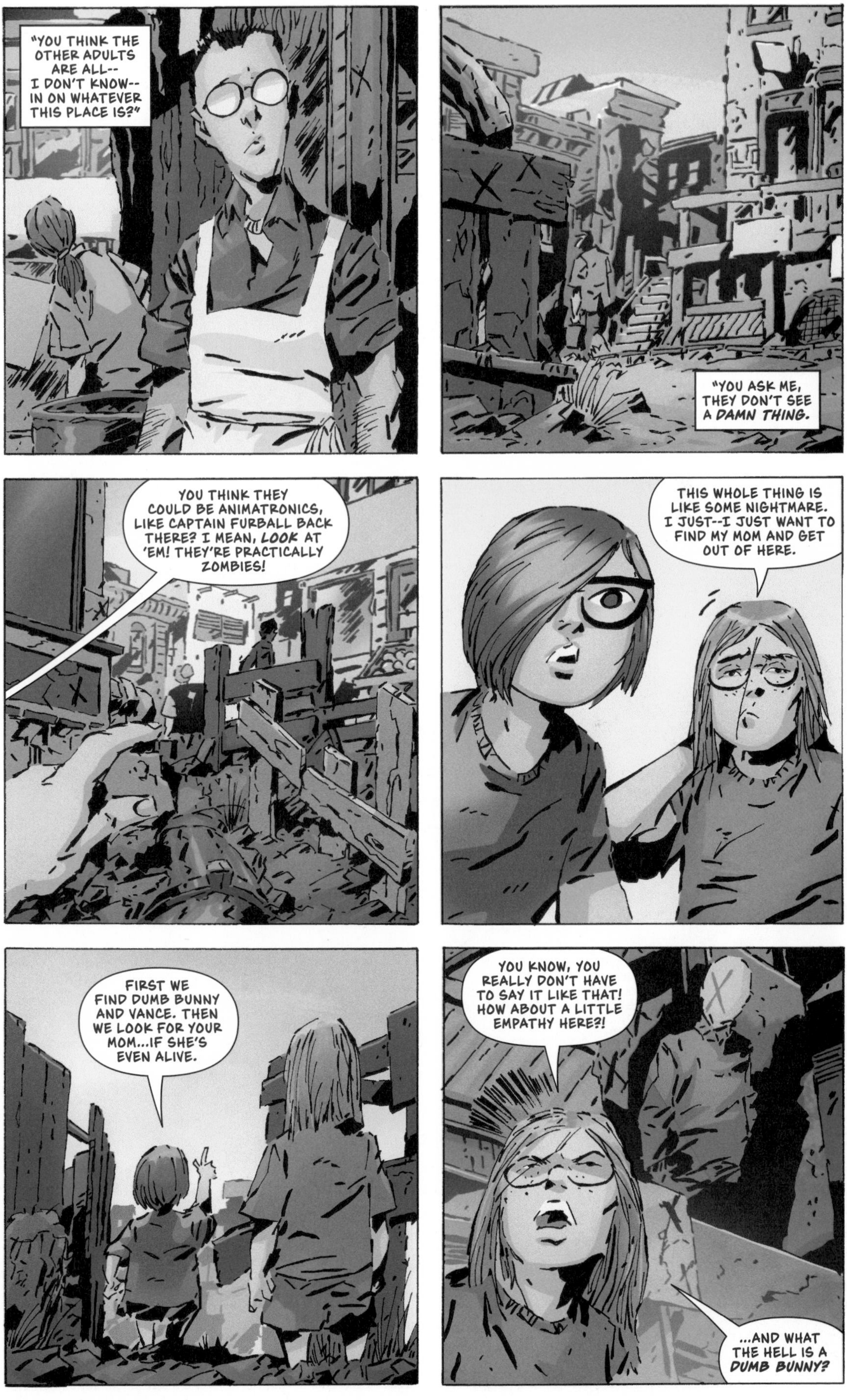
"YOU THINK THE OTHER ADULTS ARE ALL-- I DON'T KNOW-- IN ON WHATEVER THIS PLACE IS?"
"YOU ASK ME, THEY DON'T SEE A DAMN THING.
YOU THINK THEY COULD BE ANIMATRONICS, LIKE CAPTAIN FURBALL BACK THERE? I MEAN, LOOK AT 'EM! THEY'RE PRACTICALLY ZOMBIES!
THIS WHOLE THING IS LIKE SOME NIGHTMARE. I JUST--I JUST WANT TO FIND MY MOM AND GET OUT OF HERE.
FIRST WE FIND DUMB BUNNY AND VANCE. THEN WE LOOK FOR YOUR MOM...IF SHE'S EVEN ALIVE.
YOU KNOW, YOU REALLY DON'T HAVE TO SAY IT LIKE THAT! HOW ABOUT A LITTLE EMPATHY HERE?!
...AND WHAT THE HELL IS A DUMB BUNNY?

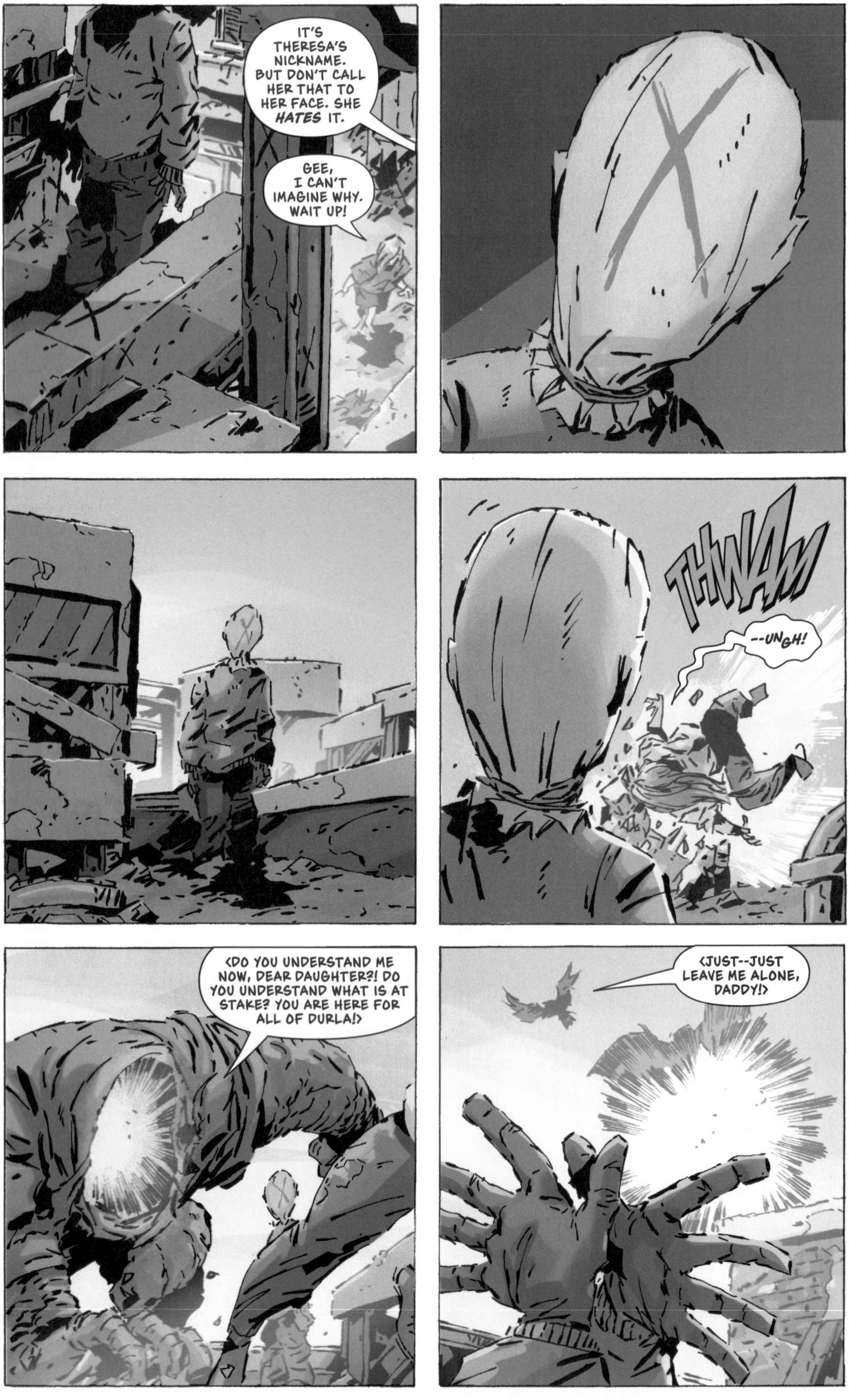
IT'S THERESA'S NICKNAME. BUT DON'T CALL HER THAT TO HER FACE. SHE HATES IT.
GEE, I CAN'T IMAGINE WHY. WAIT UP!
THWAM
--UNGH!
<DO YOU UNDERSTAND ME NOW, DEAR DAUGHTER?! DO YOU UNDERSTAND WHAT IS AT STAKE? YOU ARE HERE FOR ALL OF DURLA!>
<JUST--JUST LEAVE ME ALONE, DADDY!>

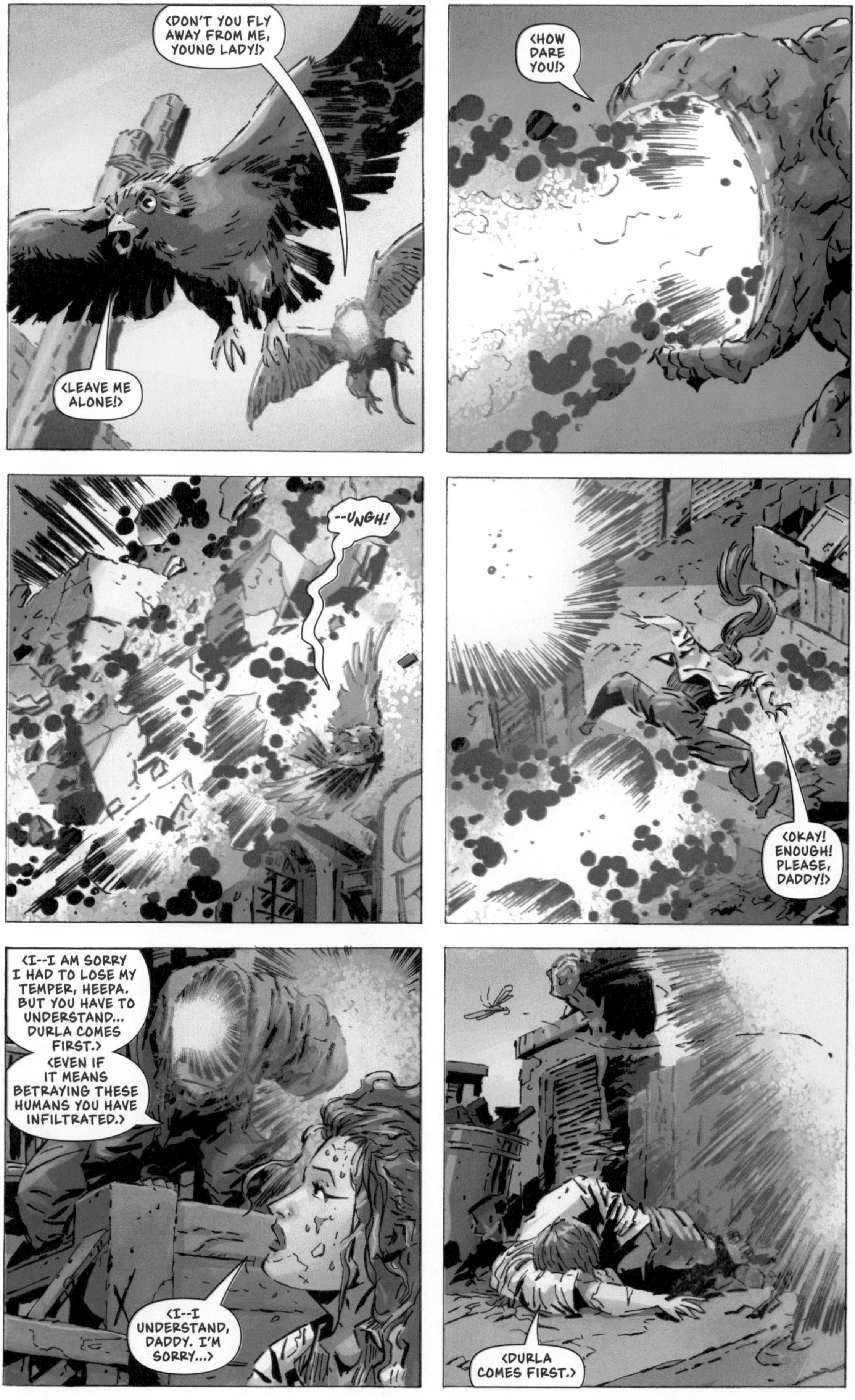
<DON'T YOU FLY AWAY FROM ME, YOUNG LADY!>
<LEAVE ME ALONE!>
<HOW DARE YOU!>
--UNGH!
<OKAY! ENOUGH! PLEASE, DADDY!>
<I--I AM SORRY I HAD TO LOSE MY TEMPER, HEEPA. BUT YOU HAVE TO UNDERSTAND... DURLA COMES FIRST.>
<EVEN IF IT MEANS BETRAYING THESE HUMANS YOU HAVE INFILTRATED.>
<I--I UNDERSTAND, DADDY. I'M SORRY...>
<DURLA COMES FIRST.>

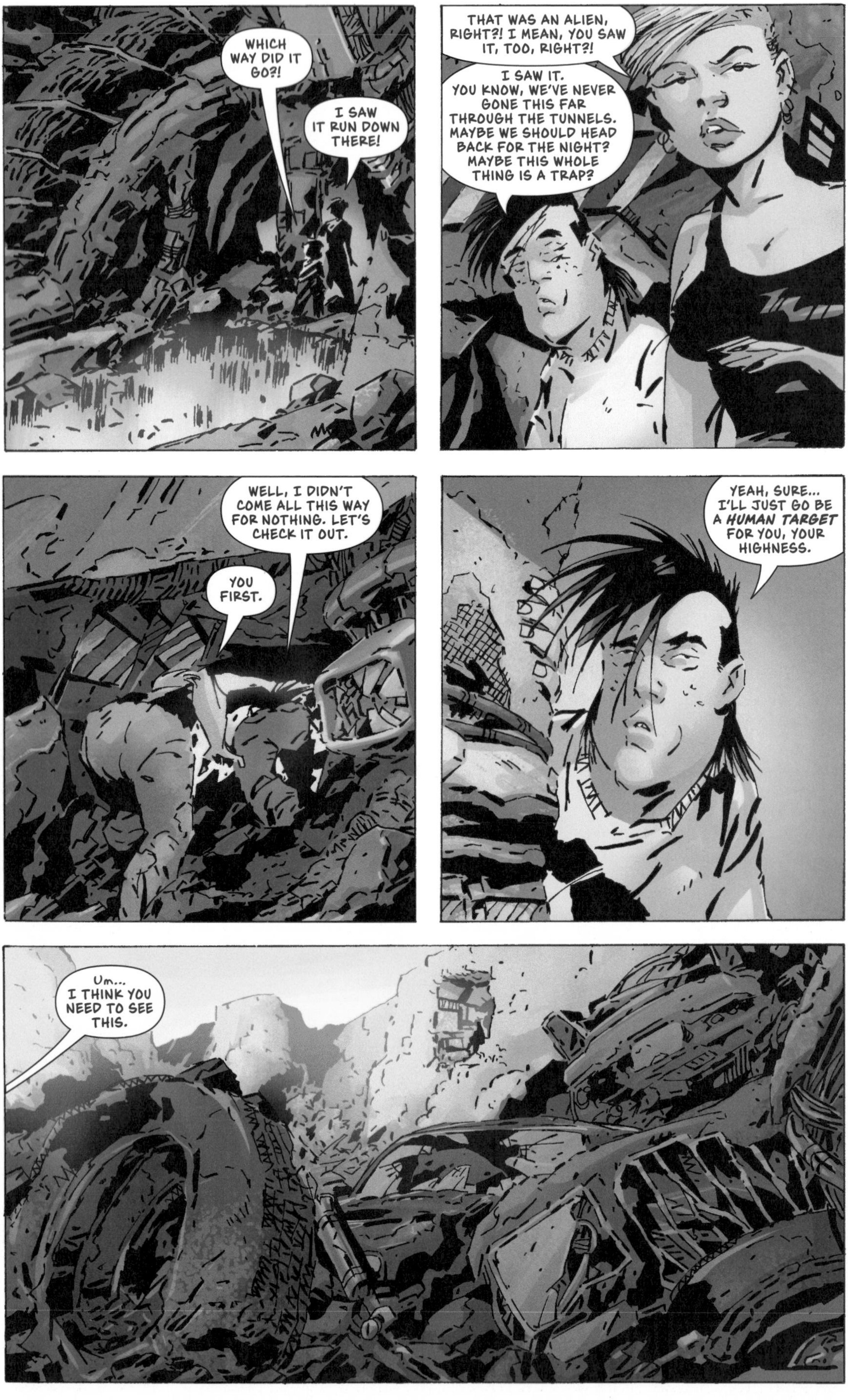
WHICH WAY DID IT GO?!
I SAW IT RUN DOWN THERE!
THAT WAS AN ALIEN, RIGHT?! I MEAN, YOU SAW IT, TOO, RIGHT?!
I SAW IT. YOU KNOW, WE'VE NEVER GONE THIS FAR THROUGH THE TUNNELS. MAYBE WE SHOULD HEAD BACK FOR THE NIGHT? MAYBE THIS WHOLE THING IS A TRAP?
WELL, I DIDN'T COME ALL THIS WAY FOR NOTHING. LET'S CHECK IT OUT.
YOU FIRST.
YEAH, SURE... I'LL JUST GO BE A *HUMAN TARGET* FOR YOU, YOUR HIGHNESS.
Um... I THINK YOU NEED TO SEE THIS.

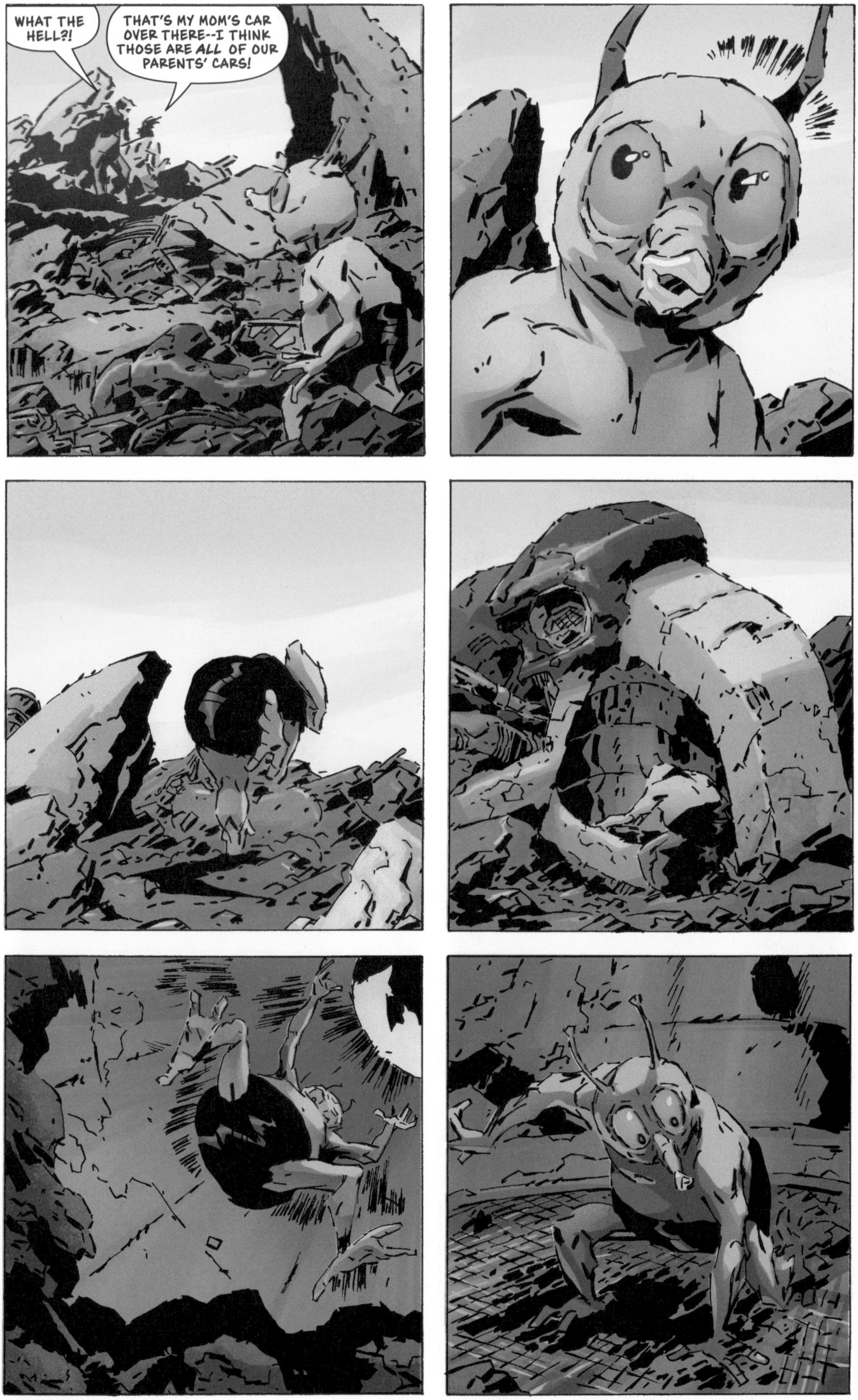
WHAT THE HELL?!
THAT'S MY MOM'S CAR OVER THERE--I THINK THOSE ARE ALL OF OUR PARENTS' CARS!

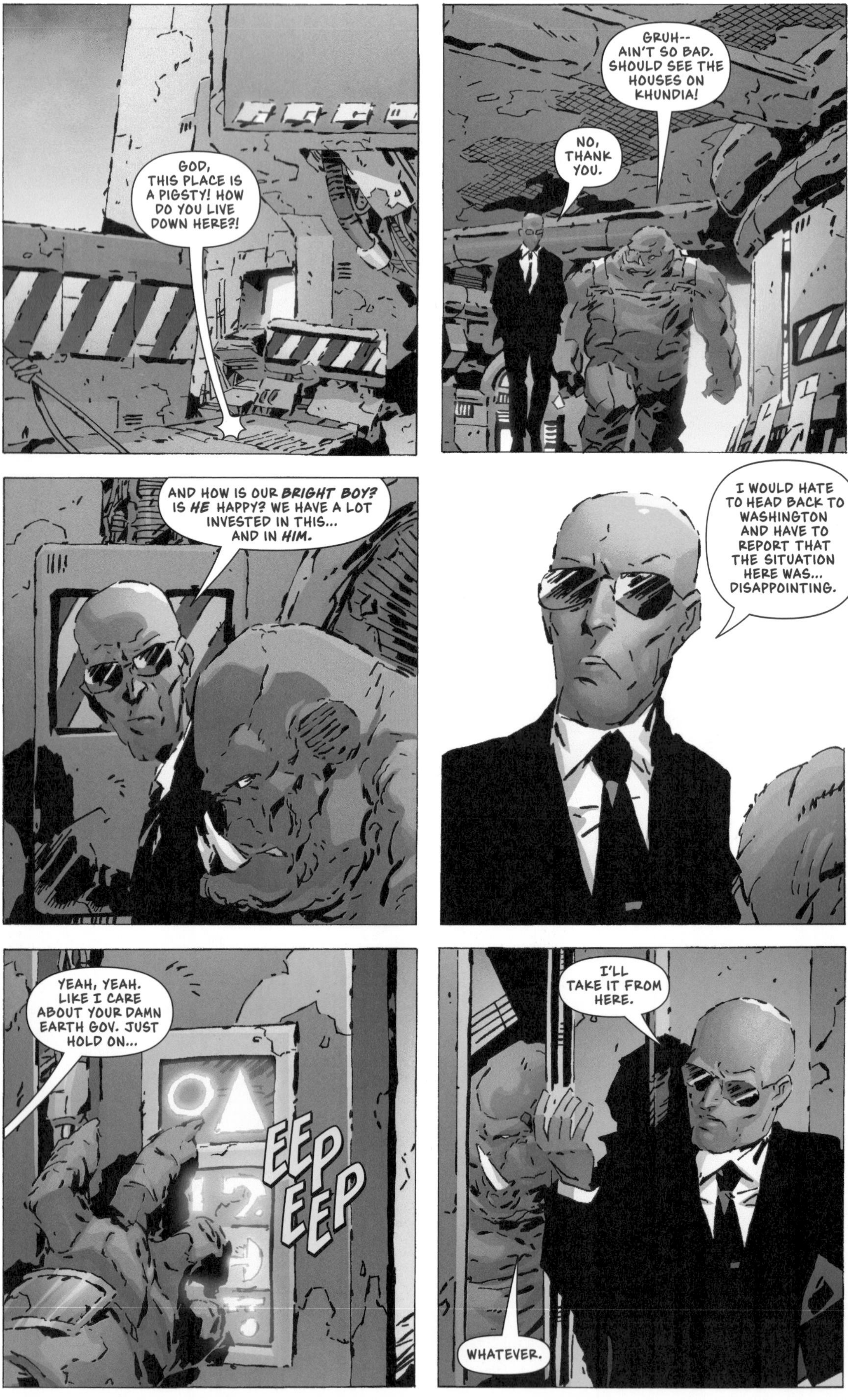
GOD, THIS PLACE IS A PIGSTY! HOW DO YOU LIVE DOWN HERE?!
GRUH-- AIN'T SO BAD. SHOULD SEE THE HOUSES ON KHUNDIA!
NO, THANK YOU.
AND HOW IS OUR *BRIGHT BOY?* IS *HE* HAPPY? WE HAVE A LOT INVESTED IN THIS... AND IN *HIM.*
I WOULD HATE TO HEAD BACK TO WASHINGTON AND HAVE TO REPORT THAT THE SITUATION HERE WAS... DISAPPOINTING.
YEAH, YEAH. LIKE I CARE ABOUT YOUR DAMN EARTH GOV. JUST HOLD ON...
EEP EEP
I'LL TAKE IT FROM HERE.
WHATEVER.

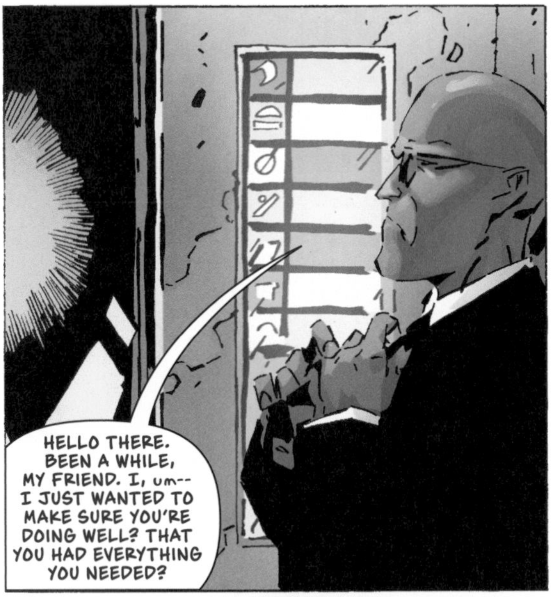
HELLO THERE. BEEN A WHILE, MY FRIEND. I, um-- I JUST WANTED TO MAKE SURE YOU'RE DOING WELL? THAT YOU HAD EVERYTHING YOU NEEDED?

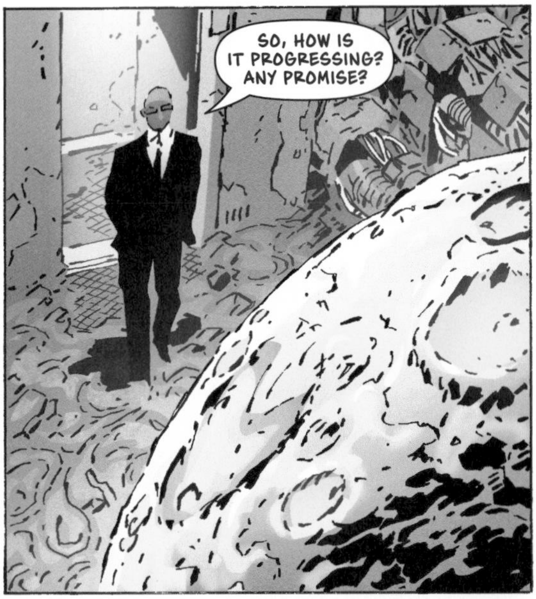
SO, HOW IS IT PROGRESSING? ANY PROMISE?

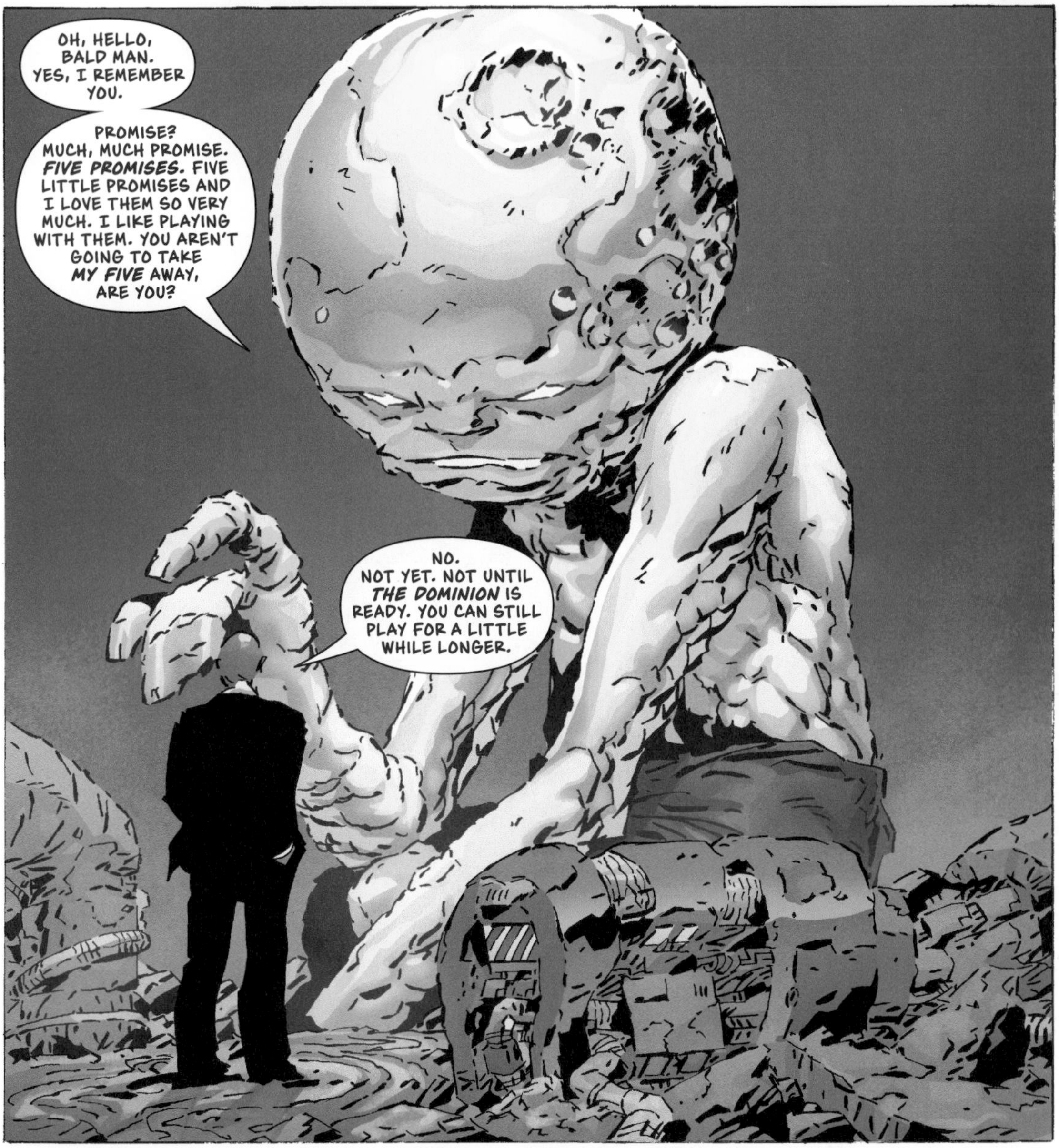
OH, HELLO, BALD MAN. YES, I REMEMBER YOU.
PROMISE? MUCH, MUCH PROMISE. *FIVE PROMISES.* FIVE LITTLE PROMISES AND I LOVE THEM SO VERY MUCH. I LIKE PLAYING WITH THEM. YOU AREN'T GOING TO TAKE *MY FIVE* AWAY, ARE YOU?
NO. NOT YET. NOT UNTIL *THE DOMINION* IS READY. YOU CAN STILL PLAY FOR A LITTLE WHILE LONGER.

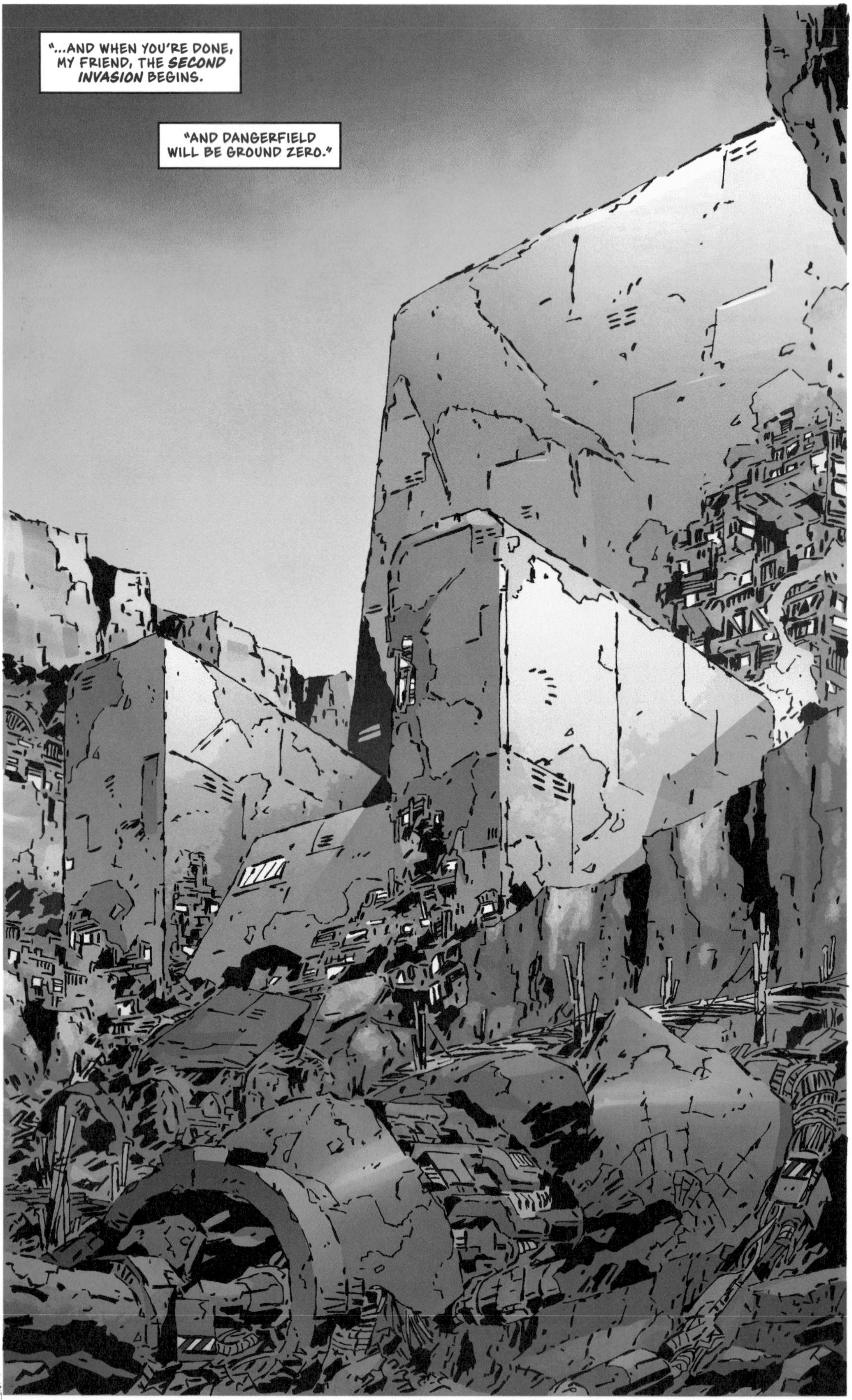
"...AND WHEN YOU'RE DONE, MY FRIEND, THE SECOND INVASION BEGINS.
"AND DANGERFIELD WILL BE GROUND ZERO."

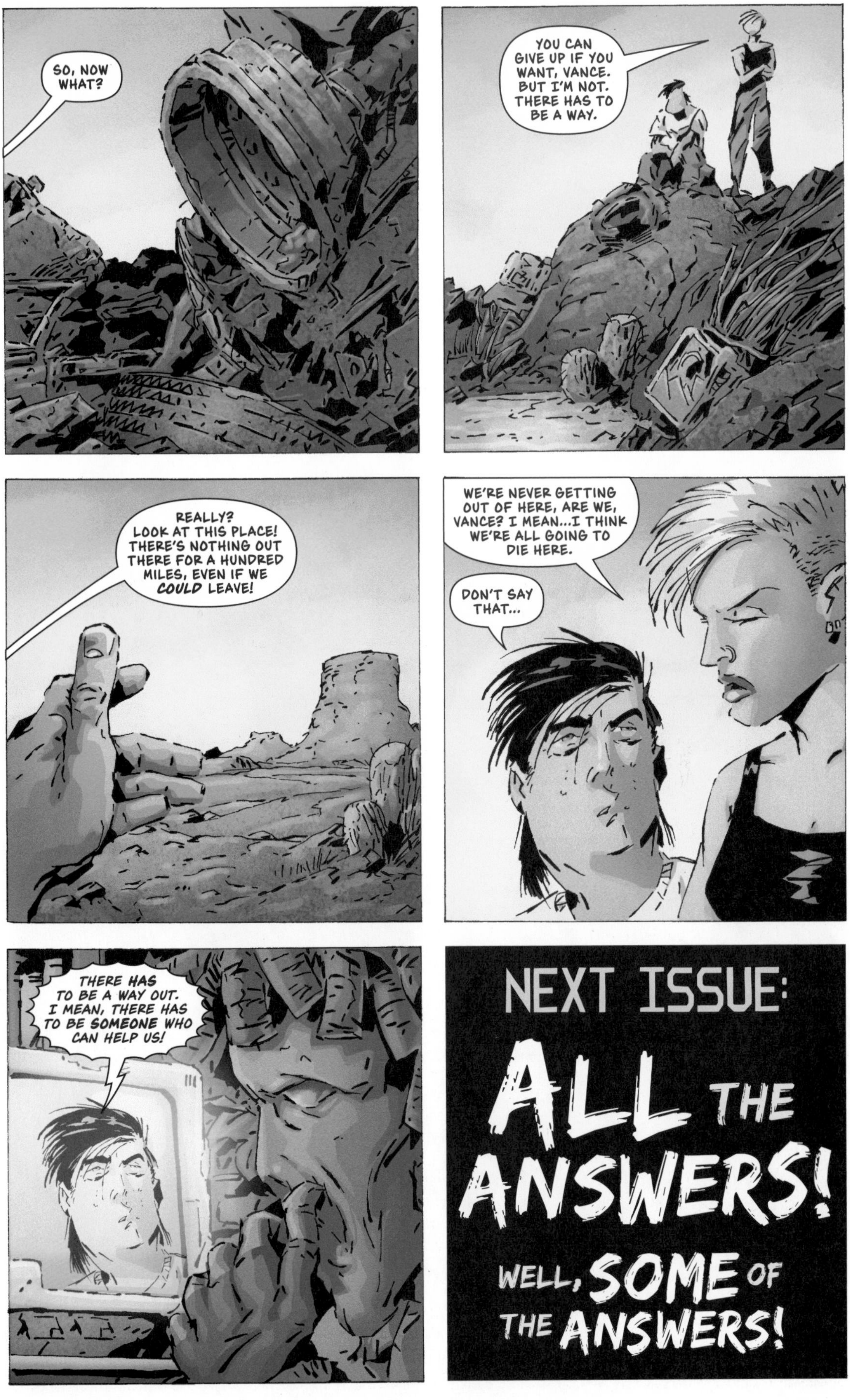
SO, NOW WHAT?
YOU CAN GIVE UP IF YOU WANT, VANCE. BUT I'M NOT. THERE HAS TO BE A WAY.
REALLY? LOOK AT THIS PLACE! THERE'S NOTHING OUT THERE FOR A HUNDRED MILES, EVEN IF WE COULD LEAVE!
WE'RE NEVER GETTING OUT OF HERE, ARE WE, VANCE? I MEAN...I THINK WE'RE ALL GOING TO DIE HERE.
DON'T SAY THAT...
THERE HAS TO BE A WAY OUT. I MEAN, THERE HAS TO BE SOMEONE WHO CAN HELP US!
NEXT ISSUE:
ALL THE ANSWERS!
WELL, SOME OF THE ANSWERS!

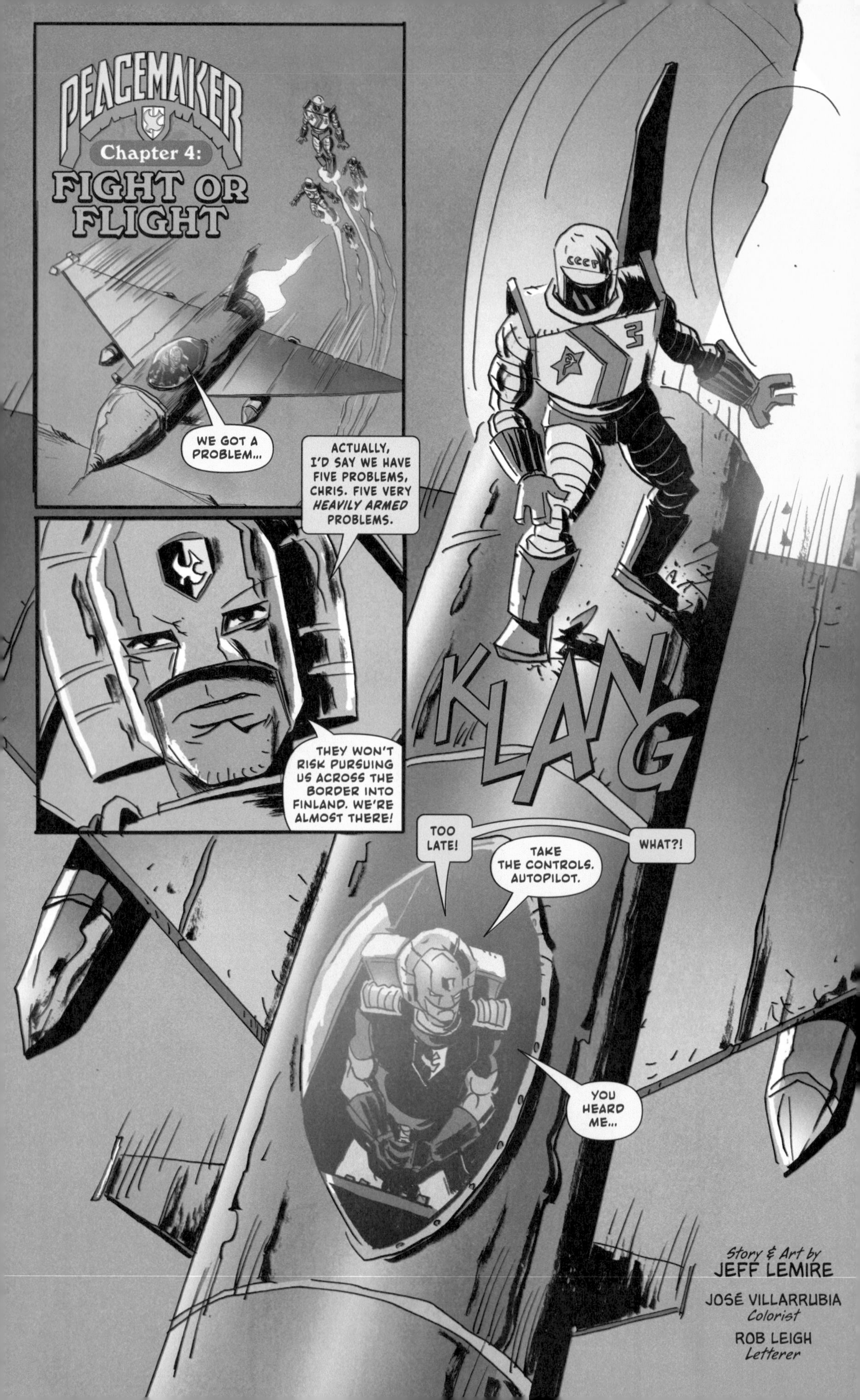
PEACEMAKER
Chapter 4:
FIGHT OR FLIGHT
WE GOT A PROBLEM...
ACTUALLY, I'D SAY WE HAVE FIVE PROBLEMS, CHRIS. FIVE VERY *HEAVILY ARMED* PROBLEMS.
THEY WON'T RISK PURSUING US ACROSS THE BORDER INTO FINLAND. WE'RE ALMOST THERE!
KLANG
TOO LATE!
WHAT?!
TAKE THE CONTROLS. AUTOPILOT.
YOU HEARD ME...
Story & Art by
JEFF LEMIRE
JOSÉ VILLARRUBIA
Colorist
ROB LEIGH
Letterer

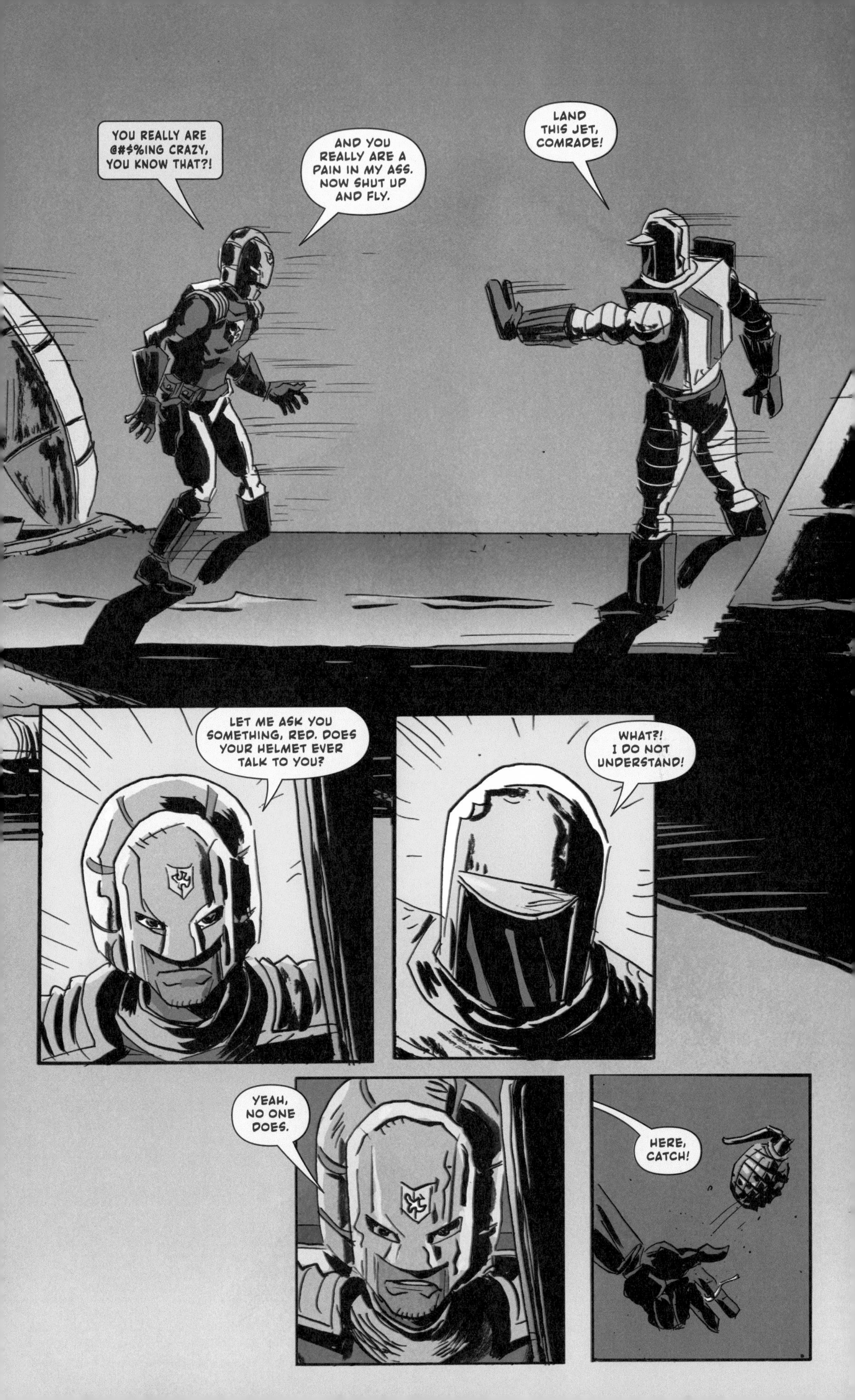
YOU REALLY ARE @#$%ING CRAZY, YOU KNOW THAT?!
AND YOU REALLY ARE A PAIN IN MY ASS. NOW SHUT UP AND FLY.
LAND THIS JET, COMRADE!
LET ME ASK YOU SOMETHING, RED. DOES YOUR HELMET EVER TALK TO YOU?
WHAT?! I DO NOT UNDERSTAND!
YEAH, NO ONE DOES.
HERE, CATCH!

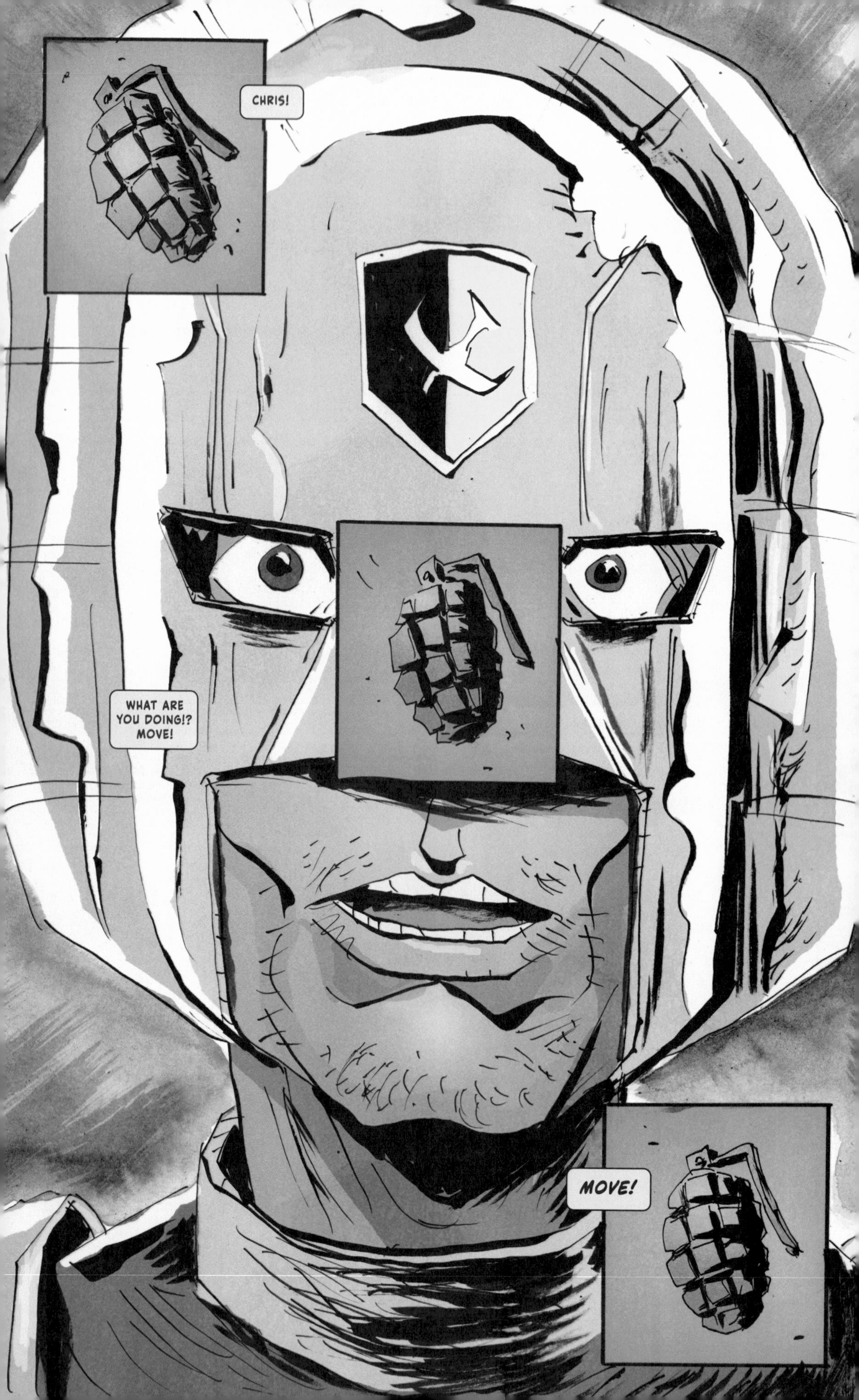
CHRIS!
WHAT ARE YOU DOING!? MOVE!
MOVE!

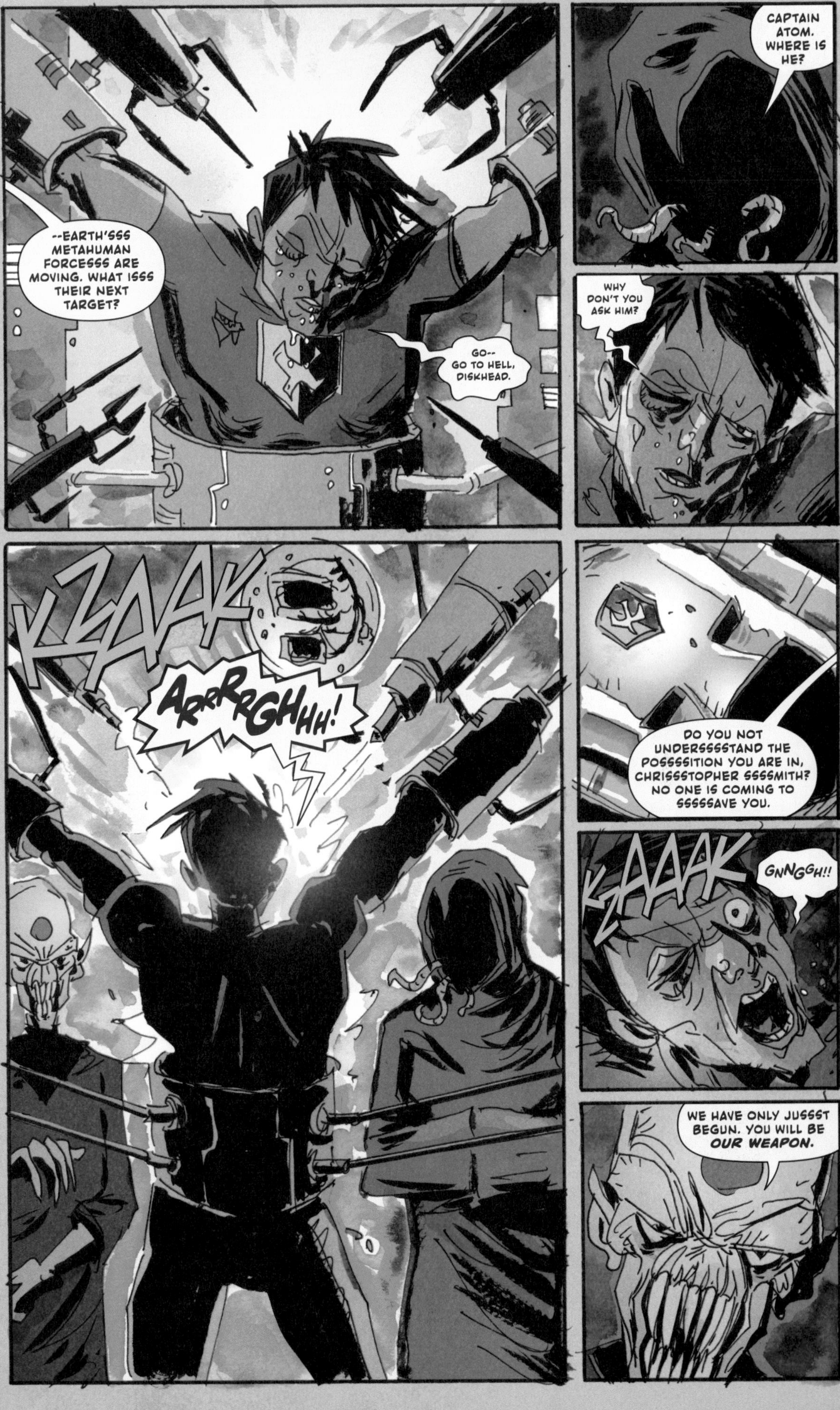
--EARTH'SSS METAHUMAN FORCESSS ARE MOVING. WHAT ISSS THEIR NEXT TARGET?
GO-- GO TO HELL, DISKHEAD.
CAPTAIN ATOM. WHERE IS HE?
WHY DON'T YOU ASK HIM?
KZAAK
ARRRRGHHH!
DO YOU NOT UNDERSSSSTAND THE POSSSSITION YOU ARE IN, CHRISSSTOPHER SSSSMITH? NO ONE IS COMING TO SSSSSAVE YOU.
KZAAAK
GNNGGH!!
WE HAVE ONLY JUSSST BEGUN. YOU WILL BE OUR WEAPON.

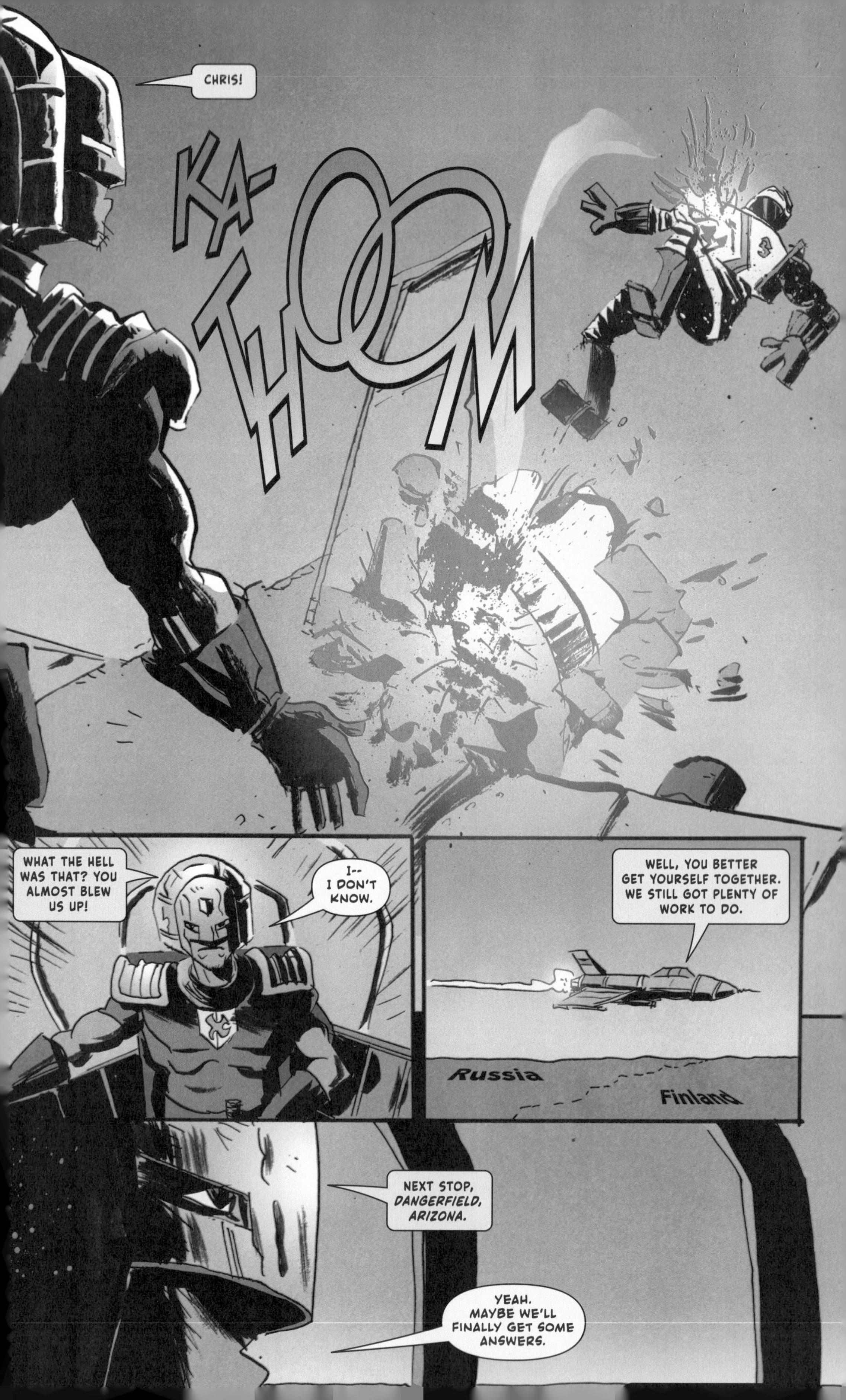
CHRIS!
KA-THOOM
WHAT THE HELL WAS THAT? YOU ALMOST BLEW US UP!
I-- I DON'T KNOW.
WELL, YOU BETTER GET YOURSELF TOGETHER. WE STILL GOT PLENTY OF WORK TO DO.
Russia
Finland
NEXT STOP, DANGERFIELD, ARIZONA.
YEAH. MAYBE WE'LL FINALLY GET SOME ANSWERS.

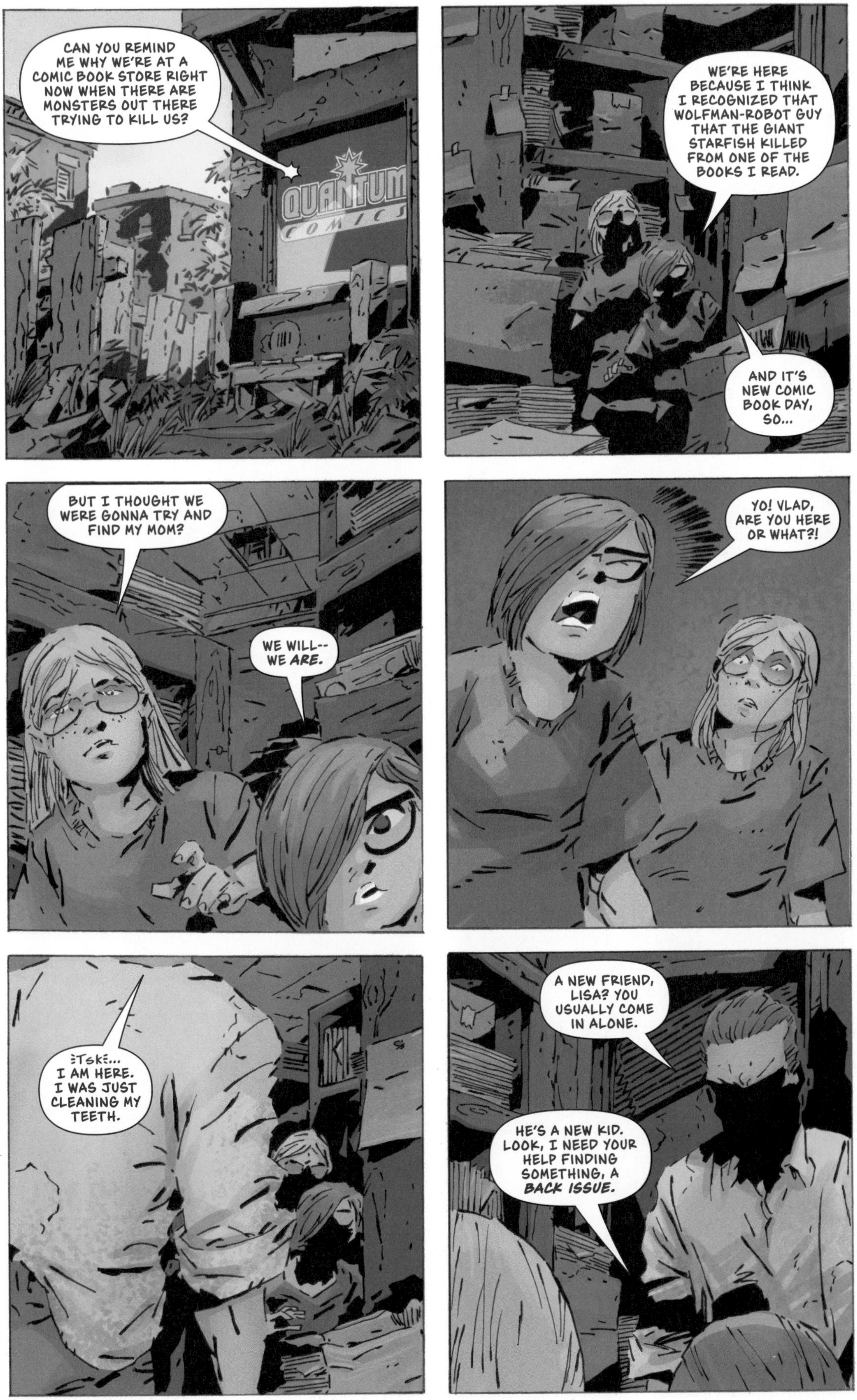
CAN YOU REMIND ME WHY WE'RE AT A COMIC BOOK STORE RIGHT NOW WHEN THERE ARE MONSTERS OUT THERE TRYING TO KILL US?
QUANTUM COMICS
WE'RE HERE BECAUSE I THINK I RECOGNIZED THAT WOLFMAN-ROBOT GUY THAT THE GIANT STARFISH KILLED FROM ONE OF THE BOOKS I READ.
AND IT'S NEW COMIC BOOK DAY, SO...
BUT I THOUGHT WE WERE GONNA TRY AND FIND MY MOM?
WE WILL-- WE *ARE*.
YO! VLAD, ARE YOU HERE OR WHAT?!
ξTSKξ... I AM HERE. I WAS JUST CLEANING MY TEETH.
A NEW FRIEND, LISA? YOU USUALLY COME IN ALONE.
HE'S A NEW KID. LOOK, I NEED YOUR HELP FINDING SOMETHING, A *BACK ISSUE*.

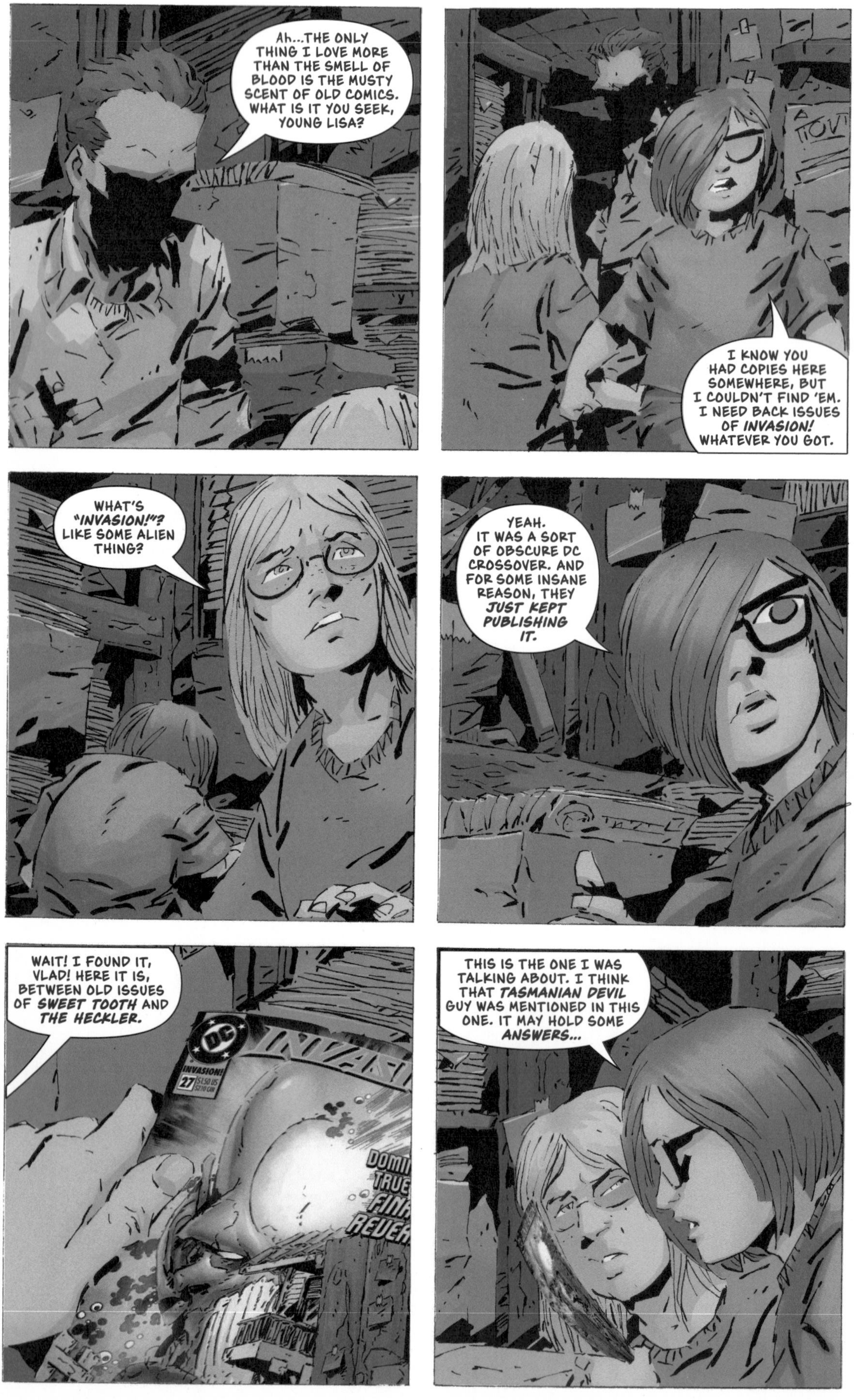
Ah...THE ONLY THING I LOVE MORE THAN THE SMELL OF BLOOD IS THE MUSTY SCENT OF OLD COMICS. WHAT IS IT YOU SEEK, YOUNG LISA?
I KNOW YOU HAD COPIES HERE SOMEWHERE, BUT I COULDN'T FIND 'EM. I NEED BACK ISSUES OF *INVASION!* WHATEVER YOU GOT.
WHAT'S *"INVASION!"*? LIKE SOME ALIEN THING?
YEAH. IT WAS A SORT OF OBSCURE DC CROSSOVER. AND FOR SOME INSANE REASON, THEY *JUST KEPT PUBLISHING IT.*
WAIT! I FOUND IT, VLAD! HERE IT IS, BETWEEN OLD ISSUES OF *SWEET TOOTH* AND *THE HECKLER.*
DC
INVASION!
27
THIS IS THE ONE I WAS TALKING ABOUT. I THINK THAT *TASMANIAN DEVIL* GUY WAS MENTIONED IN THIS ONE. IT MAY HOLD SOME *ANSWERS...*

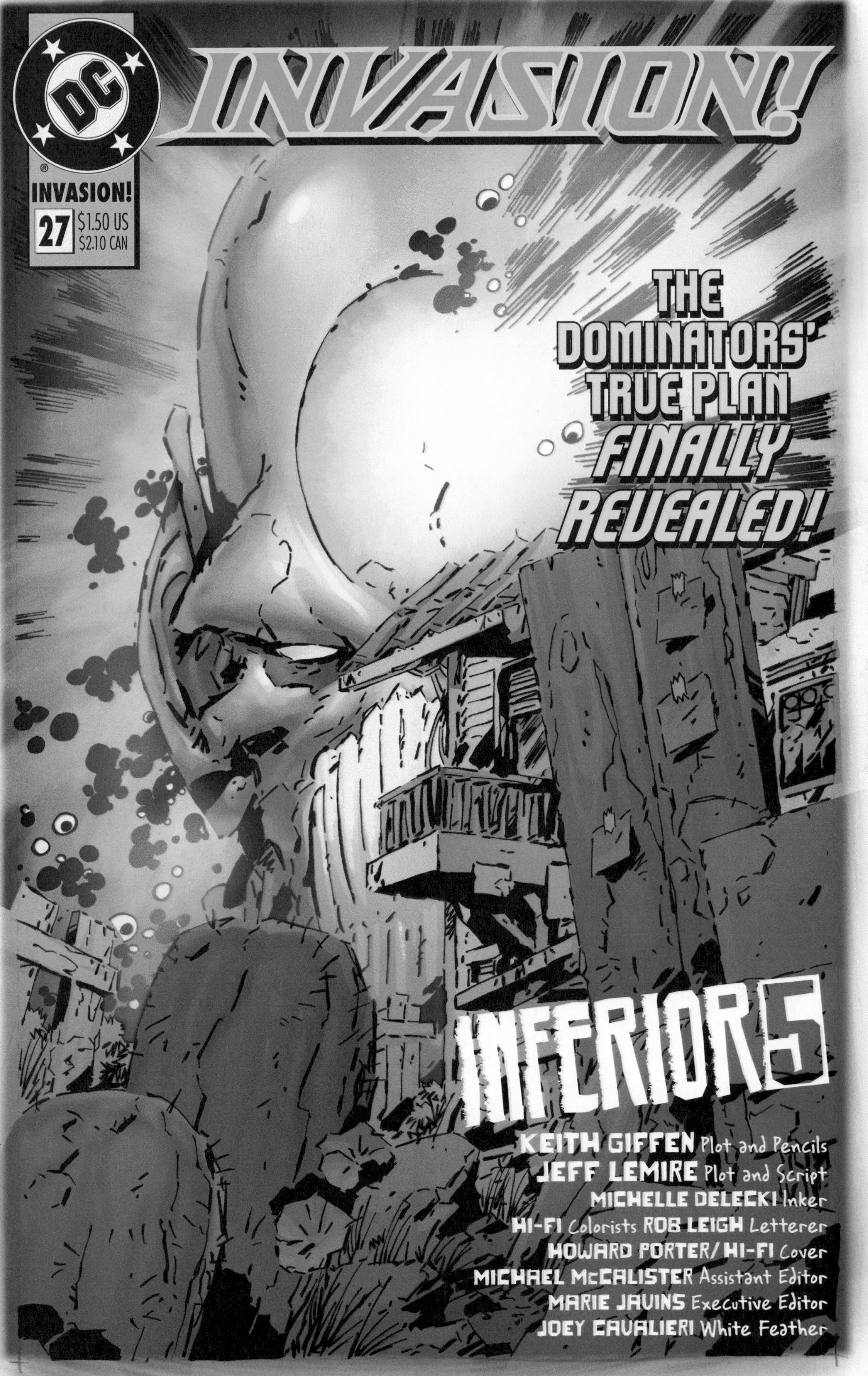

DC
INVASION!
INVASION!
27 $1.50 US $2.10 CAN
THE DOMINATORS' TRUE PLAN FINALLY REVEALED!
INFERIOR 5
KEITH GIFFEN Plot and Pencils
JEFF LEMIRE Plot and Script
MICHELLE DELECKI Inker
HI-FI Colorists ROB LEIGH Letterer
HOWARD PORTER/ HI-FI Cover
MICHAEL McCALISTER Assistant Editor
MARIE JAVINS Executive Editor
JOEY CAVALIERI White Feather

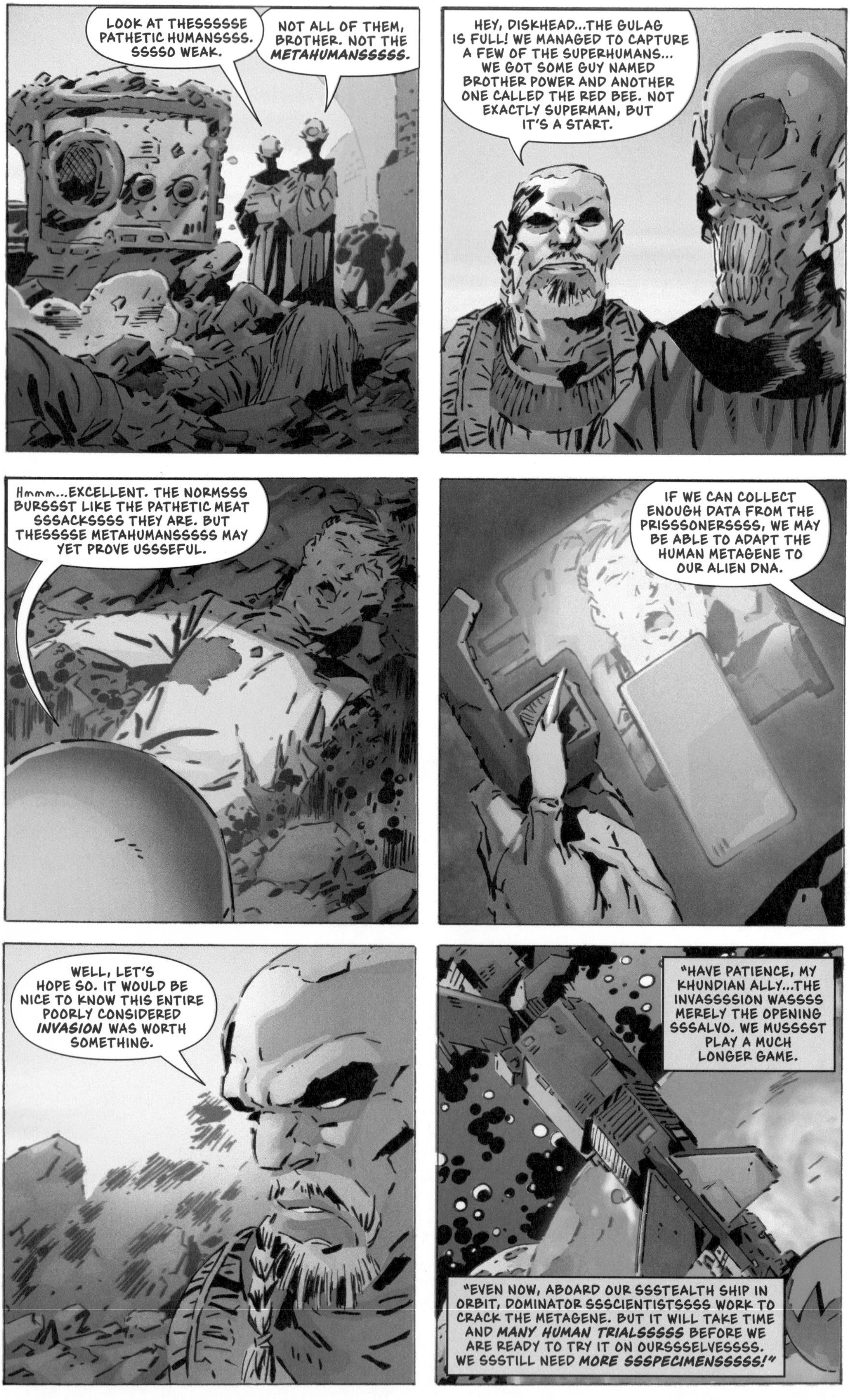

LOOK AT THESSSSSE PATHETIC HUMANSSSS. SSSSO WEAK.
NOT ALL OF THEM, BROTHER. NOT THE *METAHUMANSSSSS.*
HEY, DISKHEAD...THE GULAG IS FULL! WE MANAGED TO CAPTURE A FEW OF THE SUPERHUMANS... WE GOT SOME GUY NAMED BROTHER POWER AND ANOTHER ONE CALLED THE RED BEE. NOT EXACTLY SUPERMAN, BUT IT'S A START.
Hmmm...EXCELLENT. THE NORMSSS BURSSST LIKE THE PATHETIC MEAT SSSACKSSSS THEY ARE. BUT THESSSSE METAHUMANSSSSS MAY YET PROVE USSSEFUL.
IF WE CAN COLLECT ENOUGH DATA FROM THE PRISSSONERSSSS, WE MAY BE ABLE TO ADAPT THE HUMAN METAGENE TO OUR ALIEN DNA.
WELL, LET'S HOPE SO. IT WOULD BE NICE TO KNOW THIS ENTIRE POORLY CONSIDERED *INVASION* WAS WORTH SOMETHING.
"HAVE PATIENCE, MY KHUNDIAN ALLY...THE INVASSSSION WASSSS MERELY THE OPENING SSSALVO. WE MUSSSST PLAY A MUCH LONGER GAME.
"EVEN NOW, ABOARD OUR SSSTEALTH SHIP IN ORBIT, DOMINATOR SSSCIENTISTSSSS WORK TO CRACK THE METAGENE. BUT IT WILL TAKE TIME AND *MANY HUMAN TRIALSSSSS* BEFORE WE ARE READY TO TRY IT ON OURSSSELVESSSS. WE SSSTILL NEED *MORE SSSPECIMENSSSSS!"*

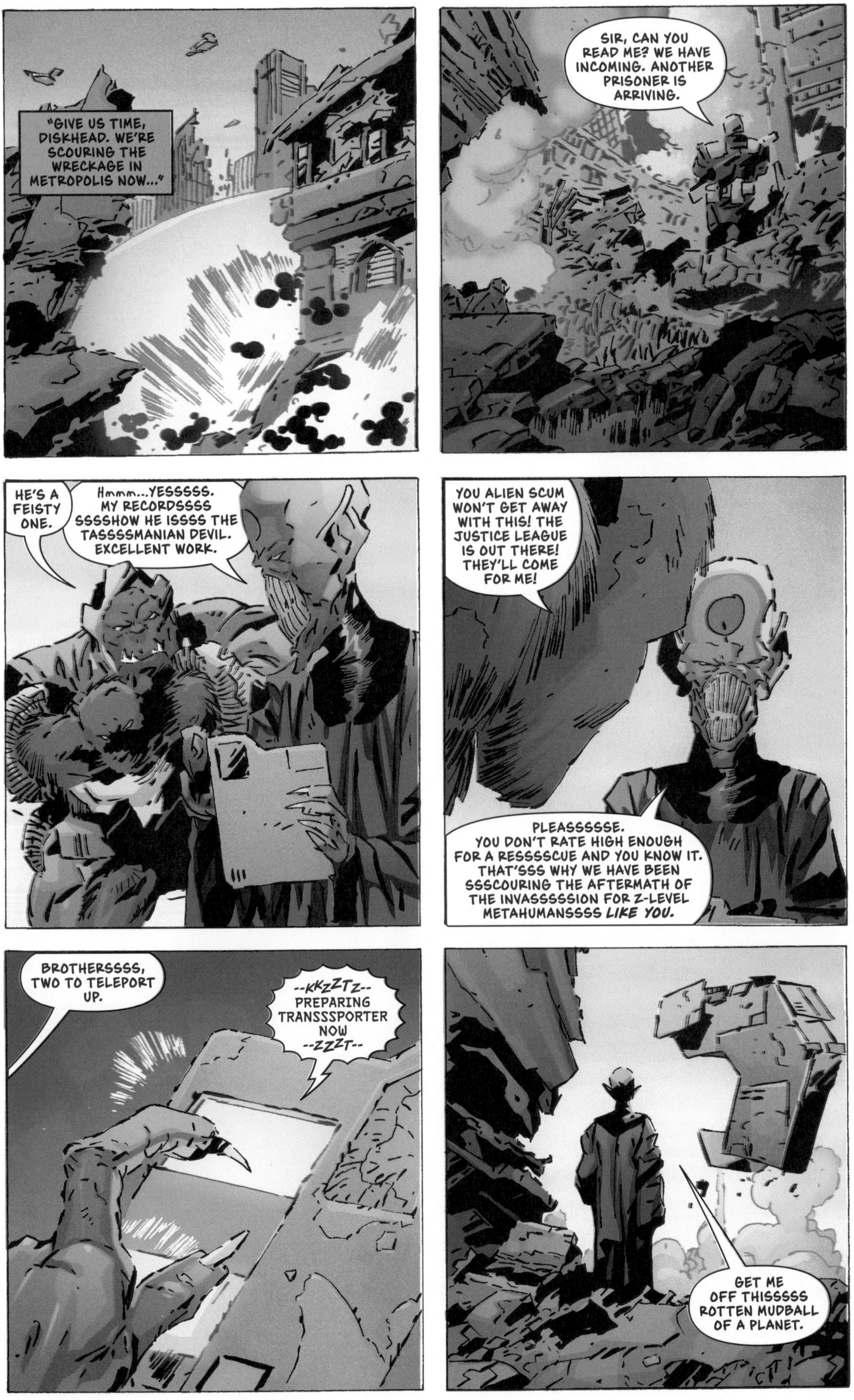
"GIVE US TIME, DISKHEAD. WE'RE SCOURING THE WRECKAGE IN METROPOLIS NOW..."
SIR, CAN YOU READ ME? WE HAVE INCOMING. ANOTHER PRISONER IS ARRIVING.
HE'S A FEISTY ONE.
Hmmm...YESSSSS. MY RECORDSSSS SSSSHOW HE ISSSS THE TASSSSMANIAN DEVIL. EXCELLENT WORK.
YOU ALIEN SCUM WON'T GET AWAY WITH THIS! THE JUSTICE LEAGUE IS OUT THERE! THEY'LL COME FOR ME!
PLEASSSSSE. YOU DON'T RATE HIGH ENOUGH FOR A RESSSSCUE AND YOU KNOW IT. THAT'SSS WHY WE HAVE BEEN SSSCOURING THE AFTERMATH OF THE INVASSSSSION FOR Z-LEVEL METAHUMANSSSS *LIKE YOU.*
BROTHERSSSS, TWO TO TELEPORT UP.
--KKZZTZ-- PREPARING TRANSSSPORTER NOW --ZZZT--
GET ME OFF THISSSSS ROTTEN MUDBALL OF A PLANET.

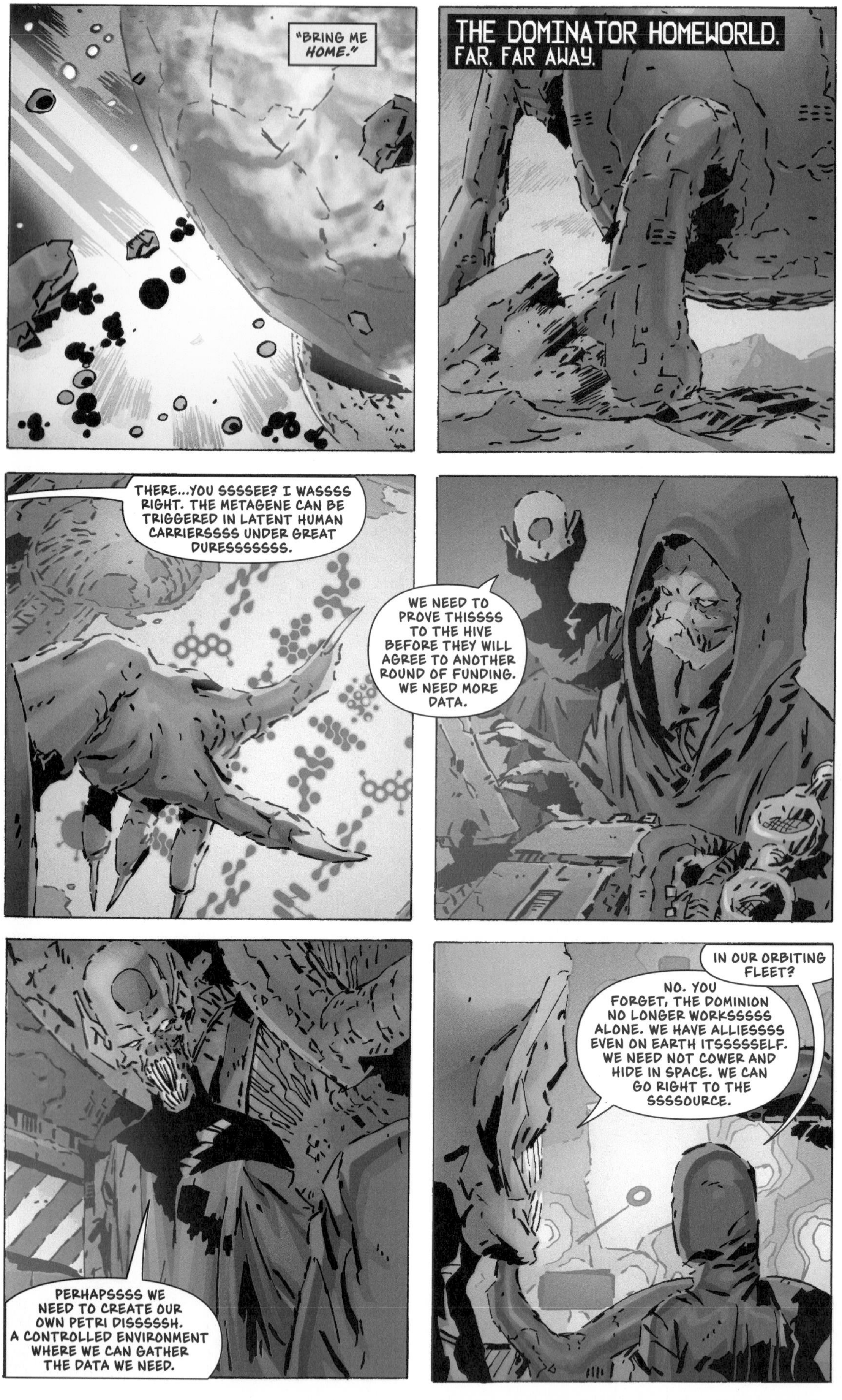
"BRING ME HOME."
THE DOMINATOR HOMEWORLD.
FAR, FAR AWAY.
THERE...YOU SSSSEE? I WASSSS RIGHT. THE METAGENE CAN BE TRIGGERED IN LATENT HUMAN CARRIERSSSS UNDER GREAT DURESSSSSSSS.
WE NEED TO PROVE THISSSS TO THE HIVE BEFORE THEY WILL AGREE TO ANOTHER ROUND OF FUNDING. WE NEED MORE DATA.
PERHAPSSSS WE NEED TO CREATE OUR OWN PETRI DISSSSSH. A CONTROLLED ENVIRONMENT WHERE WE CAN GATHER THE DATA WE NEED.
IN OUR ORBITING FLEET?
NO. YOU FORGET, THE DOMINION NO LONGER WORKSSSSS ALONE. WE HAVE ALLIESSSS EVEN ON EARTH ITSSSSSELF. WE NEED NOT COWER AND HIDE IN SPACE. WE CAN GO RIGHT TO THE SSSSOURCE.

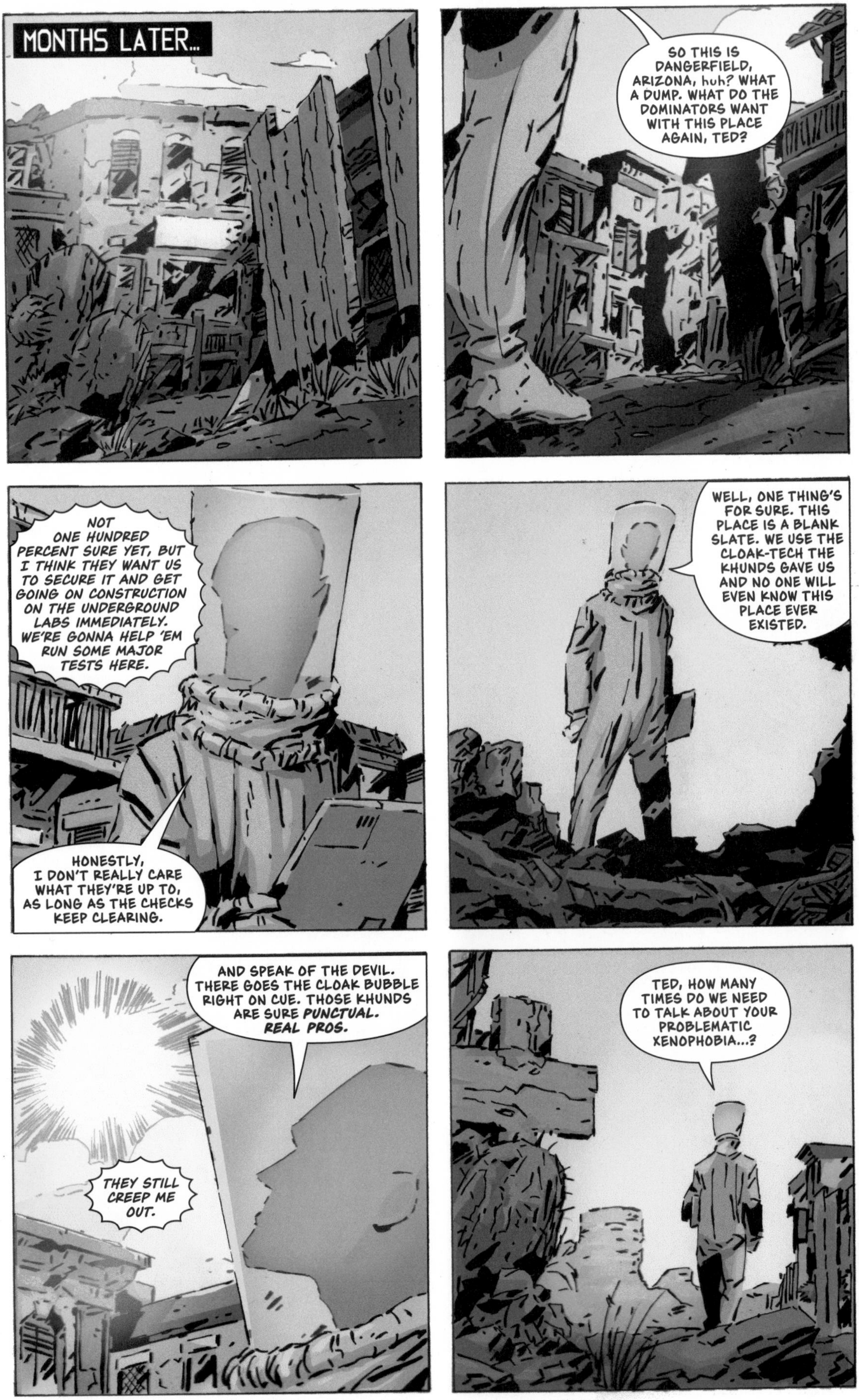
MONTHS LATER...
SO THIS IS DANGERFIELD, ARIZONA, huh? WHAT A DUMP. WHAT DO THE DOMINATORS WANT WITH THIS PLACE AGAIN, TED?
NOT ONE HUNDRED PERCENT SURE YET, BUT I THINK THEY WANT US TO SECURE IT AND GET GOING ON CONSTRUCTION ON THE UNDERGROUND LABS IMMEDIATELY. WE'RE GONNA HELP 'EM RUN SOME MAJOR TESTS HERE.
HONESTLY, I DON'T REALLY CARE WHAT THEY'RE UP TO, AS LONG AS THE CHECKS KEEP CLEARING.
WELL, ONE THING'S FOR SURE. THIS PLACE IS A BLANK SLATE. WE USE THE CLOAK-TECH THE KHUNDS GAVE US AND NO ONE WILL EVEN KNOW THIS PLACE EVER EXISTED.
AND SPEAK OF THE DEVIL. THERE GOES THE CLOAK BUBBLE RIGHT ON CUE. THOSE KHUNDS ARE SURE *PUNCTUAL.* *REAL PROS.*
THEY STILL CREEP ME OUT.
TED, HOW MANY TIMES DO WE NEED TO TALK ABOUT YOUR PROBLEMATIC XENOPHOBIA...?

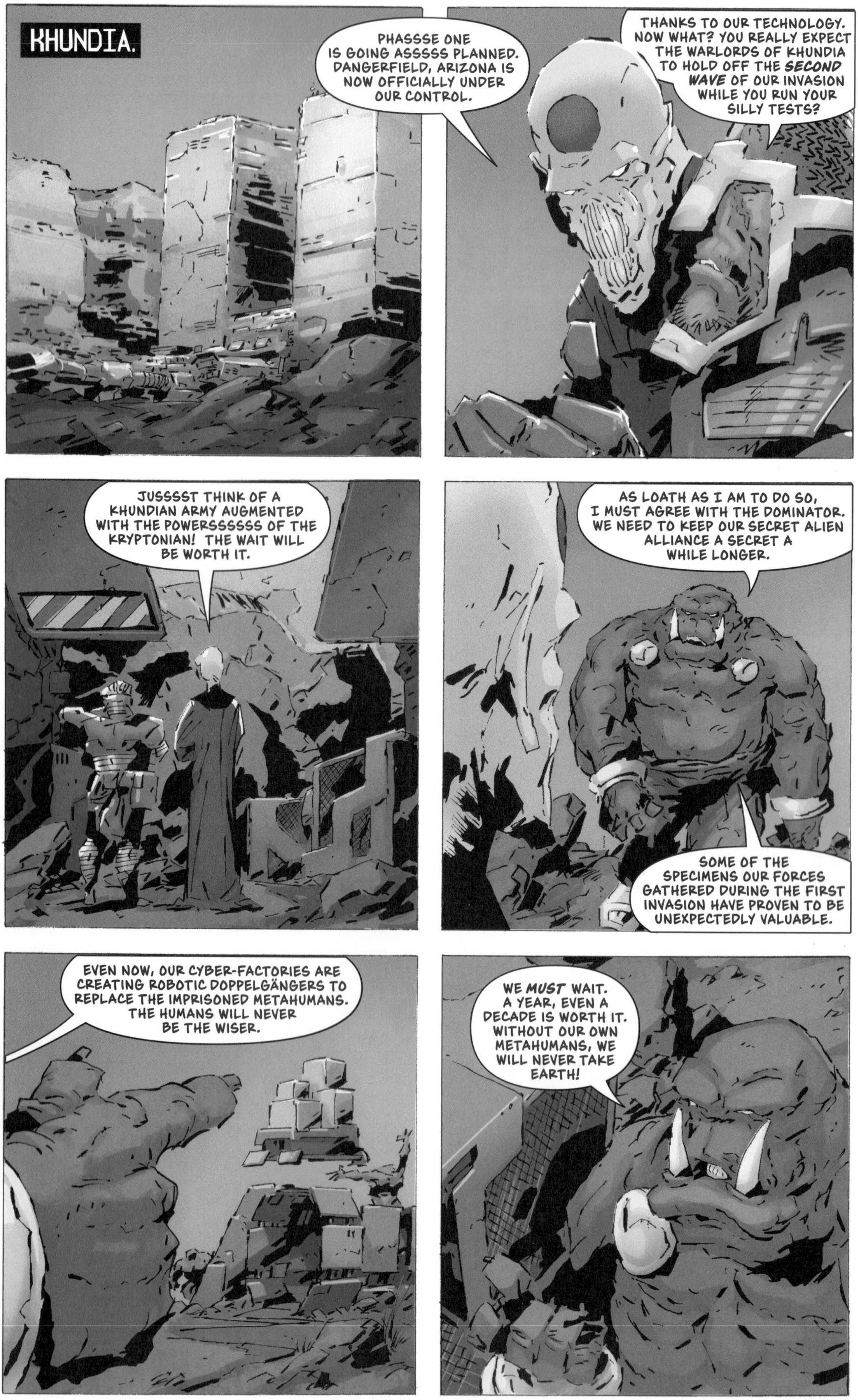
KHUNDIA.
PHASSSE ONE IS GOING ASSSSS PLANNED. DANGERFIELD, ARIZONA IS NOW OFFICIALLY UNDER OUR CONTROL.
THANKS TO OUR TECHNOLOGY. NOW WHAT? YOU REALLY EXPECT THE WARLORDS OF KHUNDIA TO HOLD OFF THE SECOND WAVE OF OUR INVASION WHILE YOU RUN YOUR SILLY TESTS?
JUSSSST THINK OF A KHUNDIAN ARMY AUGMENTED WITH THE POWERSSSSSS OF THE KRYPTONIAN! THE WAIT WILL BE WORTH IT.
AS LOATH AS I AM TO DO SO, I MUST AGREE WITH THE DOMINATOR. WE NEED TO KEEP OUR SECRET ALIEN ALLIANCE A SECRET A WHILE LONGER.
SOME OF THE SPECIMENS OUR FORCES GATHERED DURING THE FIRST INVASION HAVE PROVEN TO BE UNEXPECTEDLY VALUABLE.
EVEN NOW, OUR CYBER-FACTORIES ARE CREATING ROBOTIC DOPPELGÄNGERS TO REPLACE THE IMPRISONED METAHUMANS. THE HUMANS WILL NEVER BE THE WISER.
WE MUST WAIT. A YEAR, EVEN A DECADE IS WORTH IT. WITHOUT OUR OWN METAHUMANS, WE WILL NEVER TAKE EARTH!

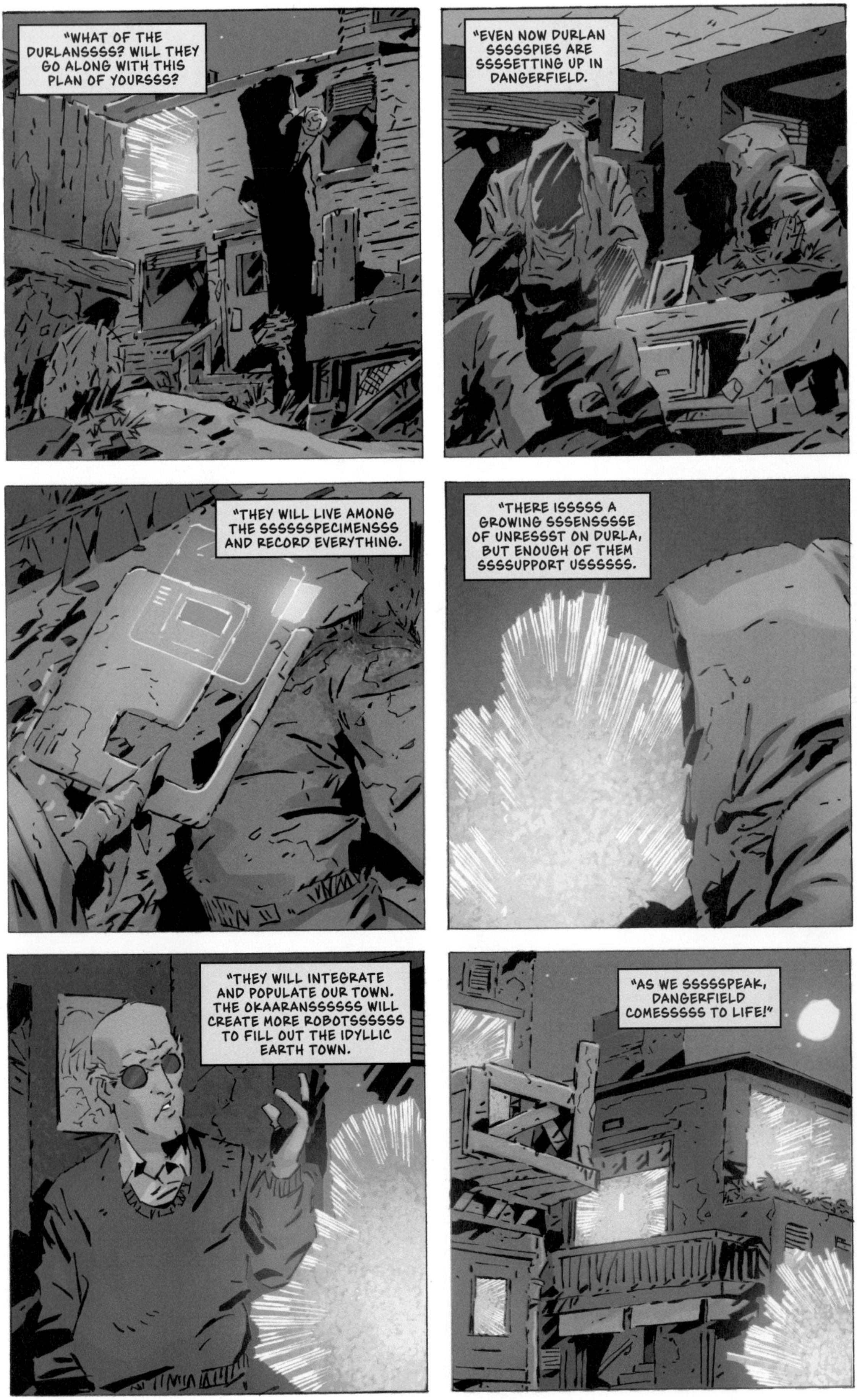
"WHAT OF THE DURLANSSSSS? WILL THEY GO ALONG WITH THIS PLAN OF YOURSSS?
"EVEN NOW DURLAN SSSSSPIES ARE SSSSETTING UP IN DANGERFIELD.
"THEY WILL LIVE AMONG THE SSSSSSPECIMENSSS AND RECORD EVERYTHING.
"THERE ISSSSS A GROWING SSSENSSSSE OF UNRESSST ON DURLA, BUT ENOUGH OF THEM SSSSUPPORT USSSSSS.
"THEY WILL INTEGRATE AND POPULATE OUR TOWN. THE OKAARANSSSSSS WILL CREATE MORE ROBOTSSSSSS TO FILL OUT THE IDYLLIC EARTH TOWN.
"AS WE SSSSSPEAK, DANGERFIELD COMESSSSS TO LIFE!"

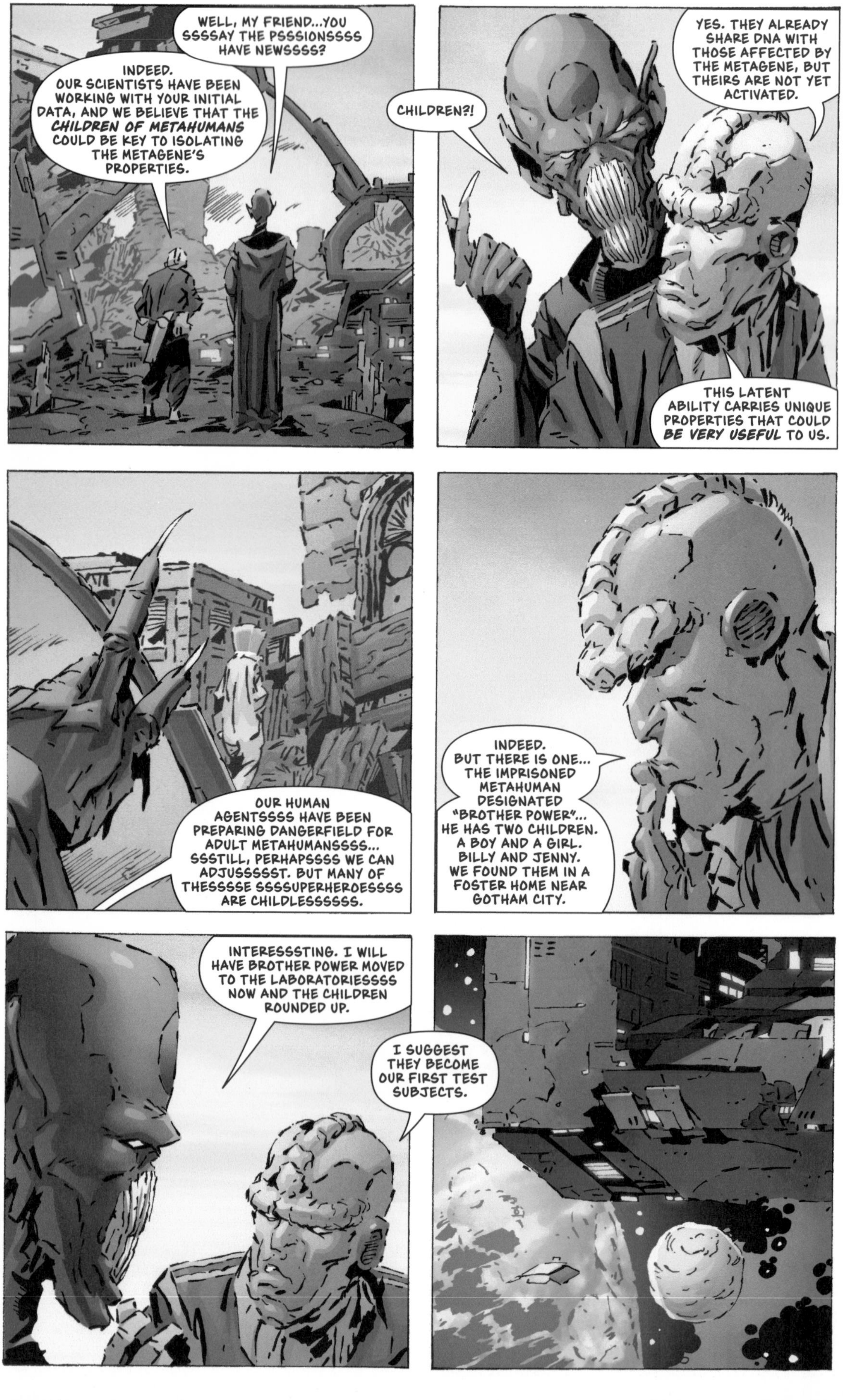
WELL, MY FRIEND...YOU SSSSAY THE PSSSIONSSSS HAVE NEWSSSS?
INDEED. OUR SCIENTISTS HAVE BEEN WORKING WITH YOUR INITIAL DATA, AND WE BELIEVE THAT THE CHILDREN OF METAHUMANS COULD BE KEY TO ISOLATING THE METAGENE'S PROPERTIES.
CHILDREN?!
YES. THEY ALREADY SHARE DNA WITH THOSE AFFECTED BY THE METAGENE, BUT THEIRS ARE NOT YET ACTIVATED.
THIS LATENT ABILITY CARRIES UNIQUE PROPERTIES THAT COULD BE VERY USEFUL TO US.
OUR HUMAN AGENTSSSS HAVE BEEN PREPARING DANGERFIELD FOR ADULT METAHUMANSSSS... SSSTILL, PERHAPSSSS WE CAN ADJUSSSSST. BUT MANY OF THESSSSE SSSSUPERHEROESSSS ARE CHILDLESSSSSS.
INDEED. BUT THERE IS ONE... THE IMPRISONED METAHUMAN DESIGNATED "BROTHER POWER"... HE HAS TWO CHILDREN. A BOY AND A GIRL. BILLY AND JENNY. WE FOUND THEM IN A FOSTER HOME NEAR GOTHAM CITY.
INTERESSSTING. I WILL HAVE BROTHER POWER MOVED TO THE LABORATORIESSSS NOW AND THE CHILDREN ROUNDED UP.
I SUGGEST THEY BECOME OUR FIRST TEST SUBJECTS.

WHAT, YOU ACTUALLY BELIEVE THIS SECOND-RATE SCI-FI CRAP?

YOU HAVE A BETTER EXPLANATION FOR EVERYTHING THAT'S HAPPENED?

IF THIS REALLY IS ALL SOME DOMINATOR EXPERIMENT AND WE'RE THE SUBJECTS...

...I GOTTA FIND HELEN!

HEY, WE MAY HAVE A PROBLEM. THE KIDS MAY BE ONTO US A BIT SOONER THAN PLANNED.

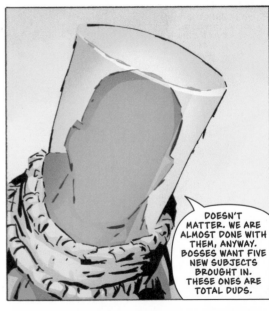

DOESN'T MATTER. WE ARE ALMOST DONE WITH THEM, ANYWAY. BOSSES WANT FIVE NEW SUBJECTS BROUGHT IN. THESE ONES ARE TOTAL DUDS.

I SAY WE KILL THEM NOW AND-- Ggk!

NOW WHAT?

SO OUR PARENTS' CARS ARE TOTALED. IT DOESN'T MEAN ANYTHING.

HEY! WHAT ARE YOU DOING?! GET OUT OF THERE, VANCE!

HOLD ON! I THINK I FOUND SOMETHING.

YOU THINK YOU ACTUALLY KNOW WHAT ANY OF THIS CRAP IS?!

ONCE... JUST ONCE, I WISH YOU'D HAVE A LITTLE FAITH IN ME, THERESA.

I HEARD SOMETHING IN HERE! IF YOU'D STOP YELLING AT ME FOR ONE SECOND--

HA! I KNEW IT! THERE'S A SECRET PASSAGE HERE!! AND I THINK THERE'S SOMEONE DOWN HERE.

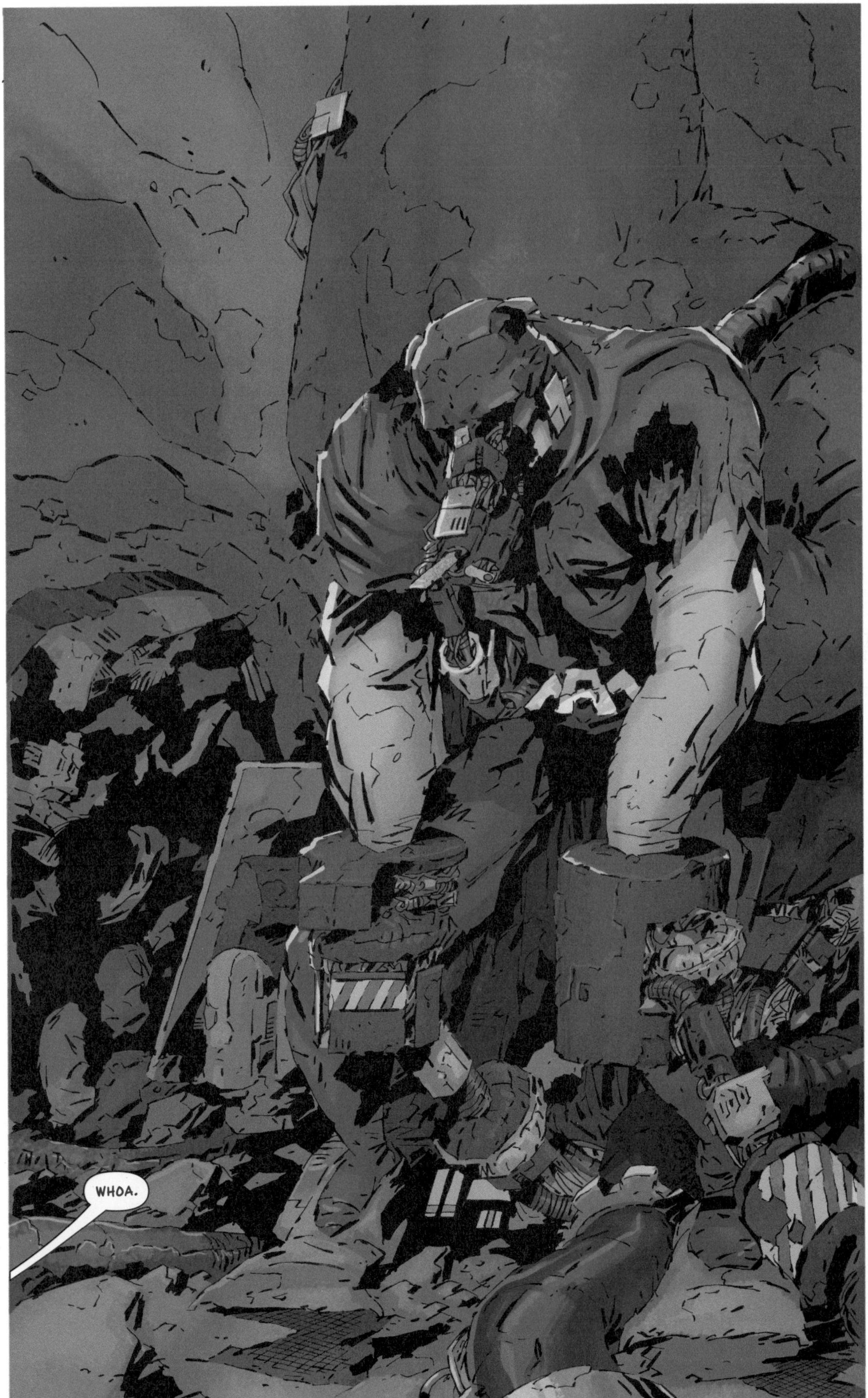
WHOA.

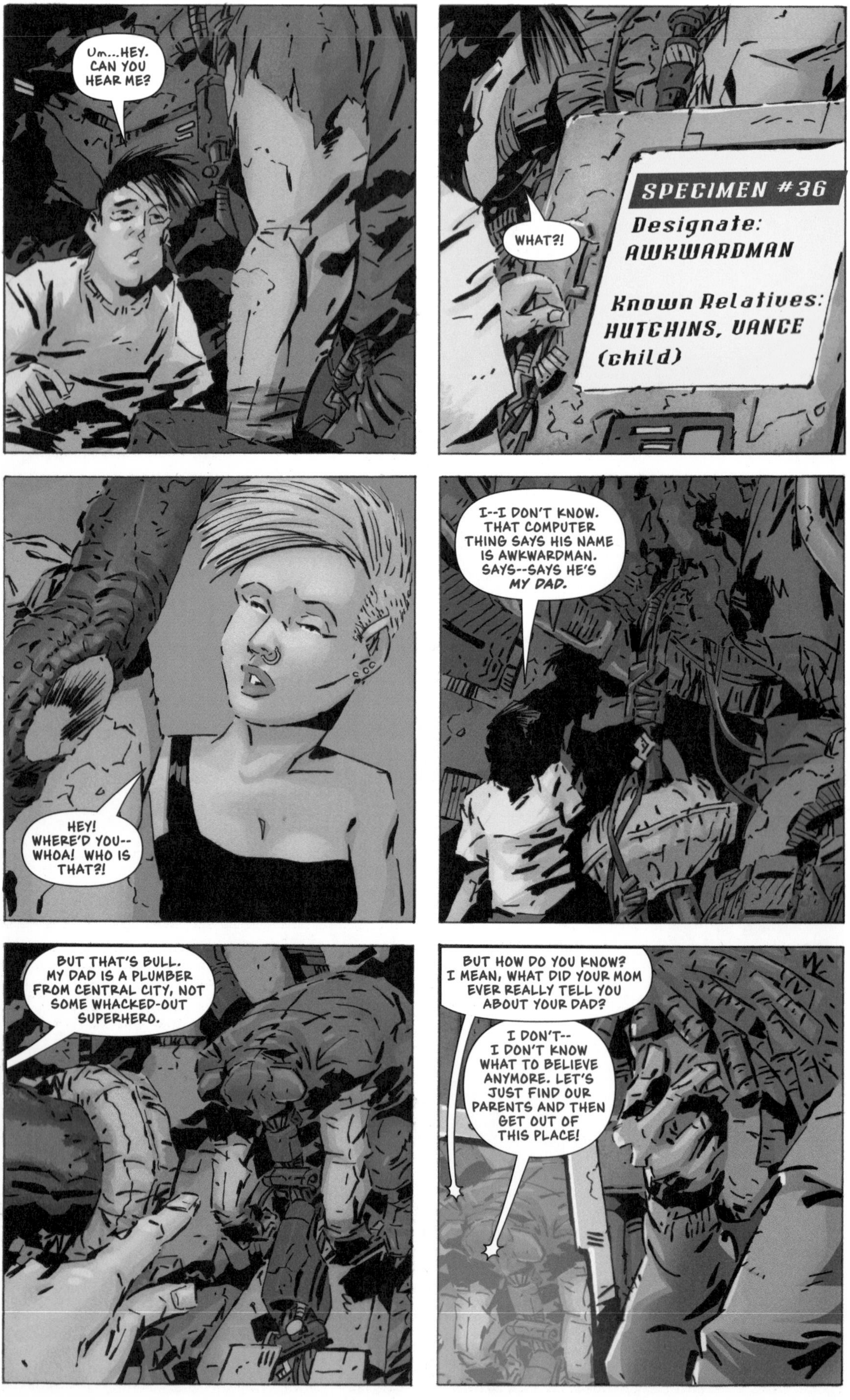
Um...HEY. CAN YOU HEAR ME?
SPECIMEN #36
Designate: AWKWARDMAN
Known Relatives: HUTCHINS, VANCE (child)
WHAT?!
HEY! WHERE'D YOU-- WHOA! WHO IS THAT?!
I--I DON'T KNOW. THAT COMPUTER THING SAYS HIS NAME IS AWKWARDMAN. SAYS--SAYS HE'S MY DAD.
BUT THAT'S BULL. MY DAD IS A PLUMBER FROM CENTRAL CITY, NOT SOME WHACKED-OUT SUPERHERO.
BUT HOW DO YOU KNOW? I MEAN, WHAT DID YOUR MOM EVER REALLY TELL YOU ABOUT YOUR DAD?
I DON'T-- I DON'T KNOW WHAT TO BELIEVE ANYMORE. LET'S JUST FIND OUR PARENTS AND THEN GET OUT OF THIS PLACE!

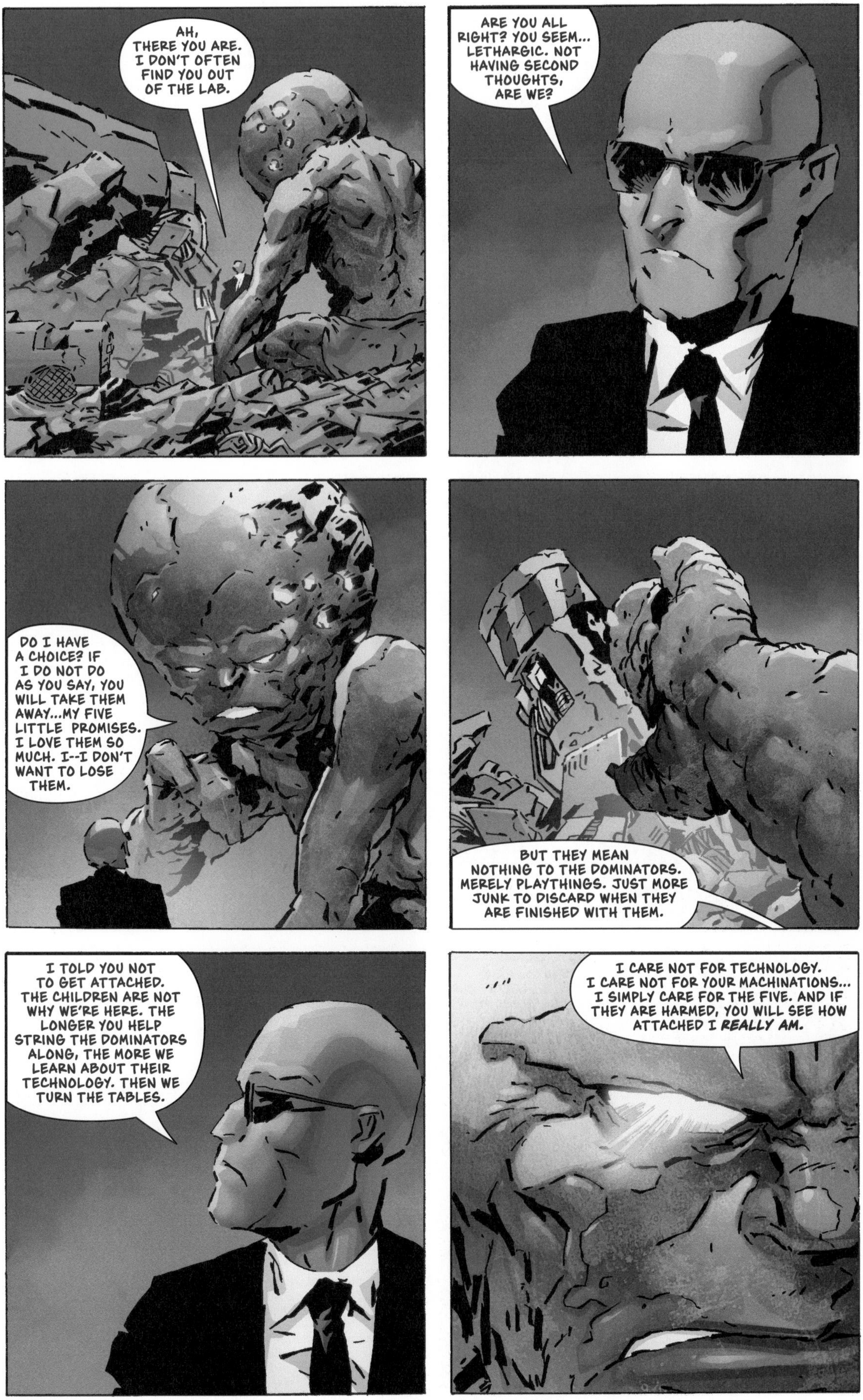
AH, THERE YOU ARE. I DON'T OFTEN FIND YOU OUT OF THE LAB.
ARE YOU ALL RIGHT? YOU SEEM... LETHARGIC. NOT HAVING SECOND THOUGHTS, ARE WE?
DO I HAVE A CHOICE? IF I DO NOT DO AS YOU SAY, YOU WILL TAKE THEM AWAY...MY FIVE LITTLE PROMISES. I LOVE THEM SO MUCH. I--I DON'T WANT TO LOSE THEM.
BUT THEY MEAN NOTHING TO THE DOMINATORS. MERELY PLAYTHINGS. JUST MORE JUNK TO DISCARD WHEN THEY ARE FINISHED WITH THEM.
I TOLD YOU NOT TO GET ATTACHED. THE CHILDREN ARE NOT WHY WE'RE HERE. THE LONGER YOU HELP STRING THE DOMINATORS ALONG, THE MORE WE LEARN ABOUT THEIR TECHNOLOGY. THEN WE TURN THE TABLES.
I CARE NOT FOR TECHNOLOGY. I CARE NOT FOR YOUR MACHINATIONS... I SIMPLY CARE FOR THE FIVE. AND IF THEY ARE HARMED, YOU WILL SEE HOW ATTACHED I *REALLY AM*.

"SSSSSOMETHING IS WRONG. THE LATESSSSST DATA MAKESSSSS NO SSSSSENSE!"

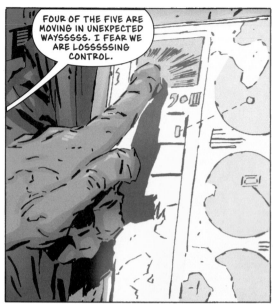

FOUR OF THE FIVE ARE MOVING IN UNEXPECTED WAYSSSSS. I FEAR WE ARE LOSSSSSING CONTROL.

YOU NEED TO BRING THEM BACK TO THE CENTER OF TOWN, BROTHER POWER. I GROW WEARY OF THESSSE GAMESSSSSS.

YOU'RE WEARY?! YOU TURNED MY CHILDREN INTO MONSTERS! THE THINGS YOU HAVE MADE ME DO! I JUST WANT OUT! I WANT IT TO END!

PATHETIC. YOUR EMOTIONSSSSS ARE YOUR WEAKNESSSSSSS. YOU COULD HAVE BEEN SSSSO FORMIDABLE. INSSSSSTEAD, JUSSSSSST A PUPPET.

YOU WILL CONTINUE TO DO AS WE SSSSSAY...

YOUR CHILDREN AND YOUR FEELINGSSSSSSS MEAN NOTHING.

WE PLAY FOR BIGGER STAKES. WE PLAY FOR THE *EARTH ITSSSELF!*

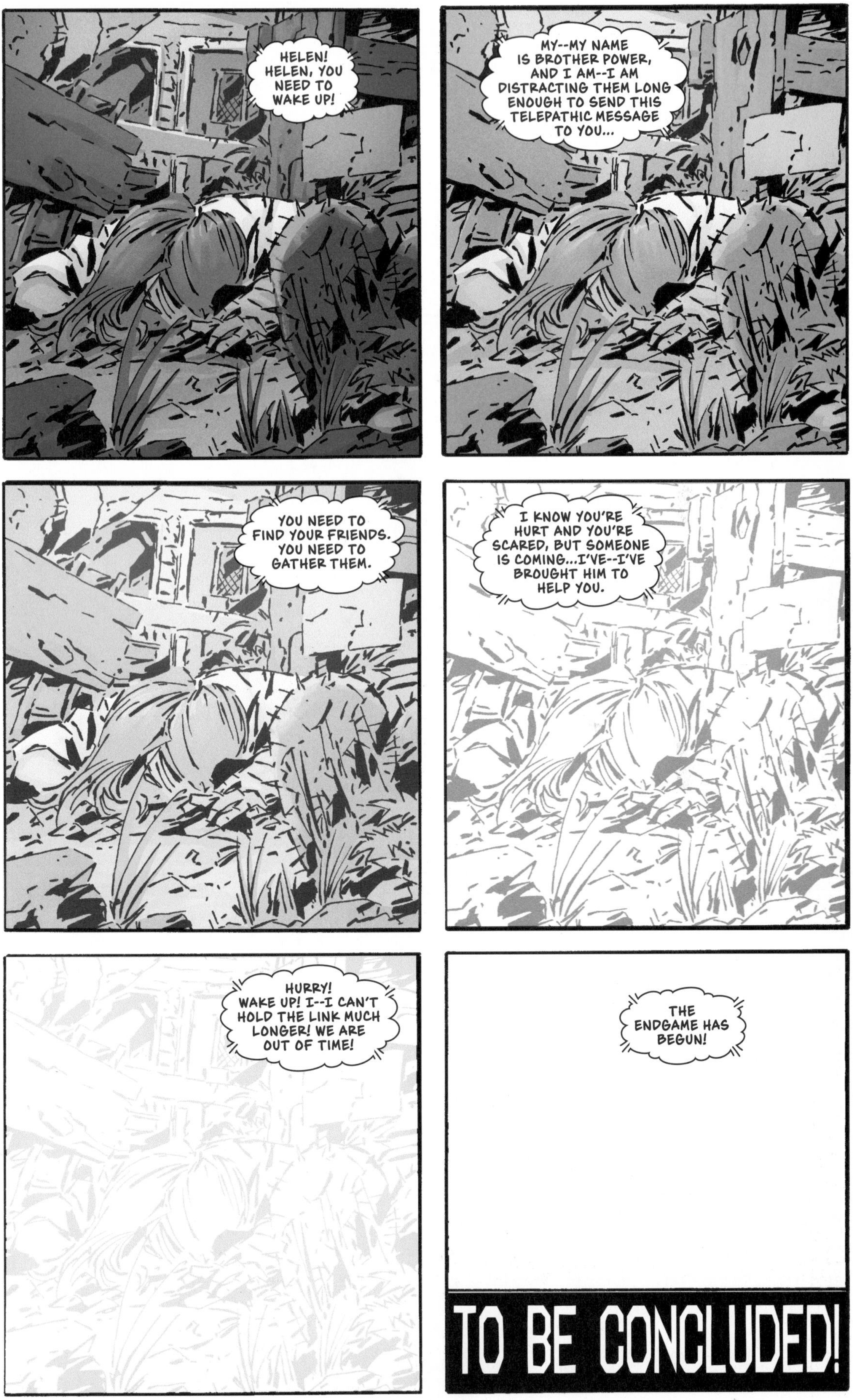
HELEN! HELEN, YOU NEED TO WAKE UP!
MY--MY NAME IS BROTHER POWER, AND I AM--I AM DISTRACTING THEM LONG ENOUGH TO SEND THIS TELEPATHIC MESSAGE TO YOU...
YOU NEED TO FIND YOUR FRIENDS. YOU NEED TO GATHER THEM.
I KNOW YOU'RE HURT AND YOU'RE SCARED, BUT SOMEONE IS COMING...I'VE--I'VE BROUGHT HIM TO HELP YOU.
HURRY! WAKE UP! I--I CAN'T HOLD THE LINK MUCH LONGER! WE ARE OUT OF TIME!
THE ENDGAME HAS BEGUN!
TO BE CONCLUDED!

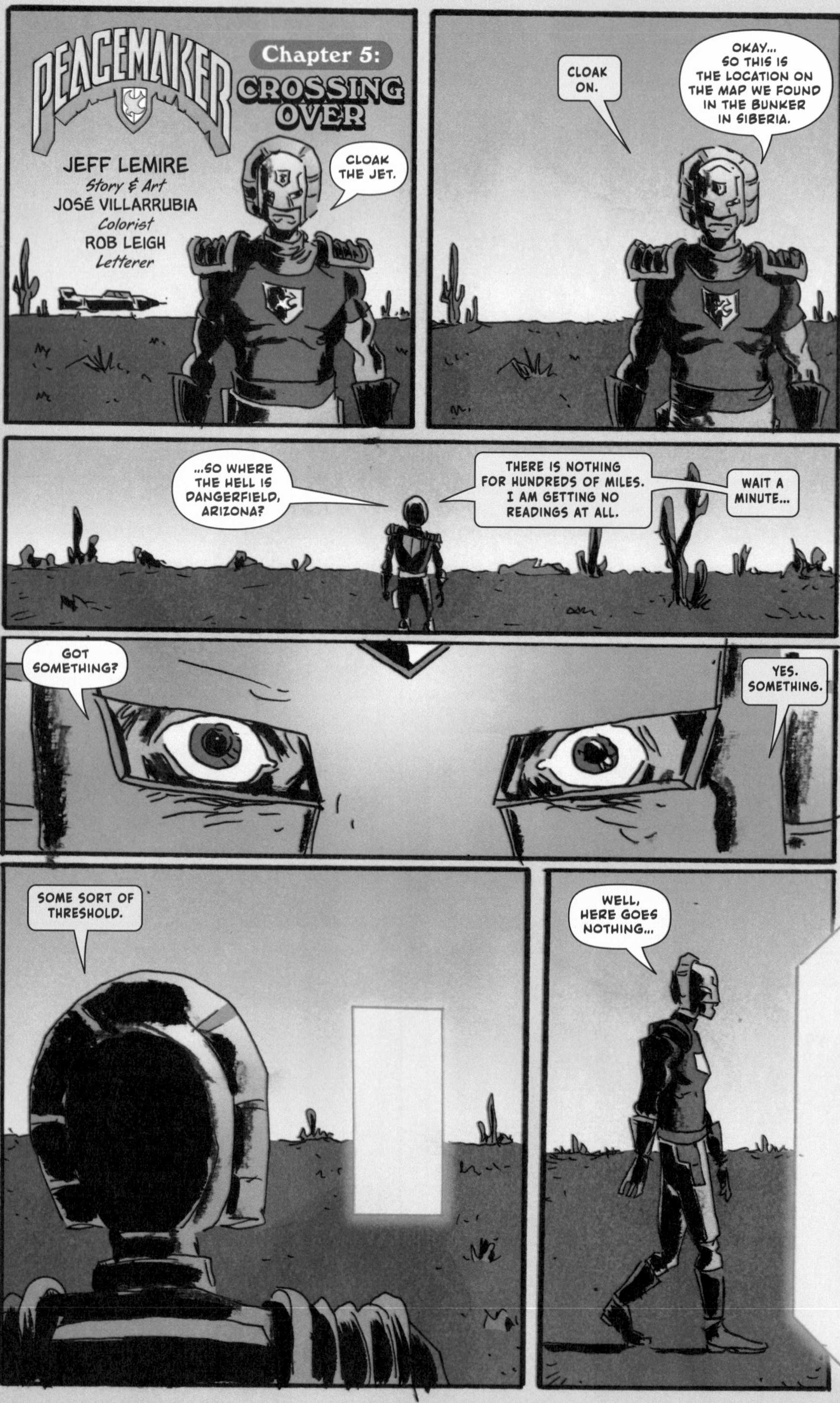
PEACEMAKER
Chapter 5:
CROSSING OVER
JEFF LEMIRE
Story & Art
JOSÉ VILLARRUBIA
Colorist
ROB LEIGH
Letterer
CLOAK THE JET.
CLOAK ON.
OKAY... SO THIS IS THE LOCATION ON THE MAP WE FOUND IN THE BUNKER IN SIBERIA.
...SO WHERE THE HELL IS DANGERFIELD, ARIZONA?
THERE IS NOTHING FOR HUNDREDS OF MILES. I AM GETTING NO READINGS AT ALL.
WAIT A MINUTE...
GOT SOMETHING?
YES. SOMETHING.
SOME SORT OF THRESHOLD.
WELL, HERE GOES NOTHING...

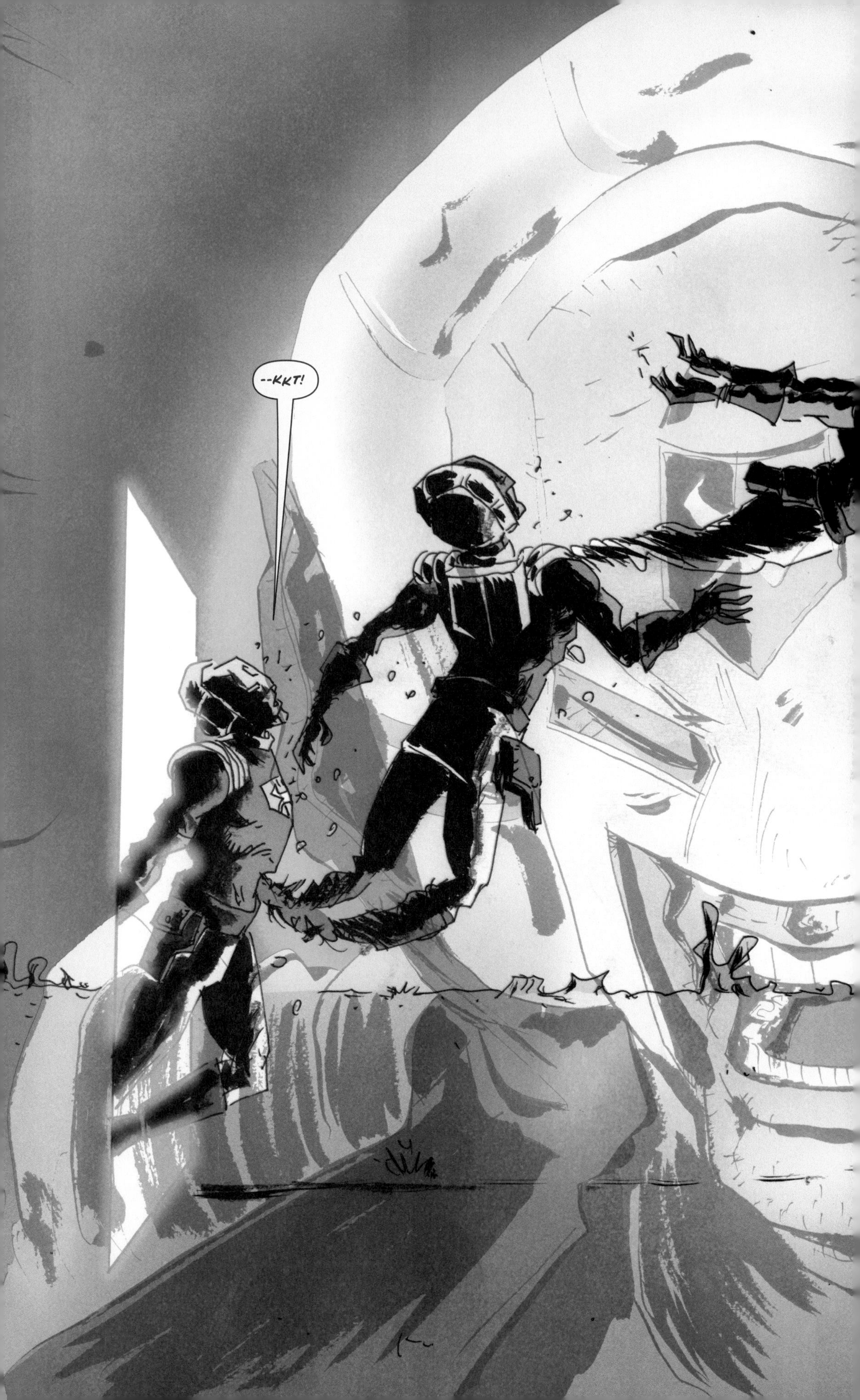
--KKT!

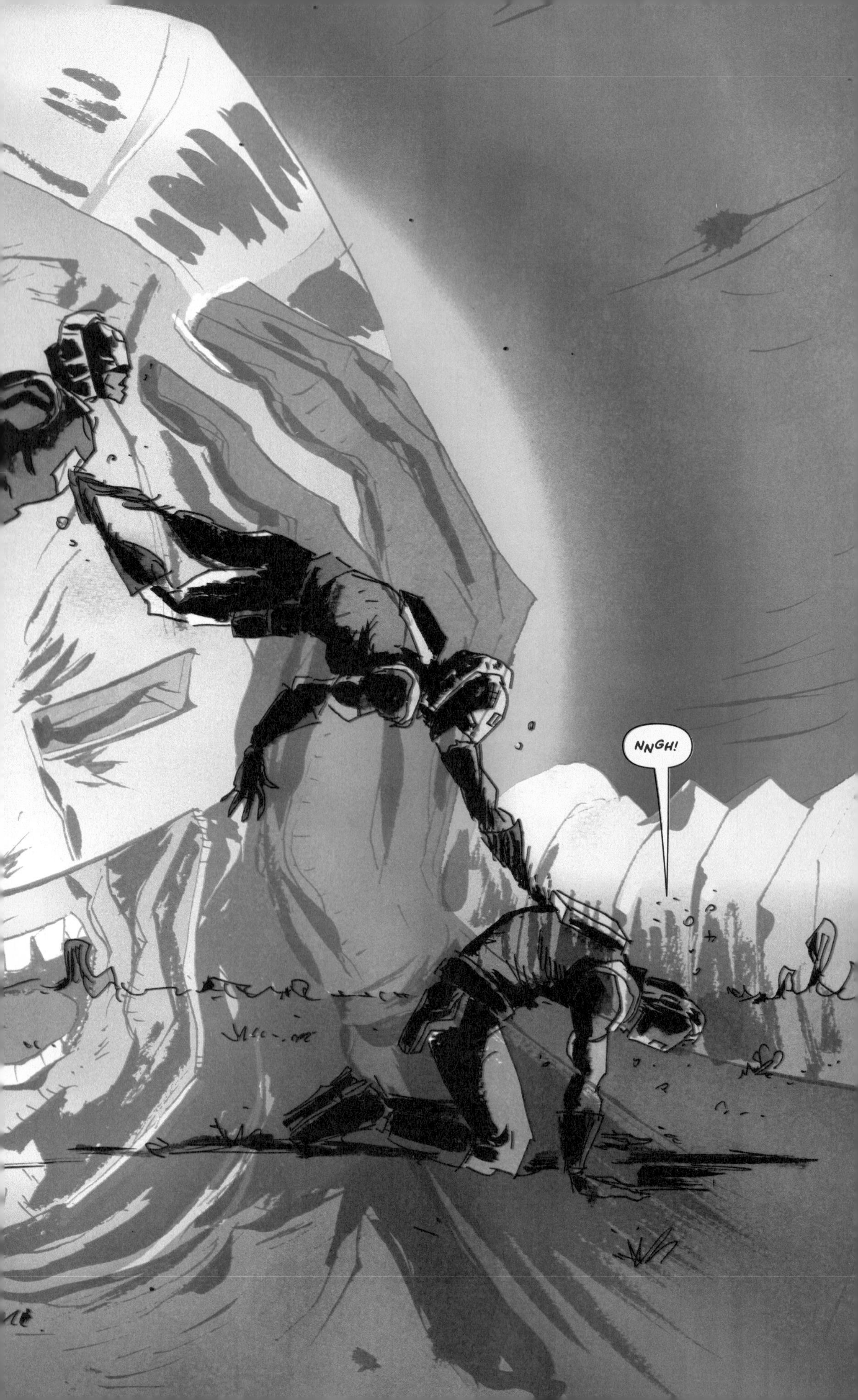
NNGH!

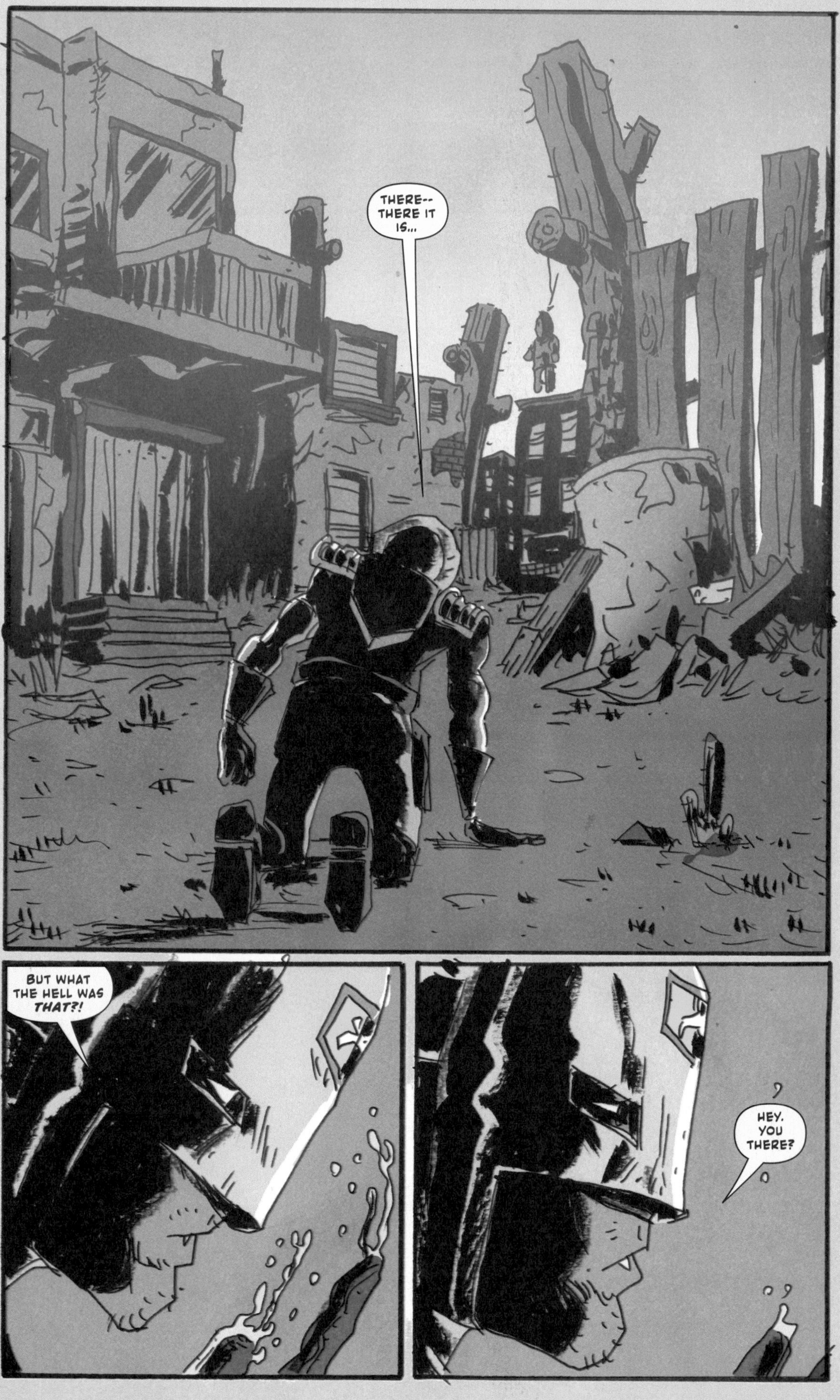
THERE--
THERE IT IS...
BUT WHAT THE HELL WAS *THAT?!*
HEY. YOU THERE?

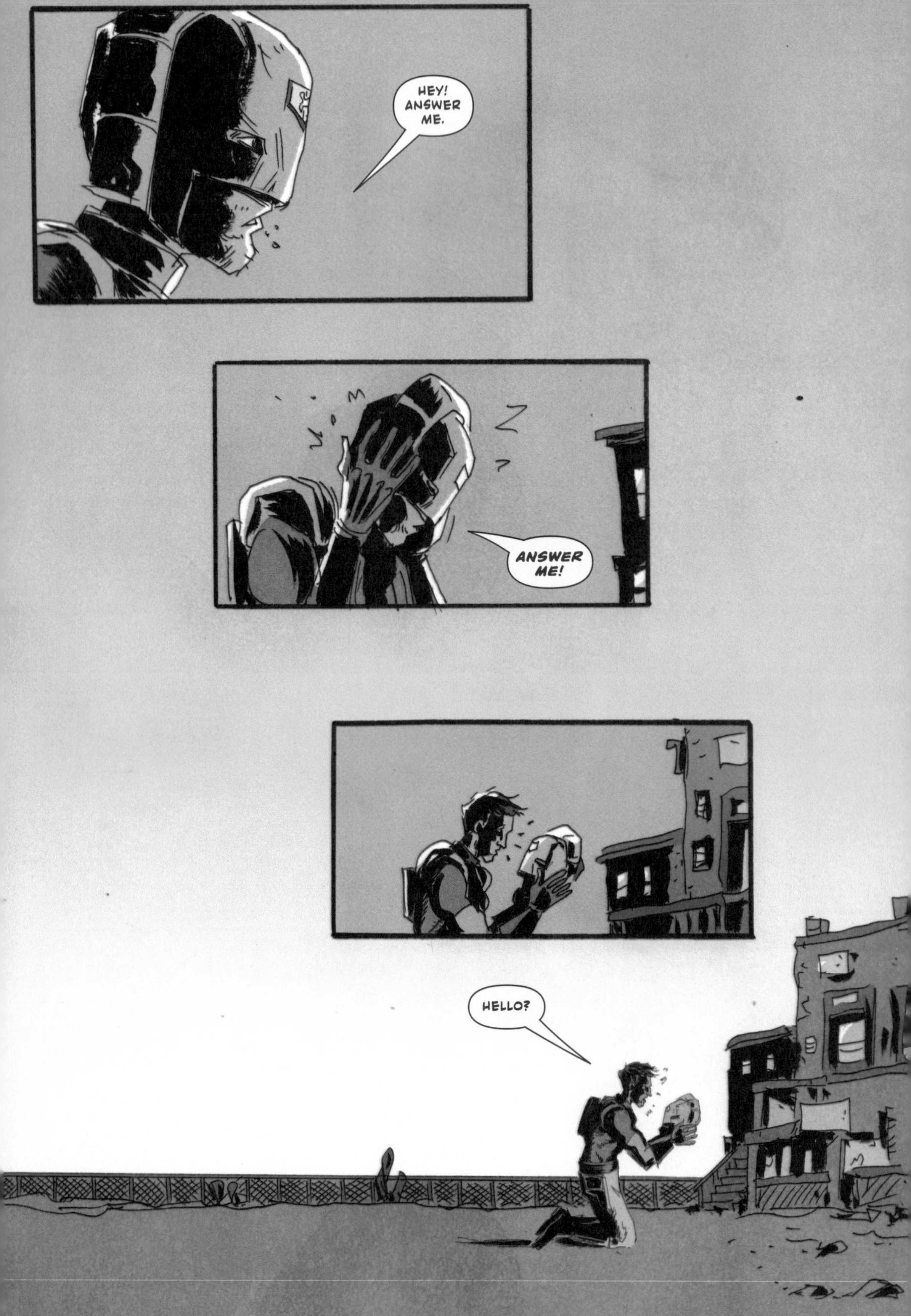
HEY! ANSWER ME.
ANSWER ME!
HELLO?
To Be Continued!

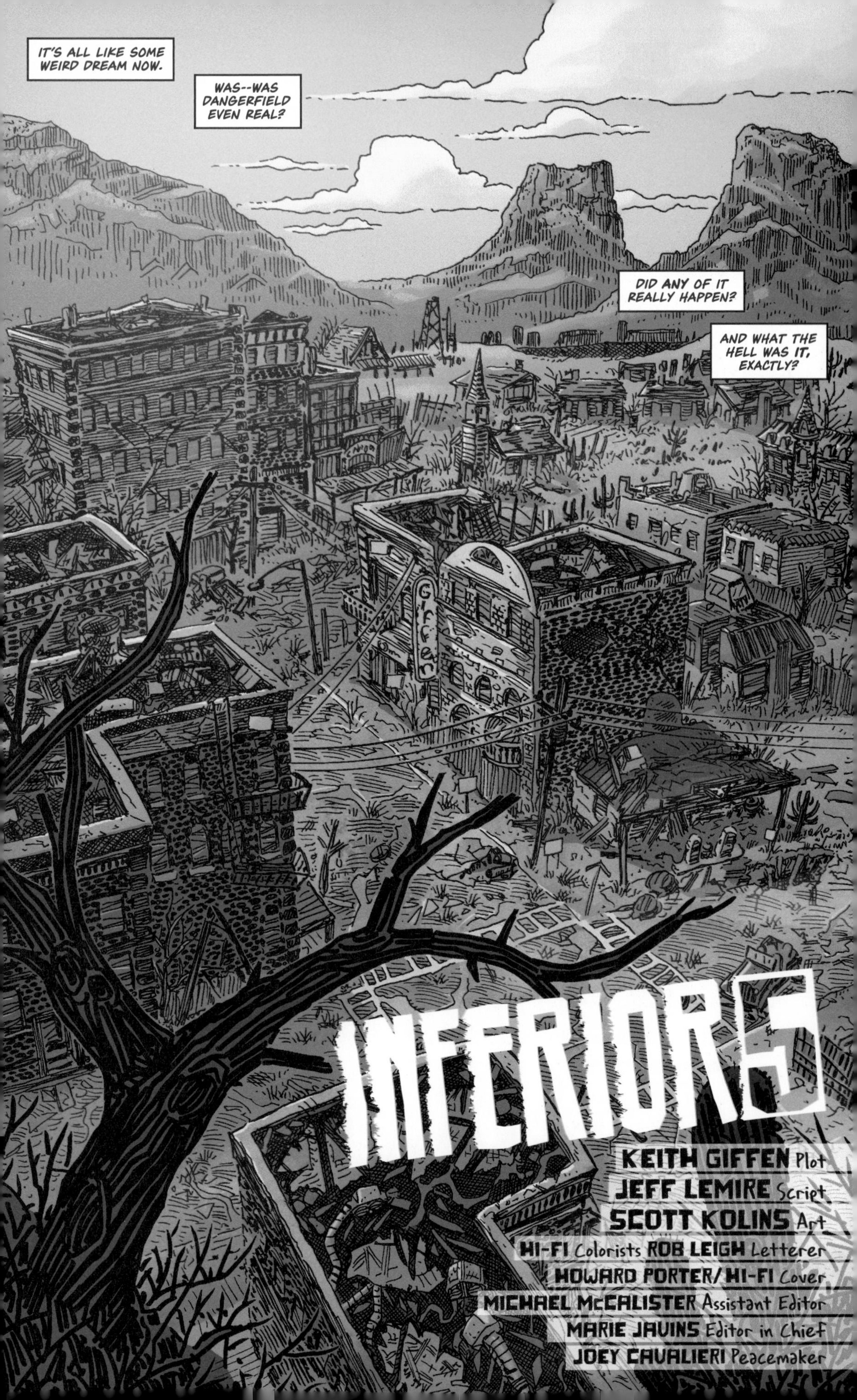
IT'S ALL LIKE SOME WEIRD DREAM NOW.
WAS--WAS DANGERFIELD EVEN REAL?
DID ANY OF IT REALLY HAPPEN?
AND WHAT THE HELL WAS IT, EXACTLY?
Giffen
INFERIOR 5
KEITH GIFFEN Plot
JEFF LEMIRE Script
SCOTT KOLINS Art
HI-FI Colorists ROB LEIGH Letterer
HOWARD PORTER/HI-FI Cover
MICHAEL McCALISTER Assistant Editor
MARIE JAVINS Editor in Chief
JOEY CAVALIERI Peacemaker

COME ON... PLEASE.

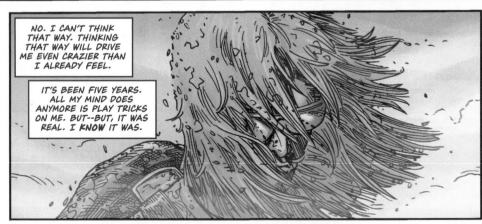

NO. I CAN'T THINK THAT WAY. THINKING THAT WAY WILL DRIVE ME EVEN CRAZIER THAN I ALREADY FEEL.

IT'S BEEN FIVE YEARS. ALL MY MIND DOES ANYMORE IS PLAY TRICKS ON ME. BUT--BUT, IT WAS REAL. I KNOW IT WAS.

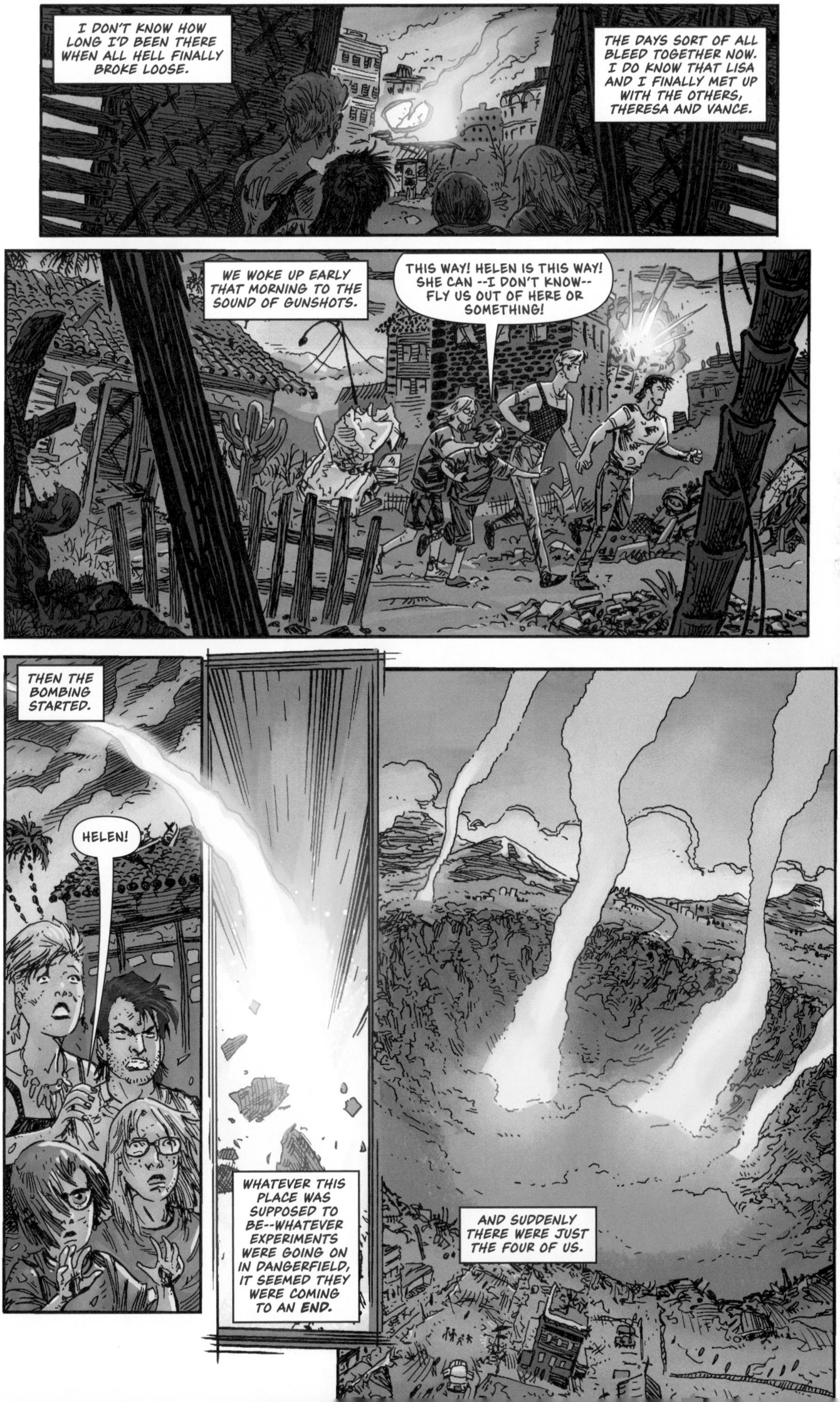
I DON'T KNOW HOW LONG I'D BEEN THERE WHEN ALL HELL FINALLY BROKE LOOSE.
THE DAYS SORT OF ALL BLEED TOGETHER NOW. I DO KNOW THAT LISA AND I FINALLY MET UP WITH THE OTHERS, THERESA AND VANCE.
WE WOKE UP EARLY THAT MORNING TO THE SOUND OF GUNSHOTS.
THIS WAY! HELEN IS THIS WAY! SHE CAN --I DON'T KNOW-- FLY US OUT OF HERE OR SOMETHING!
THEN THE BOMBING STARTED.
HELEN!
WHATEVER THIS PLACE WAS SUPPOSED TO BE--WHATEVER EXPERIMENTS WERE GOING ON IN DANGERFIELD, IT SEEMED THEY WERE COMING TO AN END.
AND SUDDENLY THERE WERE JUST THE FOUR OF US.

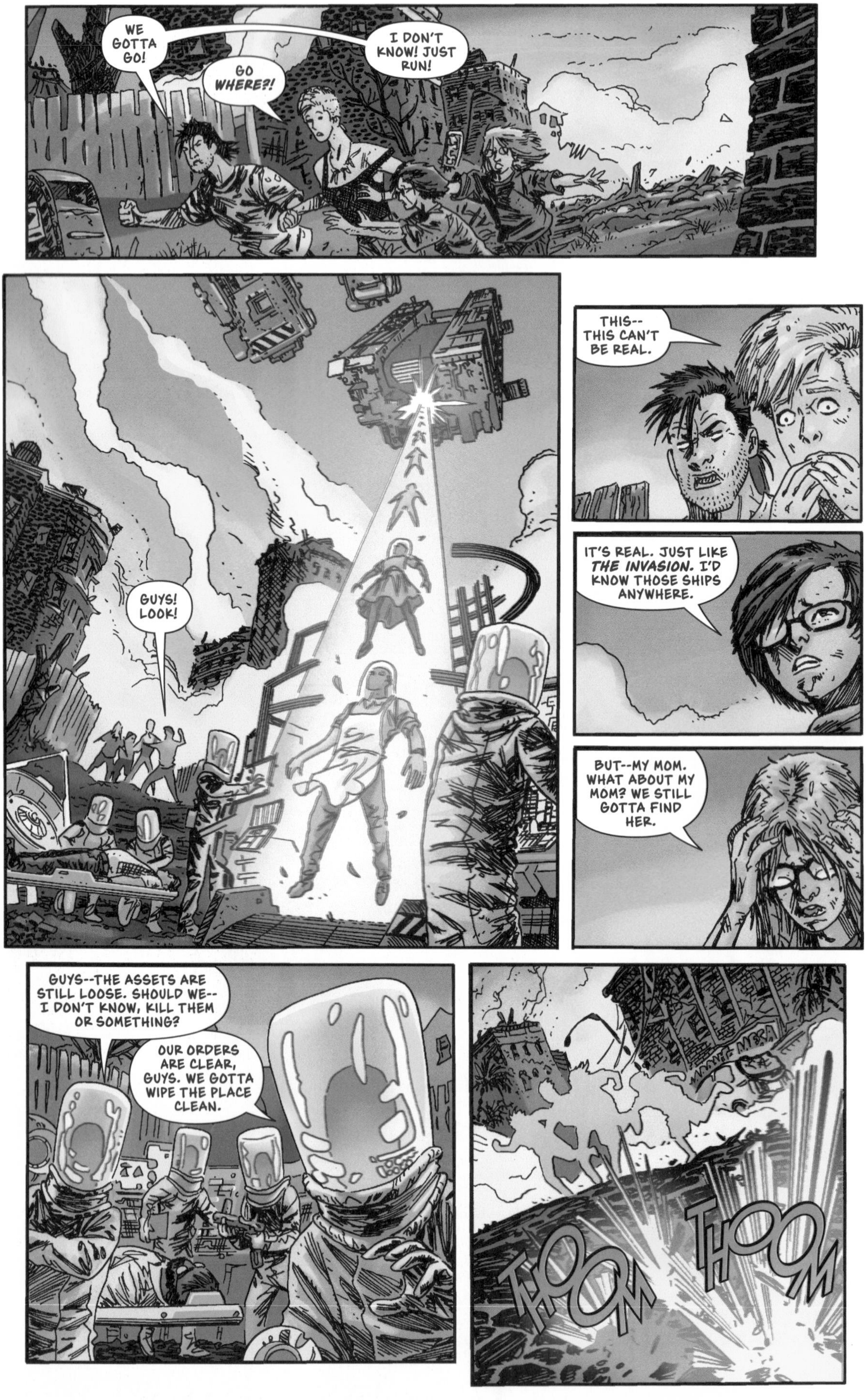
WE GOTTA GO!
GO WHERE?!
I DON'T KNOW! JUST RUN!
GUYS! LOOK!
THIS-- THIS CAN'T BE REAL.
IT'S REAL. JUST LIKE THE INVASION. I'D KNOW THOSE SHIPS ANYWHERE.
BUT--MY MOM. WHAT ABOUT MY MOM? WE STILL GOTTA FIND HER.
GUYS--THE ASSETS ARE STILL LOOSE. SHOULD WE-- I DON'T KNOW, KILL THEM OR SOMETHING?
OUR ORDERS ARE CLEAR, GUYS. WE GOTTA WIPE THE PLACE CLEAN.
THOOM
THOOM

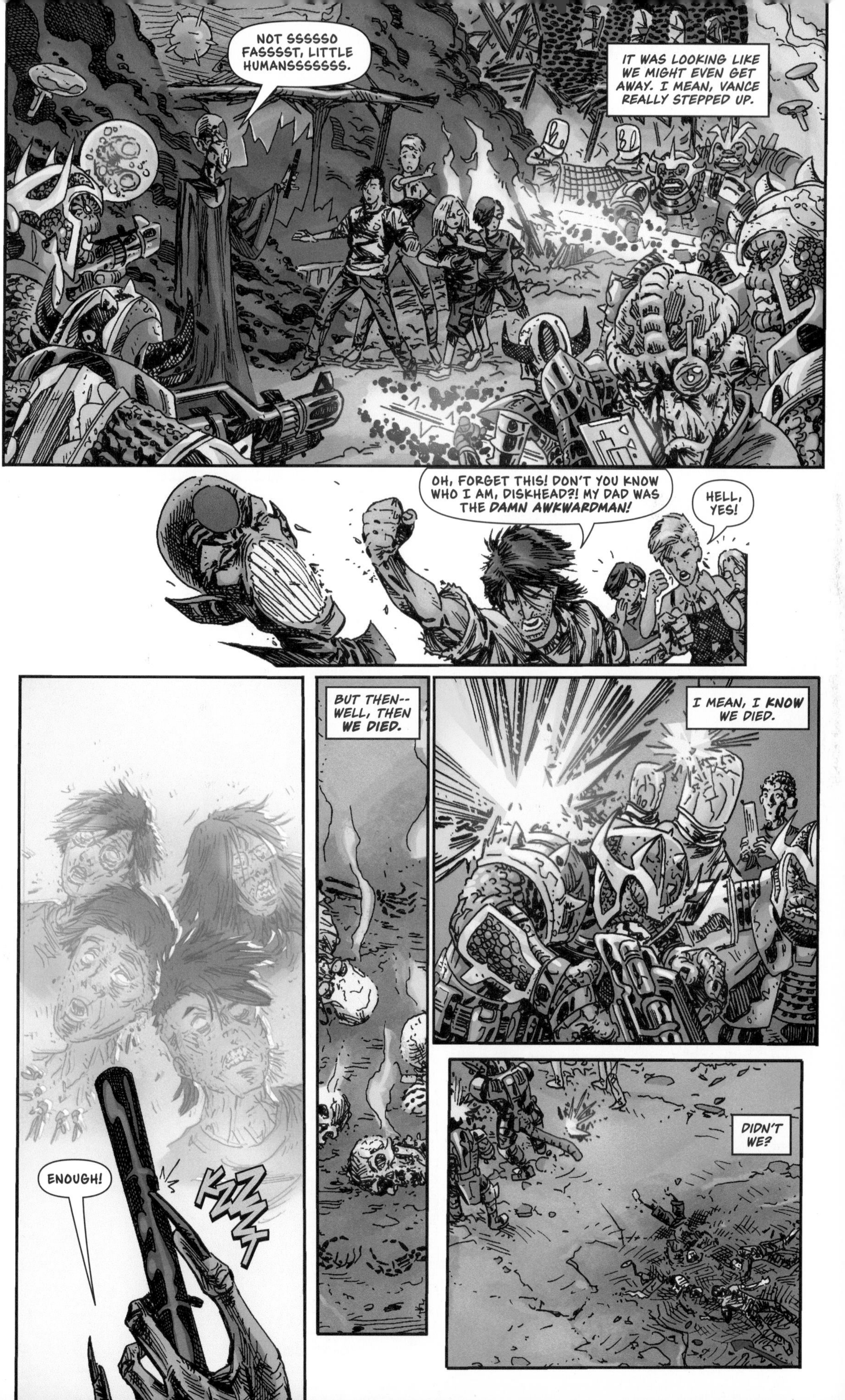
NOT SSSSSO FASSSST, LITTLE HUMANSSSSSSS.
IT WAS LOOKING LIKE WE MIGHT EVEN GET AWAY. I MEAN, VANCE REALLY STEPPED UP.
OH, FORGET THIS! DON'T YOU KNOW WHO I AM, DISKHEAD?! MY DAD WAS THE DAMN AWKWARDMAN!
HELL, YES!
ENOUGH!
KZZZZK
BUT THEN-- WELL, THEN WE DIED.
I MEAN, I KNOW WE DIED.
DIDN'T WE?

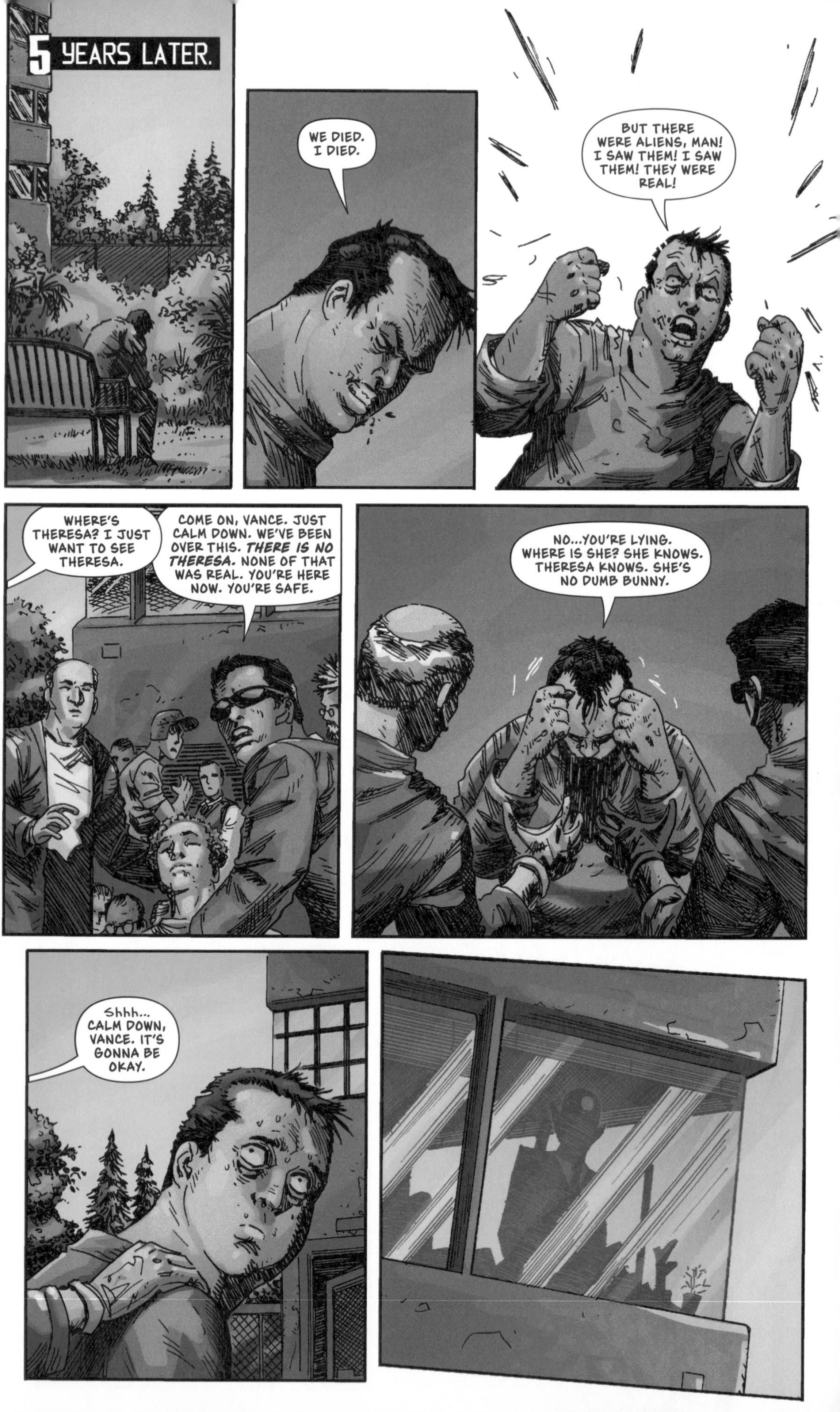
5 YEARS LATER.
WE DIED. I DIED.
BUT THERE WERE ALIENS, MAN! I SAW THEM! I SAW THEM! THEY WERE REAL!
WHERE'S THERESA? I JUST WANT TO SEE THERESA.
COME ON, VANCE. JUST CALM DOWN. WE'VE BEEN OVER THIS. THERE IS NO THERESA. NONE OF THAT WAS REAL. YOU'RE HERE NOW. YOU'RE SAFE.
NO...YOU'RE LYING. WHERE IS SHE? SHE KNOWS. THERESA KNOWS. SHE'S NO DUMB BUNNY.
Shhh... CALM DOWN, VANCE. IT'S GONNA BE OKAY.

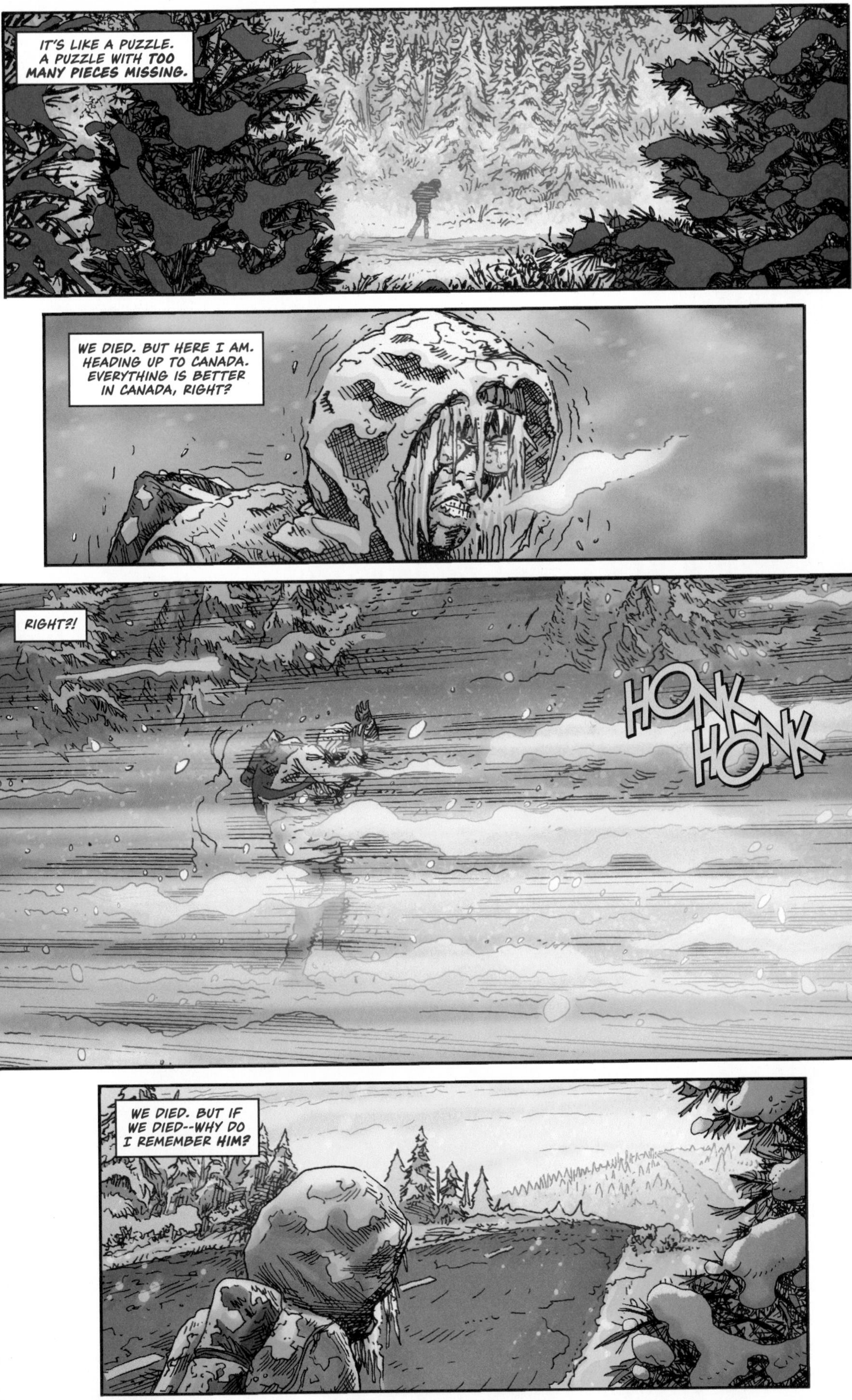
IT'S LIKE A PUZZLE. A PUZZLE WITH TOO MANY PIECES MISSING.
WE DIED. BUT HERE I AM. HEADING UP TO CANADA. EVERYTHING IS BETTER IN CANADA, RIGHT?
RIGHT?!
HONK HONK
WE DIED. BUT IF WE DIED--WHY DO I REMEMBER HIM?

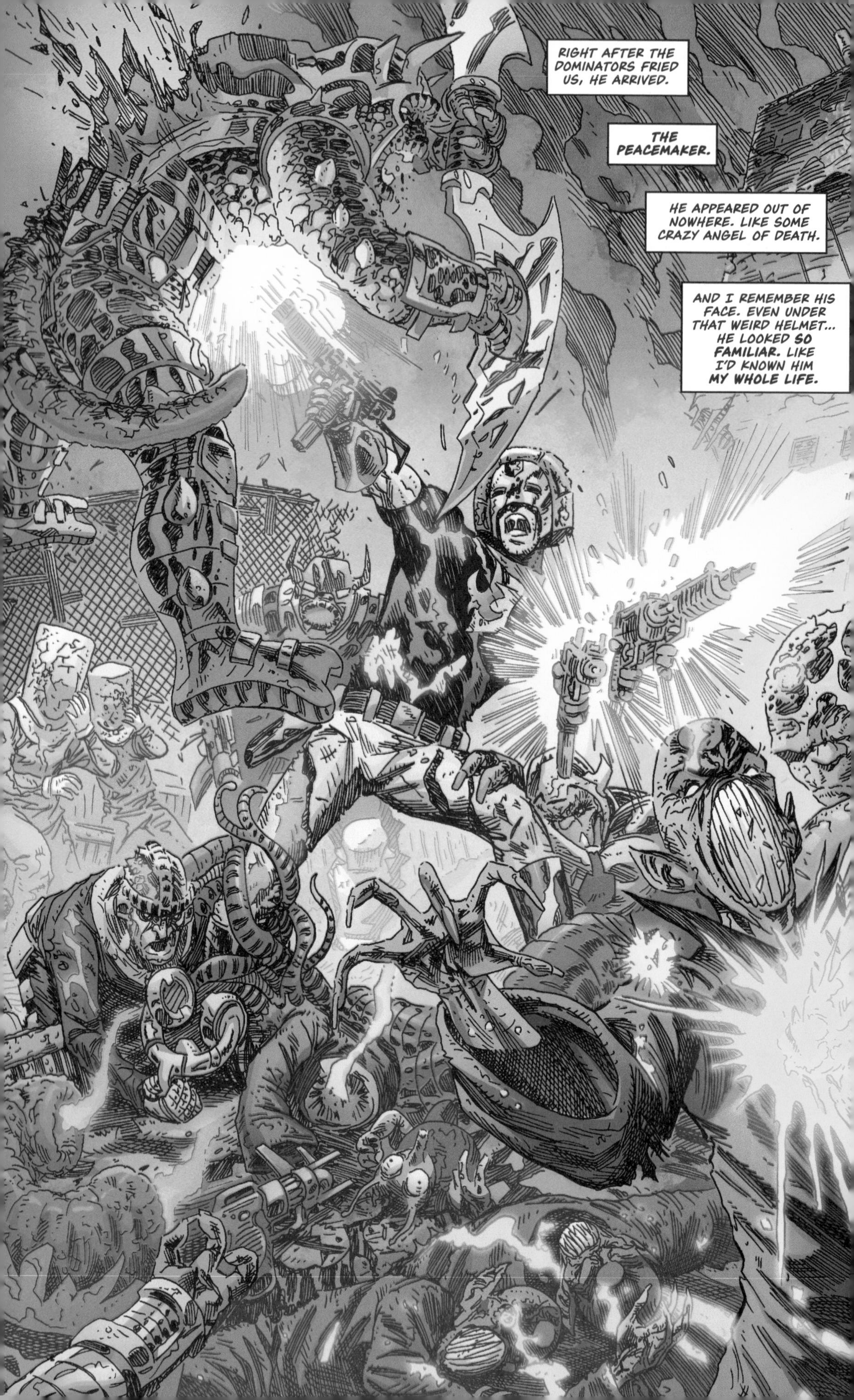
RIGHT AFTER THE DOMINATORS FRIED US, HE ARRIVED.
THE PEACEMAKER.
HE APPEARED OUT OF NOWHERE. LIKE SOME CRAZY ANGEL OF DEATH.
AND I REMEMBER HIS FACE. EVEN UNDER THAT WEIRD HELMET... HE LOOKED SO FAMILIAR. LIKE I'D KNOWN HIM MY WHOLE LIFE.

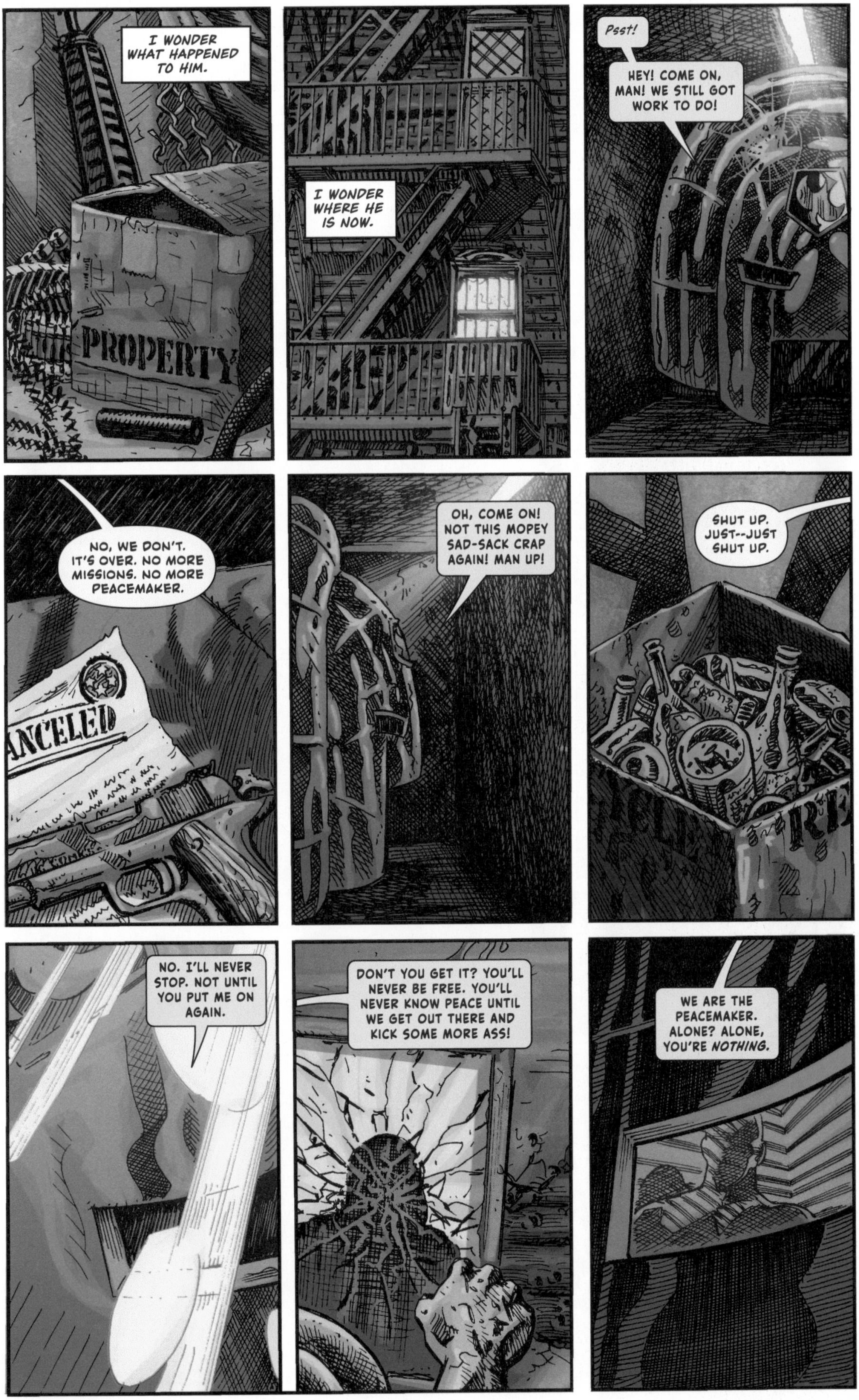
I WONDER WHAT HAPPENED TO HIM.
PROPERTY
I WONDER WHERE HE IS NOW.
Psst!
HEY! COME ON, MAN! WE STILL GOT WORK TO DO!
NO, WE DON'T. IT'S OVER. NO MORE MISSIONS. NO MORE PEACEMAKER.
ANCELED
OH, COME ON! NOT THIS MOPEY SAD-SACK CRAP AGAIN! MAN UP!
SHUT UP. JUST--JUST SHUT UP.
NO. I'LL NEVER STOP. NOT UNTIL YOU PUT ME ON AGAIN.
DON'T YOU GET IT? YOU'LL NEVER BE FREE. YOU'LL NEVER KNOW PEACE UNTIL WE GET OUT THERE AND KICK SOME MORE ASS!
WE ARE THE PEACEMAKER. ALONE? ALONE, YOU'RE *NOTHING*.

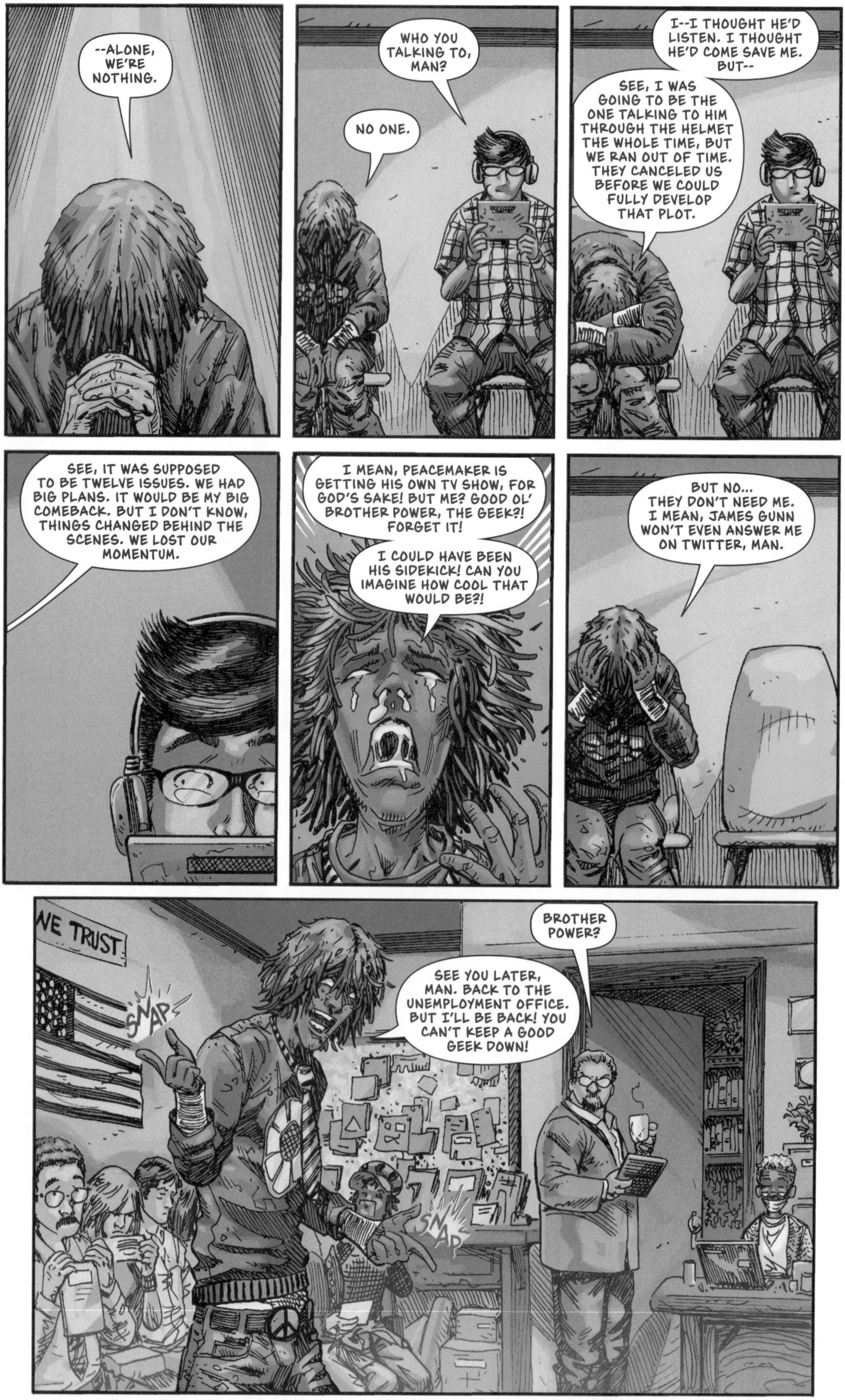
--ALONE, WE'RE NOTHING.
WHO YOU TALKING TO, MAN?
NO ONE.
I--I THOUGHT HE'D LISTEN. I THOUGHT HE'D COME SAVE ME. BUT--
SEE, I WAS GOING TO BE THE ONE TALKING TO HIM THROUGH THE HELMET THE WHOLE TIME, BUT WE RAN OUT OF TIME. THEY CANCELED US BEFORE WE COULD FULLY DEVELOP THAT PLOT.
SEE, IT WAS SUPPOSED TO BE TWELVE ISSUES. WE HAD BIG PLANS. IT WOULD BE MY BIG COMEBACK. BUT I DON'T KNOW, THINGS CHANGED BEHIND THE SCENES. WE LOST OUR MOMENTUM.
I MEAN, PEACEMAKER IS GETTING HIS OWN TV SHOW, FOR GOD'S SAKE! BUT ME? GOOD OL' BROTHER POWER, THE GEEK?! FORGET IT!
I COULD HAVE BEEN HIS SIDEKICK! CAN YOU IMAGINE HOW COOL THAT WOULD BE?!
BUT NO... THEY DON'T NEED ME. I MEAN, JAMES GUNN WON'T EVEN ANSWER ME ON TWITTER, MAN.
WE TRUST
SNAP
BROTHER POWER?
SEE YOU LATER, MAN. BACK TO THE UNEMPLOYMENT OFFICE. BUT I'LL BE BACK! YOU CAN'T KEEP A GOOD GEEK DOWN!
SNAP

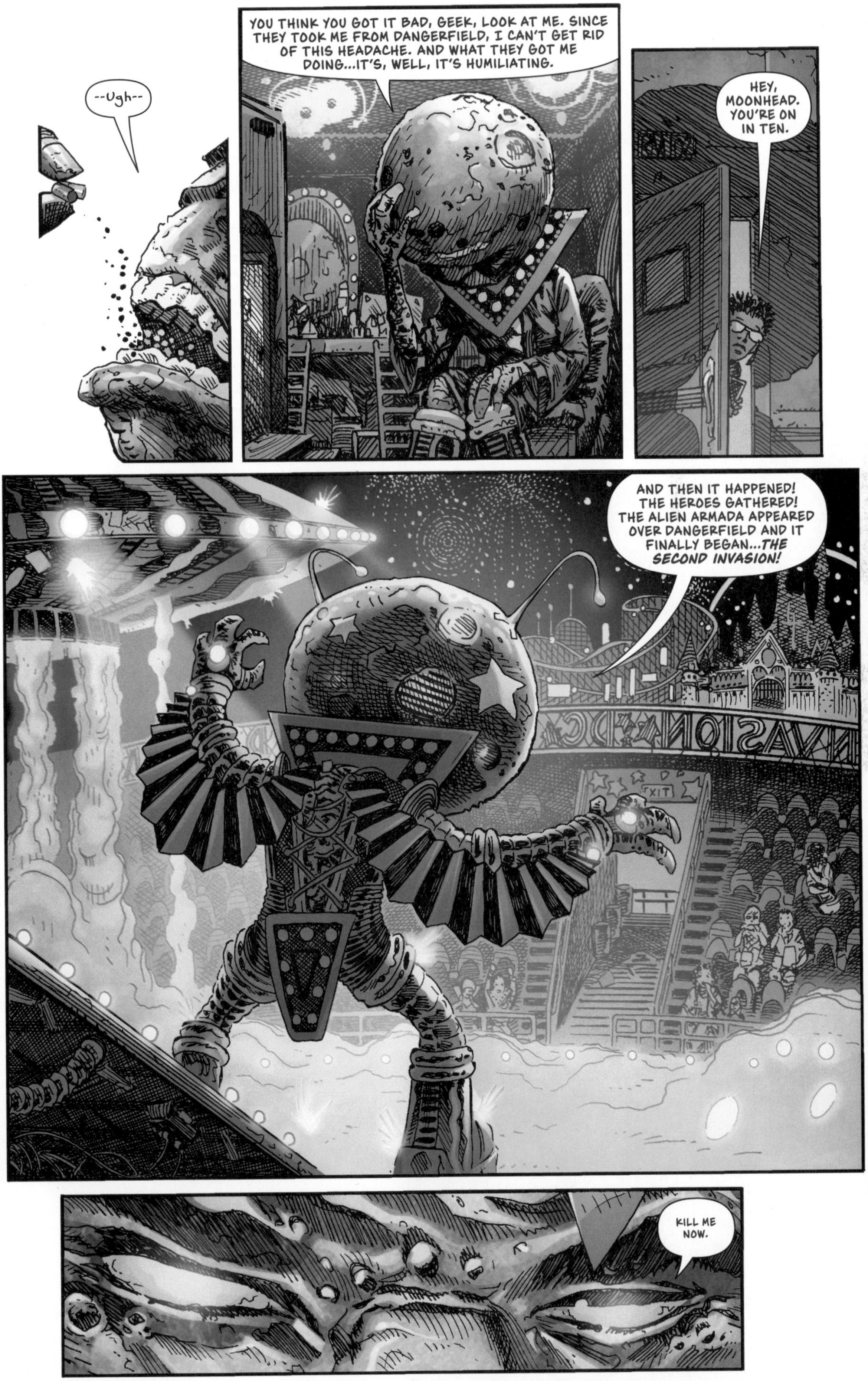

--Ugh--
YOU THINK YOU GOT IT BAD, GEEK, LOOK AT ME. SINCE THEY TOOK ME FROM DANGERFIELD, I CAN'T GET RID OF THIS HEADACHE. AND WHAT THEY GOT ME DOING...IT'S, WELL, IT'S HUMILIATING.
HEY, MOONHEAD. YOU'RE ON IN TEN.
AND THEN IT HAPPENED! THE HEROES GATHERED! THE ALIEN ARMADA APPEARED OVER DANGERFIELD AND IT FINALLY BEGAN...*THE SECOND INVASION!*
EXIT
INVASION
KILL ME NOW.

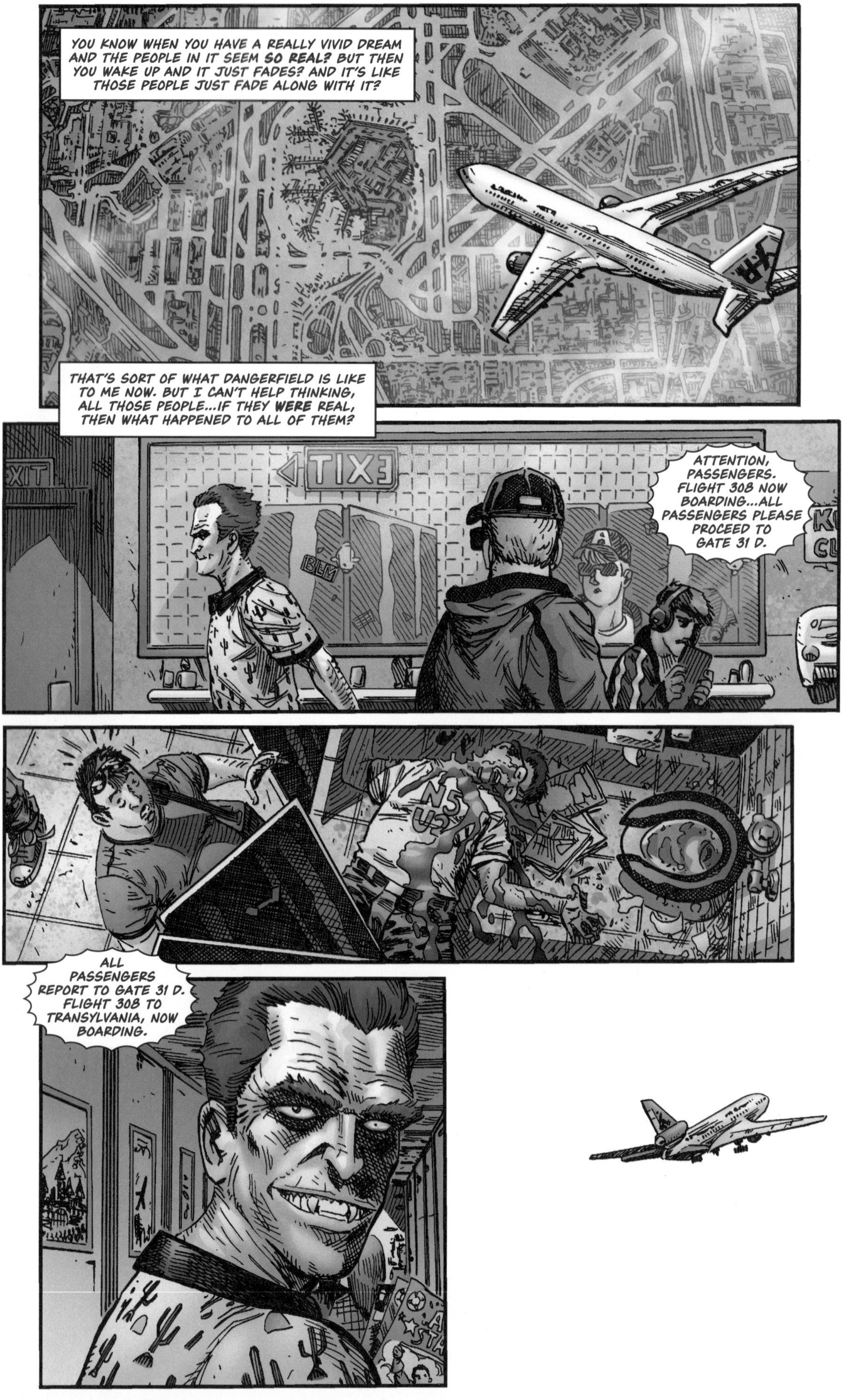
YOU KNOW WHEN YOU HAVE A REALLY VIVID DREAM AND THE PEOPLE IN IT SEEM SO REAL? BUT THEN YOU WAKE UP AND IT JUST FADES? AND IT'S LIKE THOSE PEOPLE JUST FADE ALONG WITH IT?
THAT'S SORT OF WHAT DANGERFIELD IS LIKE TO ME NOW. BUT I CAN'T HELP THINKING, ALL THOSE PEOPLE...IF THEY WERE REAL, THEN WHAT HAPPENED TO ALL OF THEM?
EXIT
ATTENTION, PASSENGERS. FLIGHT 308 NOW BOARDING...ALL PASSENGERS PLEASE PROCEED TO GATE 31 D.
ALL PASSENGERS REPORT TO GATE 31 D. FLIGHT 308 TO TRANSYLVANIA, NOW BOARDING.

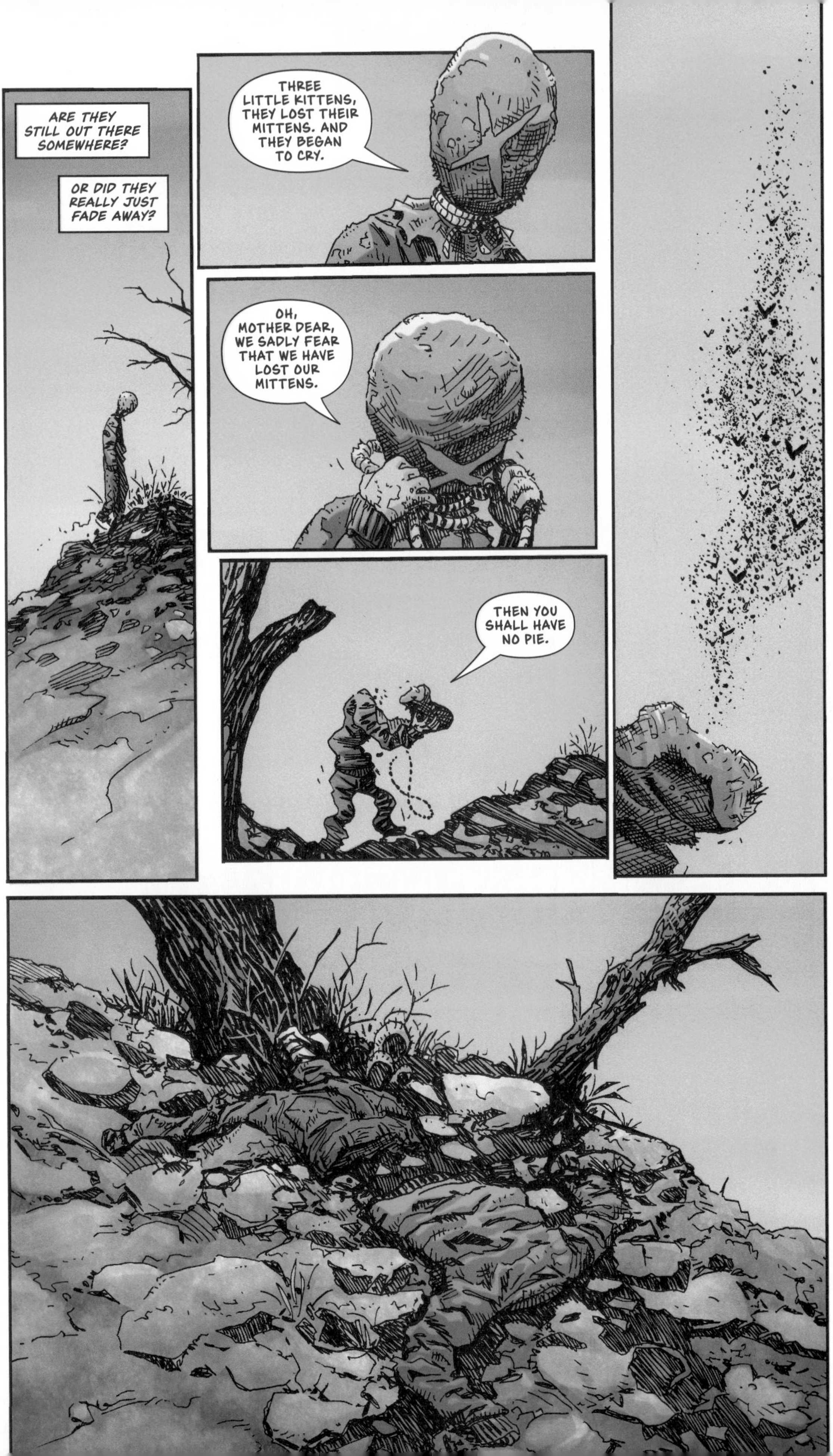
ARE THEY STILL OUT THERE SOMEWHERE?
OR DID THEY REALLY JUST FADE AWAY?
THREE LITTLE KITTENS, THEY LOST THEIR MITTENS. AND THEY BEGAN TO CRY.
OH, MOTHER DEAR, WE SADLY FEAR THAT WE HAVE LOST OUR MITTENS.
THEN YOU SHALL HAVE NO PIE.

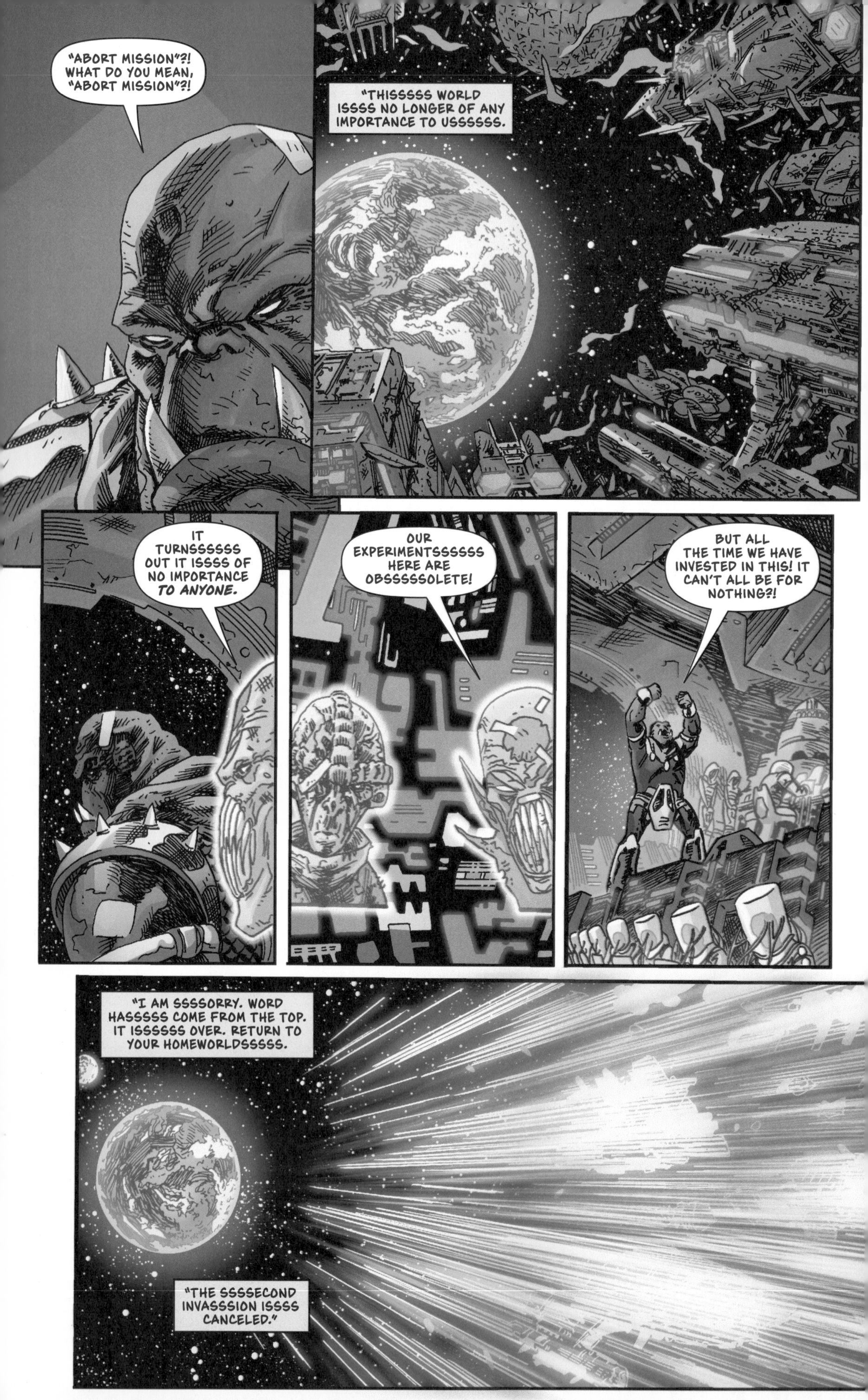
"ABORT MISSION"?! WHAT DO YOU MEAN, "ABORT MISSION"?!
"THISSSSS WORLD ISSSS NO LONGER OF ANY IMPORTANCE TO USSSSSS.
IT TURNSSSSSS OUT IT ISSSS OF NO IMPORTANCE TO ANYONE.
OUR EXPERIMENTSSSSSS HERE ARE OBSSSSSOLETE!
BUT ALL THE TIME WE HAVE INVESTED IN THIS! IT CAN'T ALL BE FOR NOTHING?!
"I AM SSSSORRY. WORD HASSSSS COME FROM THE TOP. IT ISSSSSS OVER. RETURN TO YOUR HOMEWORLDSSSSS.
"THE SSSSECOND INVASSSION ISSSS CANCELED."

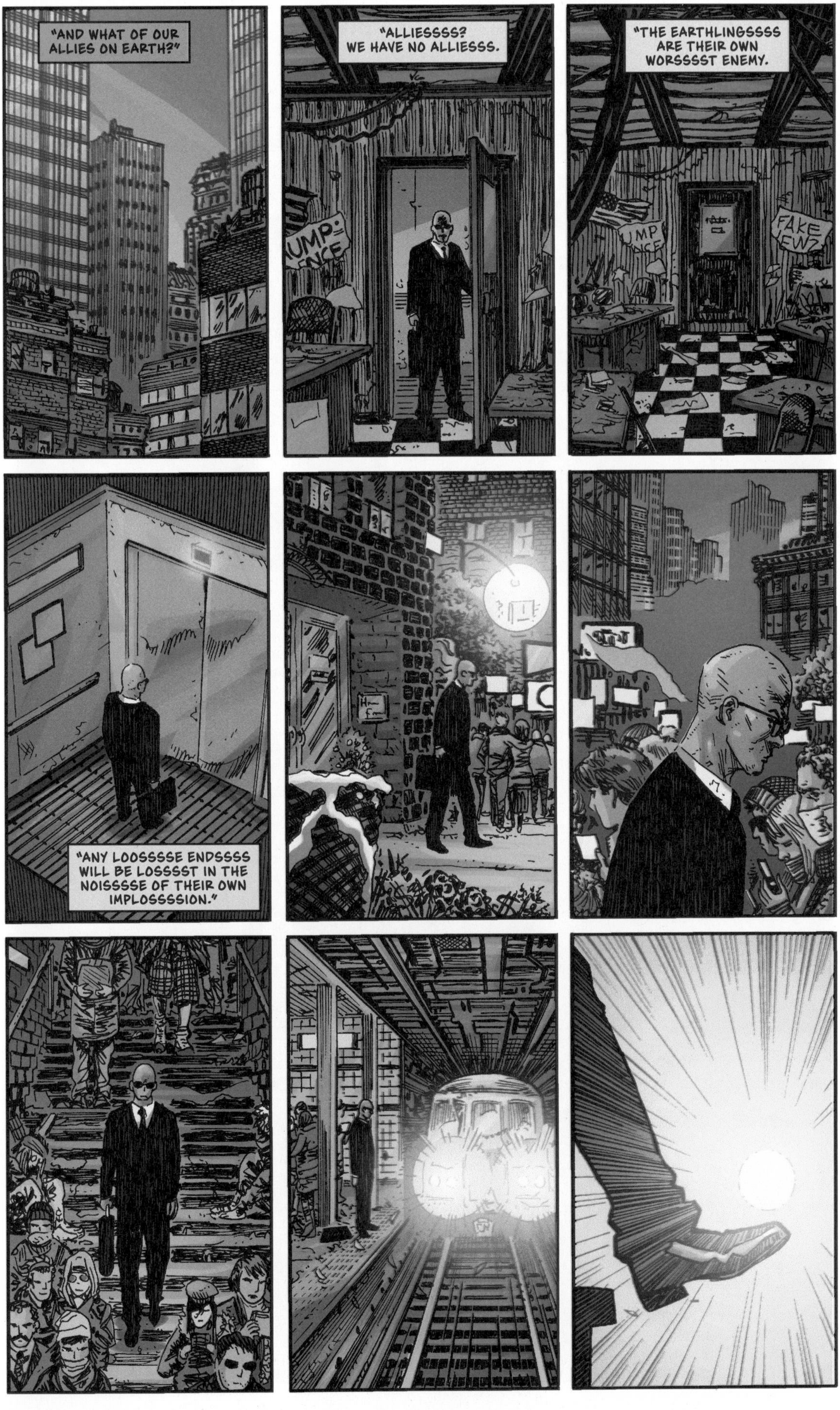
"AND WHAT OF OUR ALLIES ON EARTH?"
"ALLIESSSS? WE HAVE NO ALLIESSS.
"THE EARTHLINGSSSS ARE THEIR OWN WORSSSST ENEMY.
"ANY LOOSSSSE ENDSSSS WILL BE LOSSSST IN THE NOISSSSE OF THEIR OWN IMPLOSSSSION."

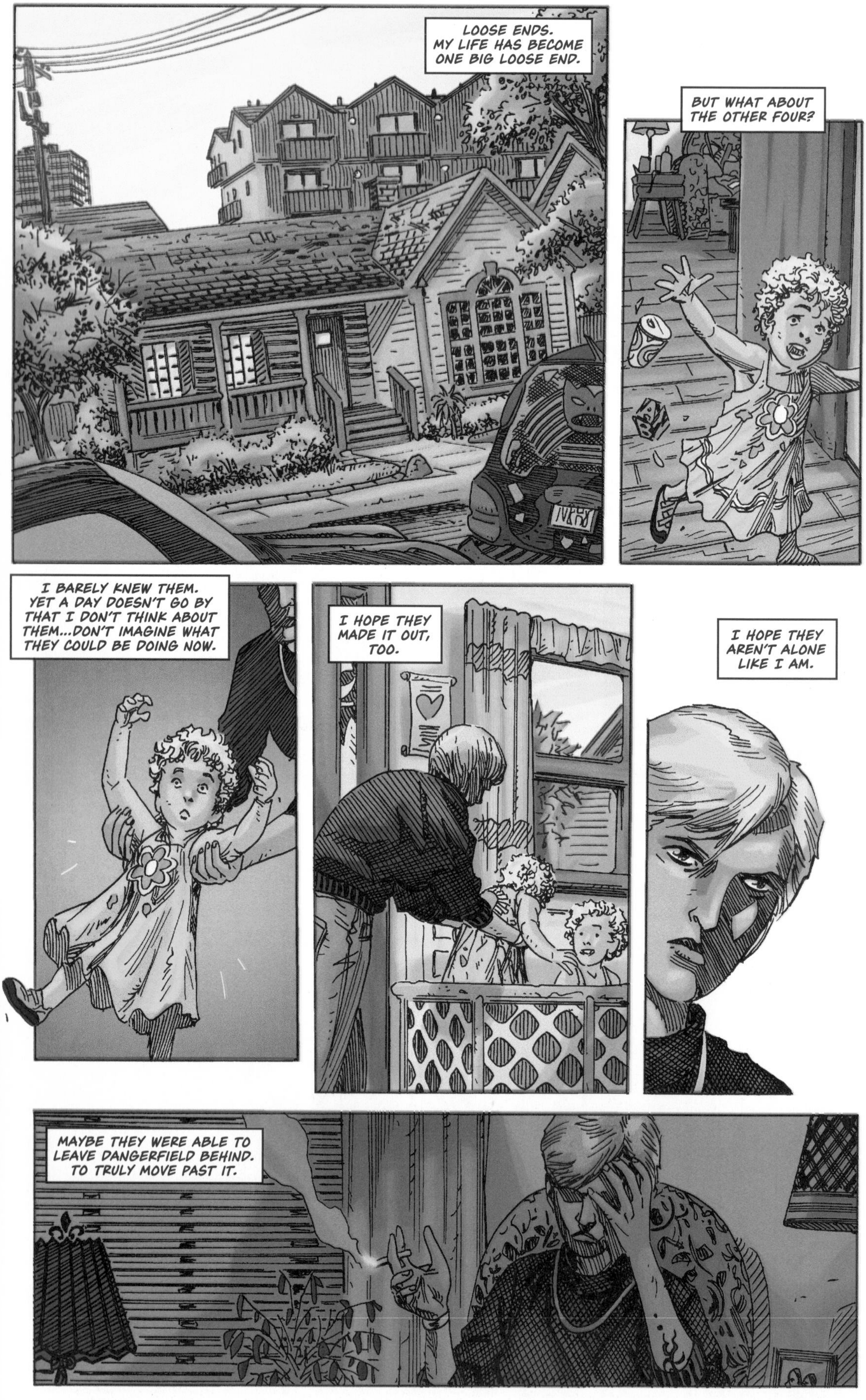
LOOSE ENDS. MY LIFE HAS BECOME ONE BIG LOOSE END.
BUT WHAT ABOUT THE OTHER FOUR?
I BARELY KNEW THEM. YET A DAY DOESN'T GO BY THAT I DON'T THINK ABOUT THEM...DON'T IMAGINE WHAT THEY COULD BE DOING NOW.
I HOPE THEY MADE IT OUT, TOO.
I HOPE THEY AREN'T ALONE LIKE I AM.
MAYBE THEY WERE ABLE TO LEAVE DANGERFIELD BEHIND. TO TRULY MOVE PAST IT.

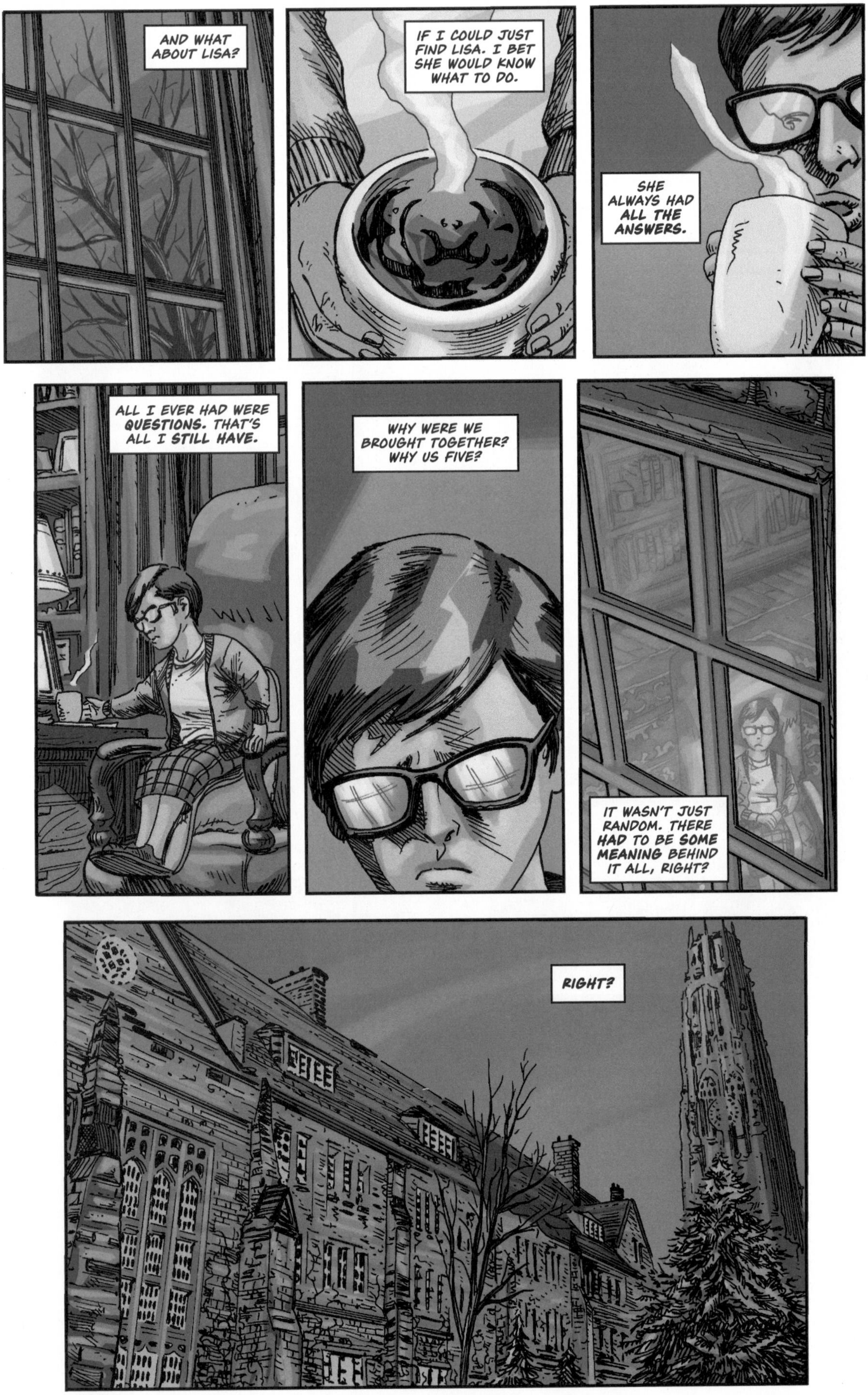
AND WHAT ABOUT LISA?
IF I COULD JUST FIND LISA. I BET SHE WOULD KNOW WHAT TO DO.
SHE ALWAYS HAD ALL THE ANSWERS.
ALL I EVER HAD WERE QUESTIONS. THAT'S ALL I STILL HAVE.
WHY WERE WE BROUGHT TOGETHER? WHY US FIVE?
IT WASN'T JUST RANDOM. THERE HAD TO BE SOME MEANING BEHIND IT ALL, RIGHT?
RIGHT?

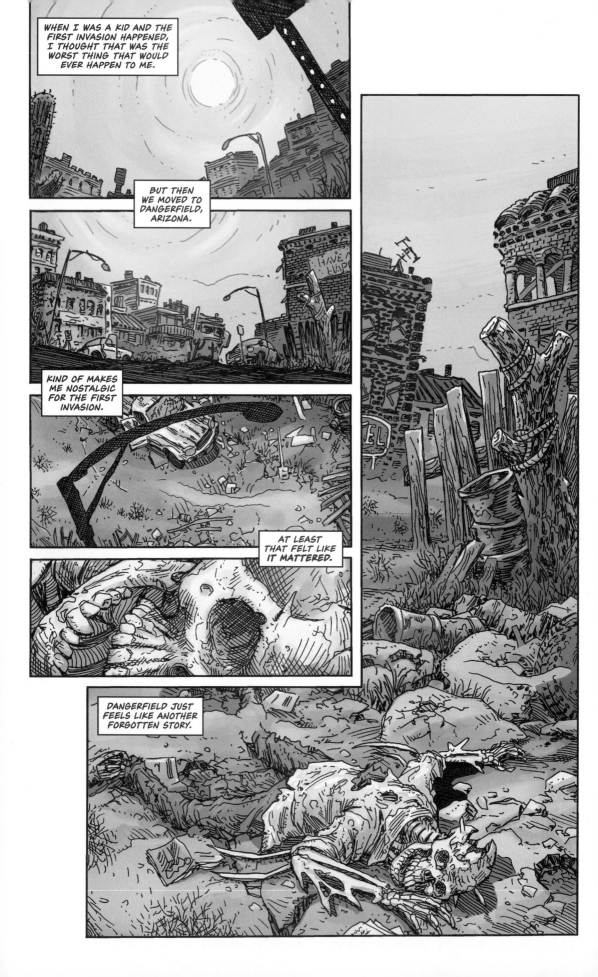

WHEN I WAS A KID AND THE FIRST INVASION HAPPENED, I THOUGHT THAT WAS THE WORST THING THAT WOULD EVER HAPPEN TO ME.

BUT THEN WE MOVED TO DANGERFIELD, ARIZONA.

KIND OF MAKES ME NOSTALGIC FOR THE FIRST INVASION.

AT LEAST THAT FELT LIKE IT MATTERED.

DANGERFIELD JUST FEELS LIKE ANOTHER FORGOTTEN STORY.

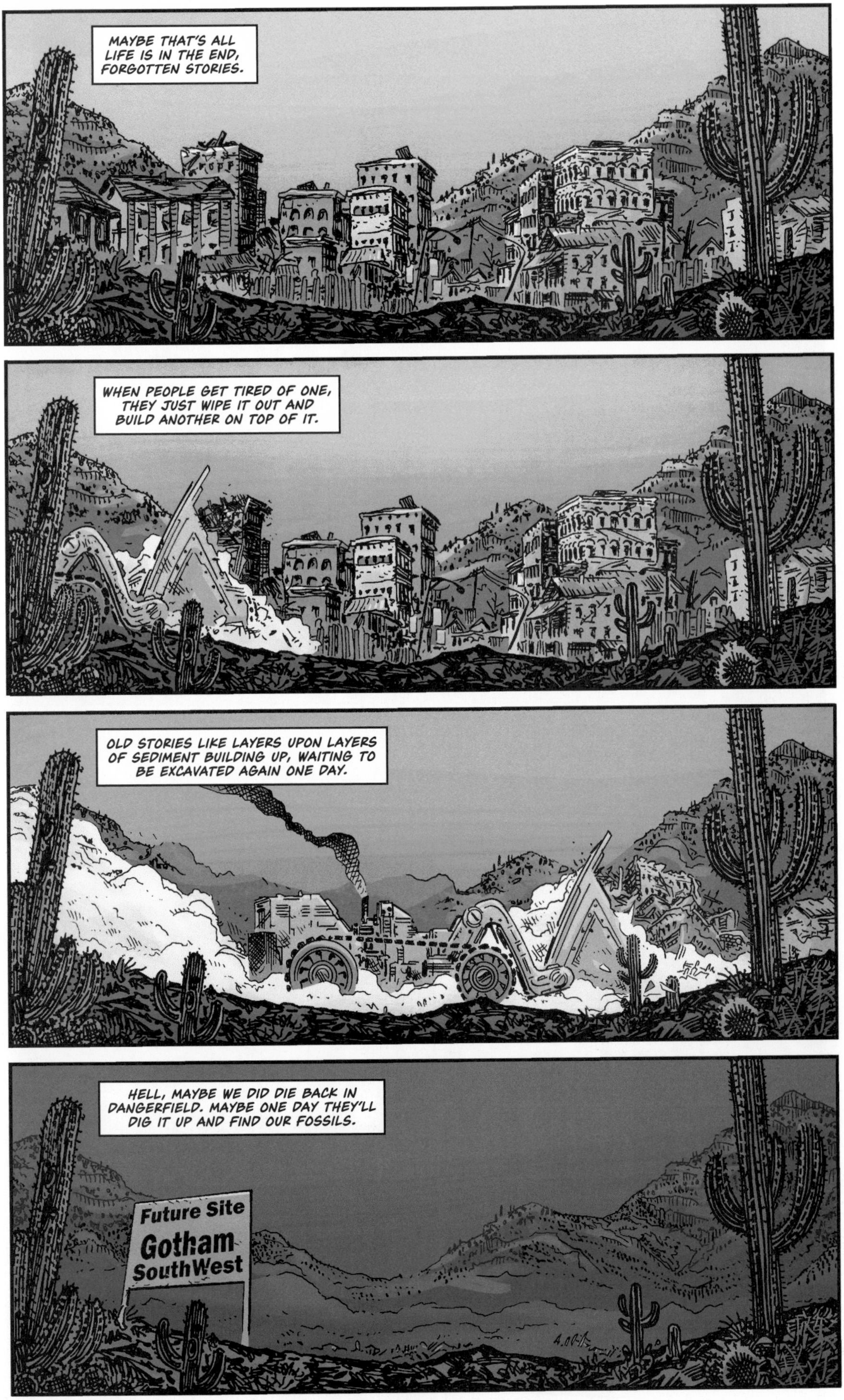
MAYBE THAT'S ALL LIFE IS IN THE END, FORGOTTEN STORIES.
WHEN PEOPLE GET TIRED OF ONE, THEY JUST WIPE IT OUT AND BUILD ANOTHER ON TOP OF IT.
OLD STORIES LIKE LAYERS UPON LAYERS OF SEDIMENT BUILDING UP, WAITING TO BE EXCAVATED AGAIN ONE DAY.
HELL, MAYBE WE DID DIE BACK IN DANGERFIELD. MAYBE ONE DAY THEY'LL DIG IT UP AND FIND OUR FOSSILS.
Future Site
Gotham
SouthWest

POWR

DUN

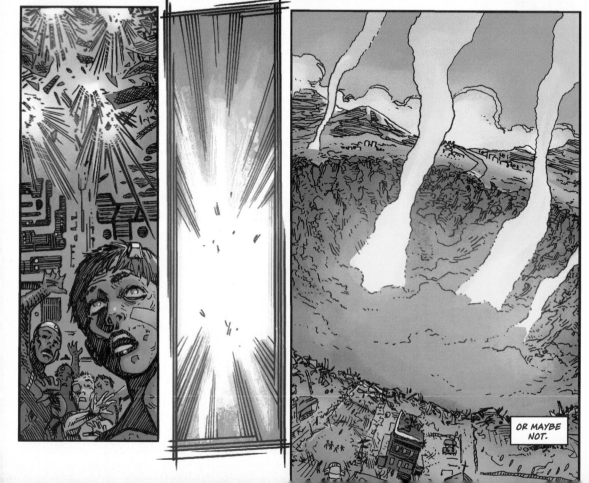

OR MAYBE NOT.

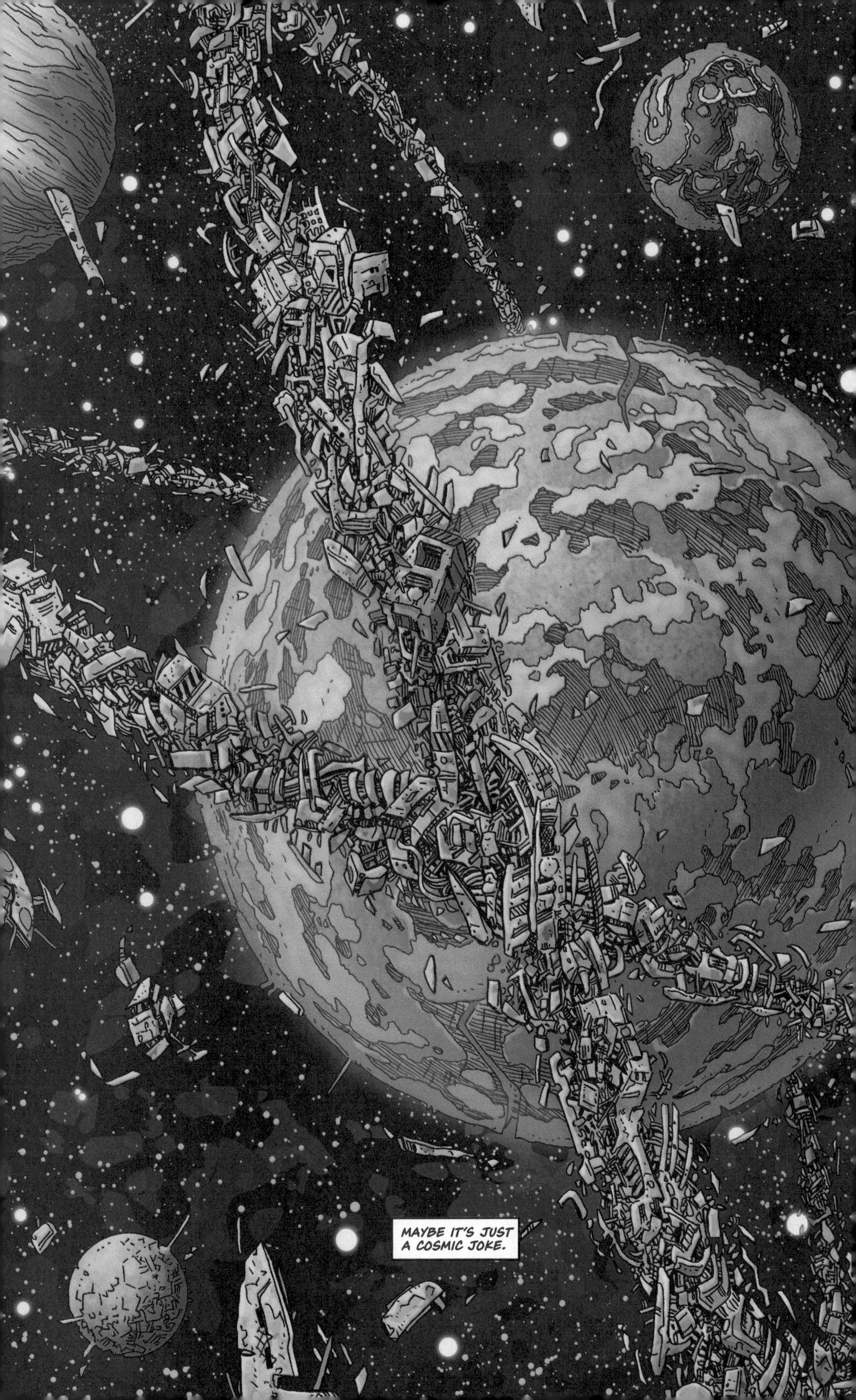
MAYBE IT'S JUST
A COSMIC JOKE.

WHAT DO YOU WANT?

BEEN LOOKING ALL OVER FOR YOU, KID.

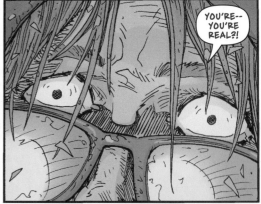

YOU'RE-- YOU'RE REAL?!

OF COURSE I AM. NOW HOP IN. WE GOT WORK TO DO.

END?

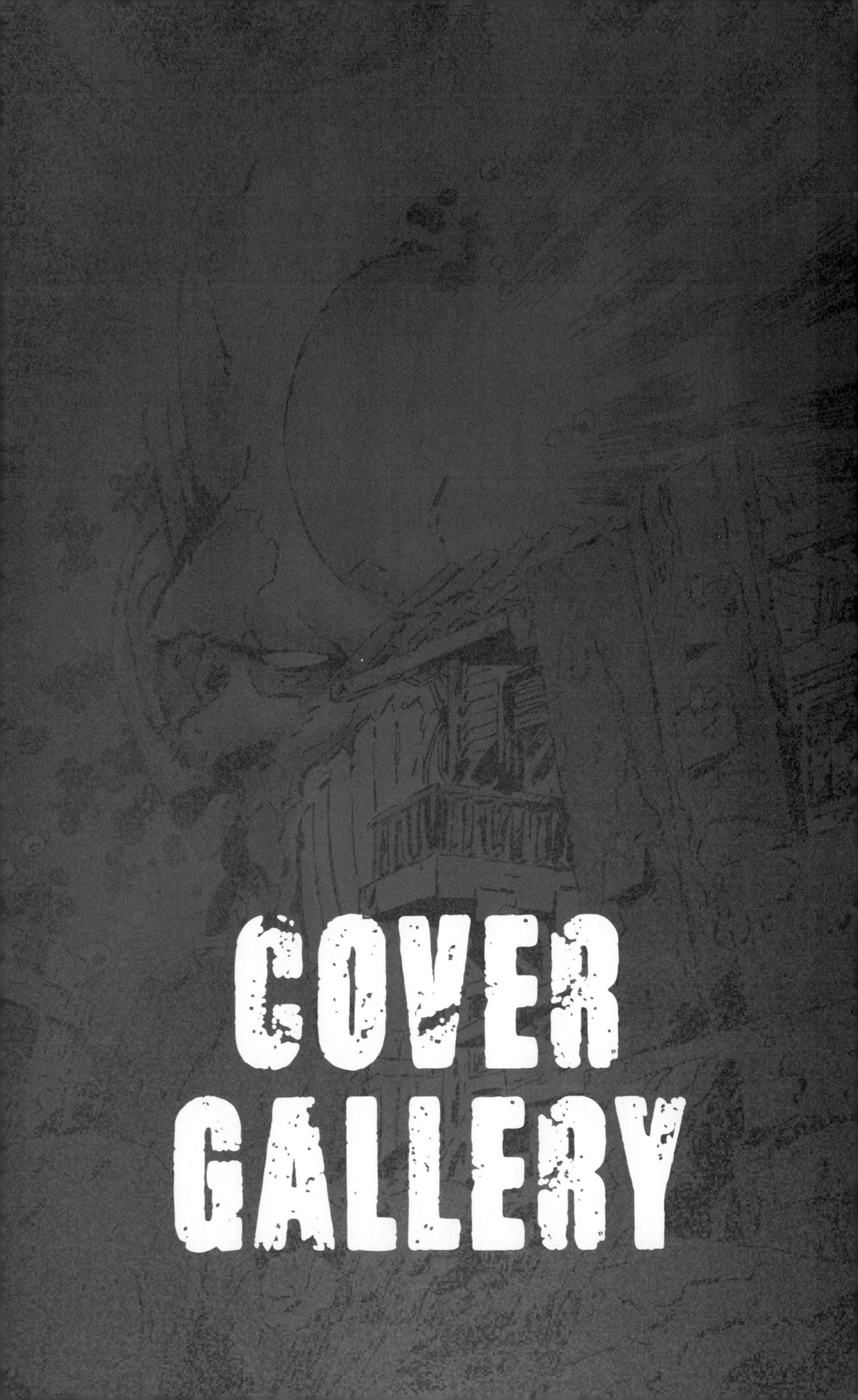

COVER GALLERY

Inferior Five #1 cover by
KEITH GIFFEN, MICHELLE DELECKI, and HI-FI

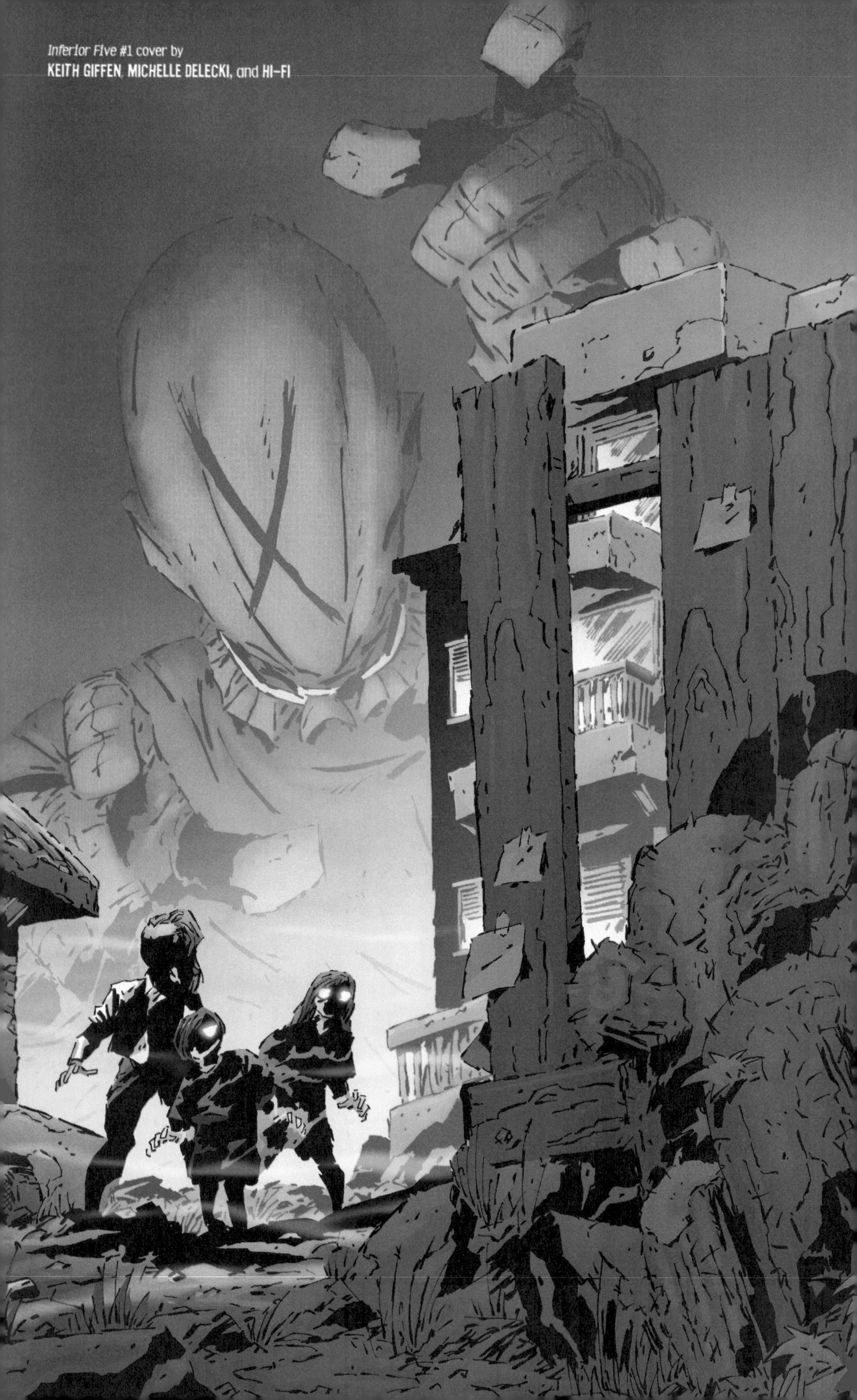

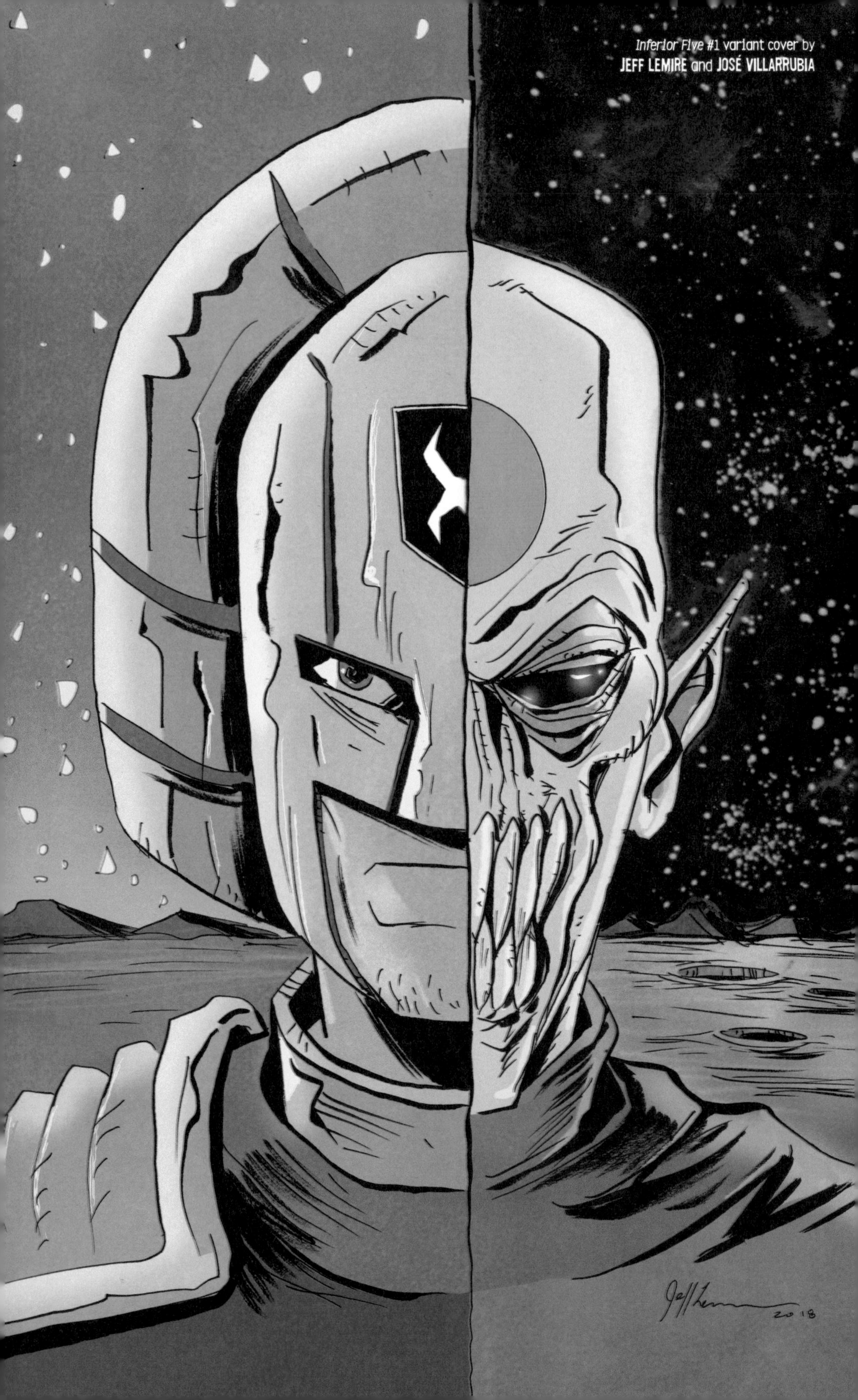

Inferior Five #1 variant cover by
JEFF LEMIRE and **JOSÉ VILLARRUBIA**

Inferior Five #2 cover by
KEITH GIFFEN, MICHELLE DELECKI, and **HI-FI**

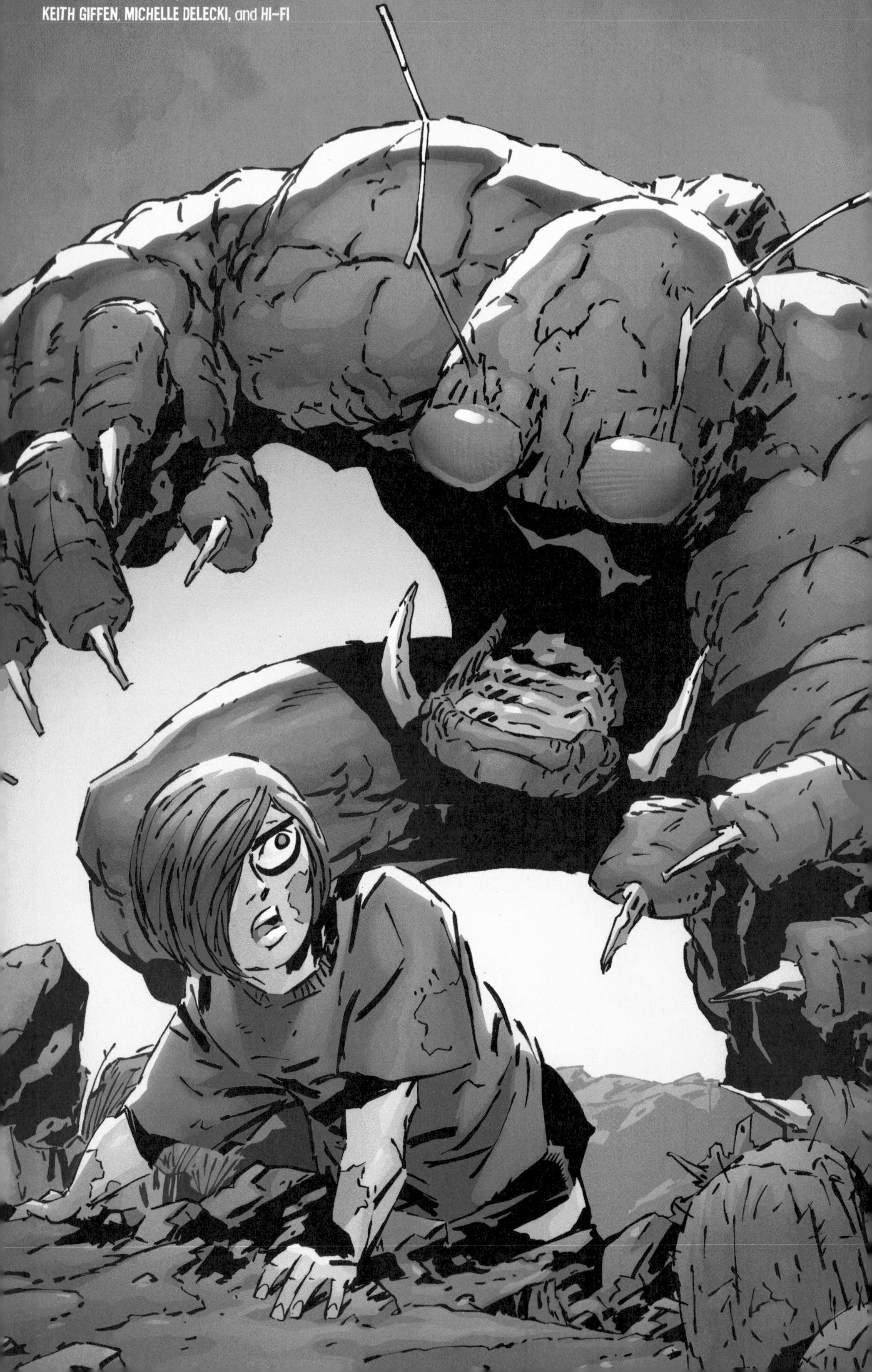

Inferior Five #3 cover by
KEITH GIFFEN, MICHELLE DELECKI, and **HI-FI**

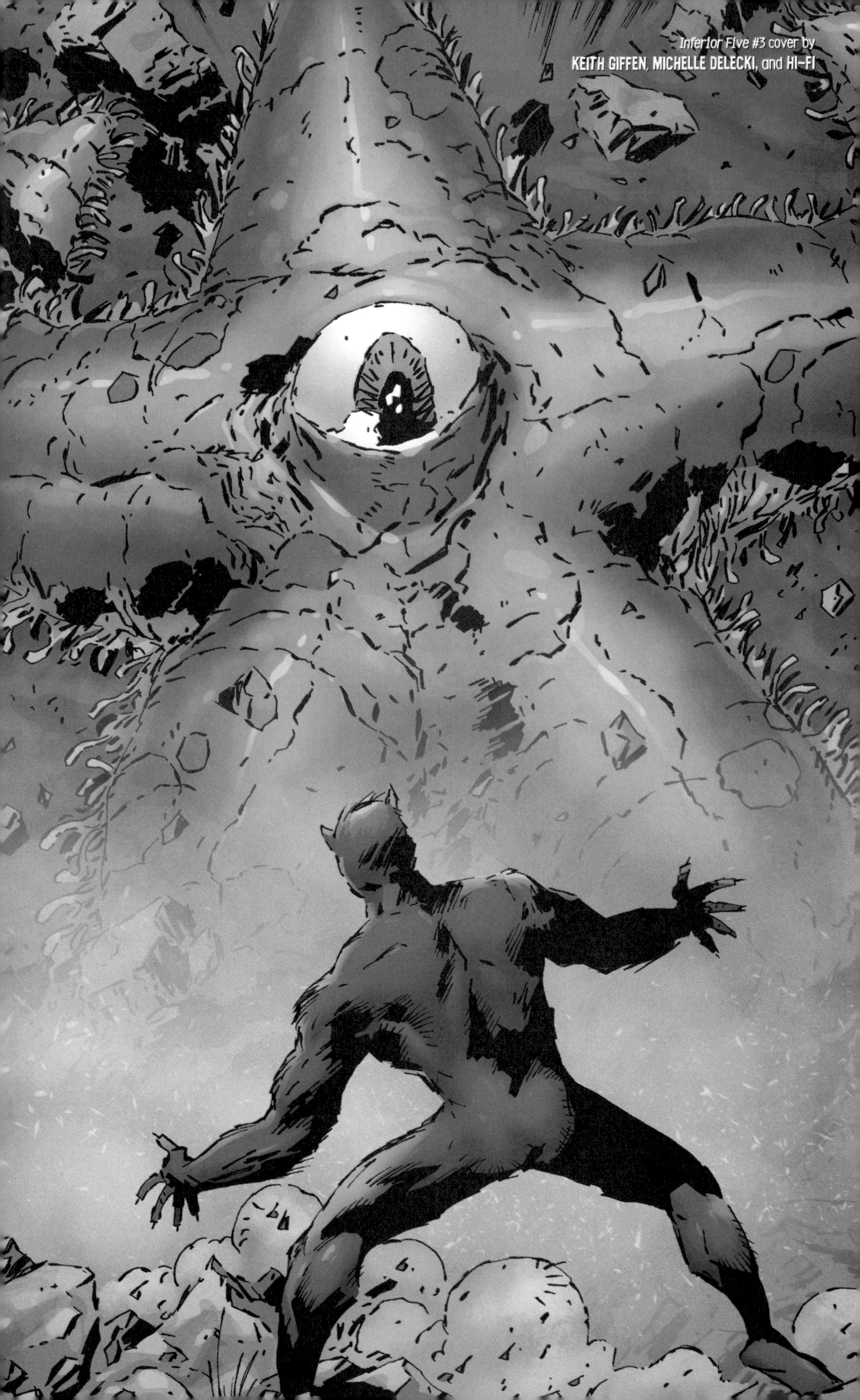

Inferior Five #4 cover by
SCOTT KOBLISH and **HI-FI**

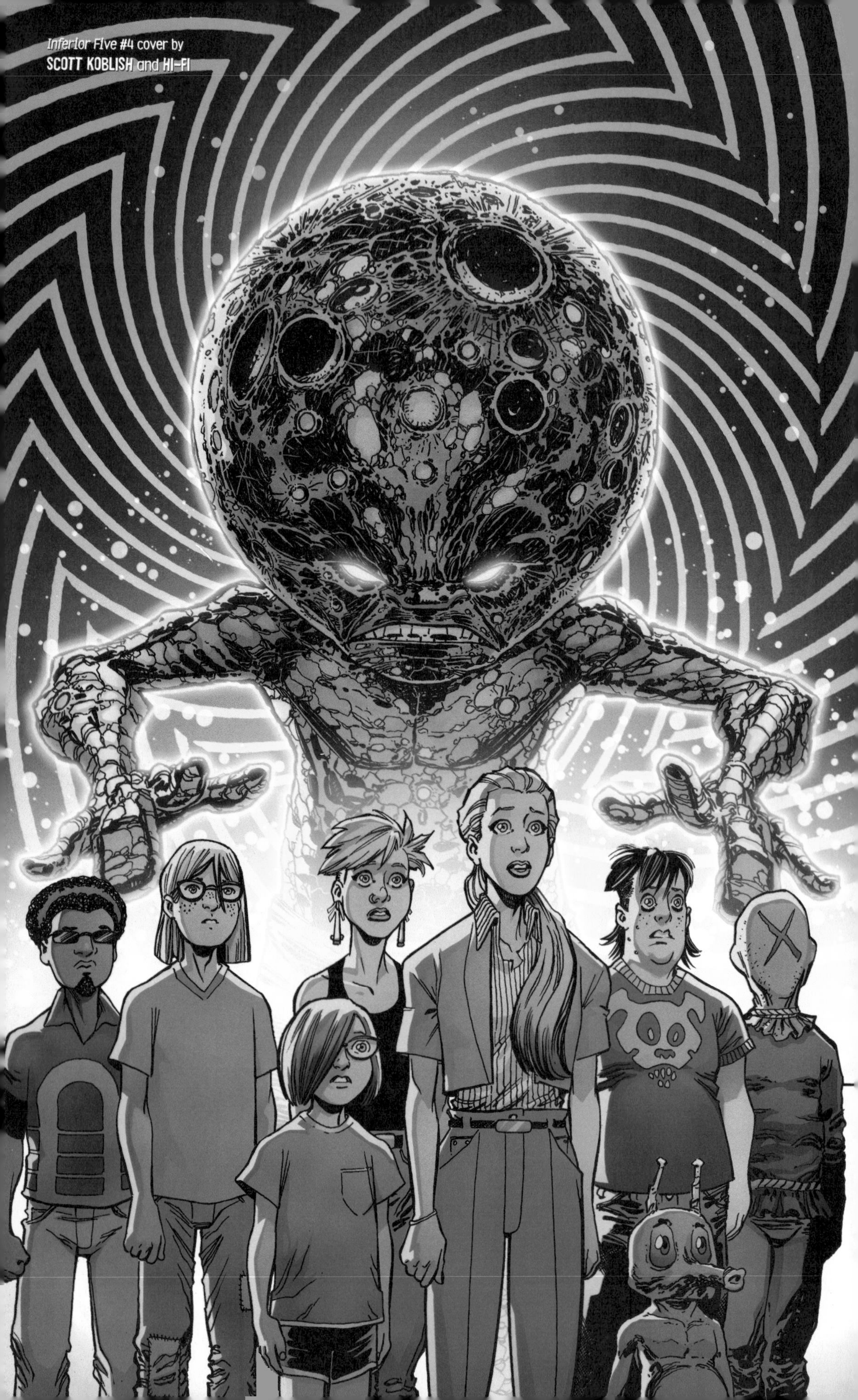

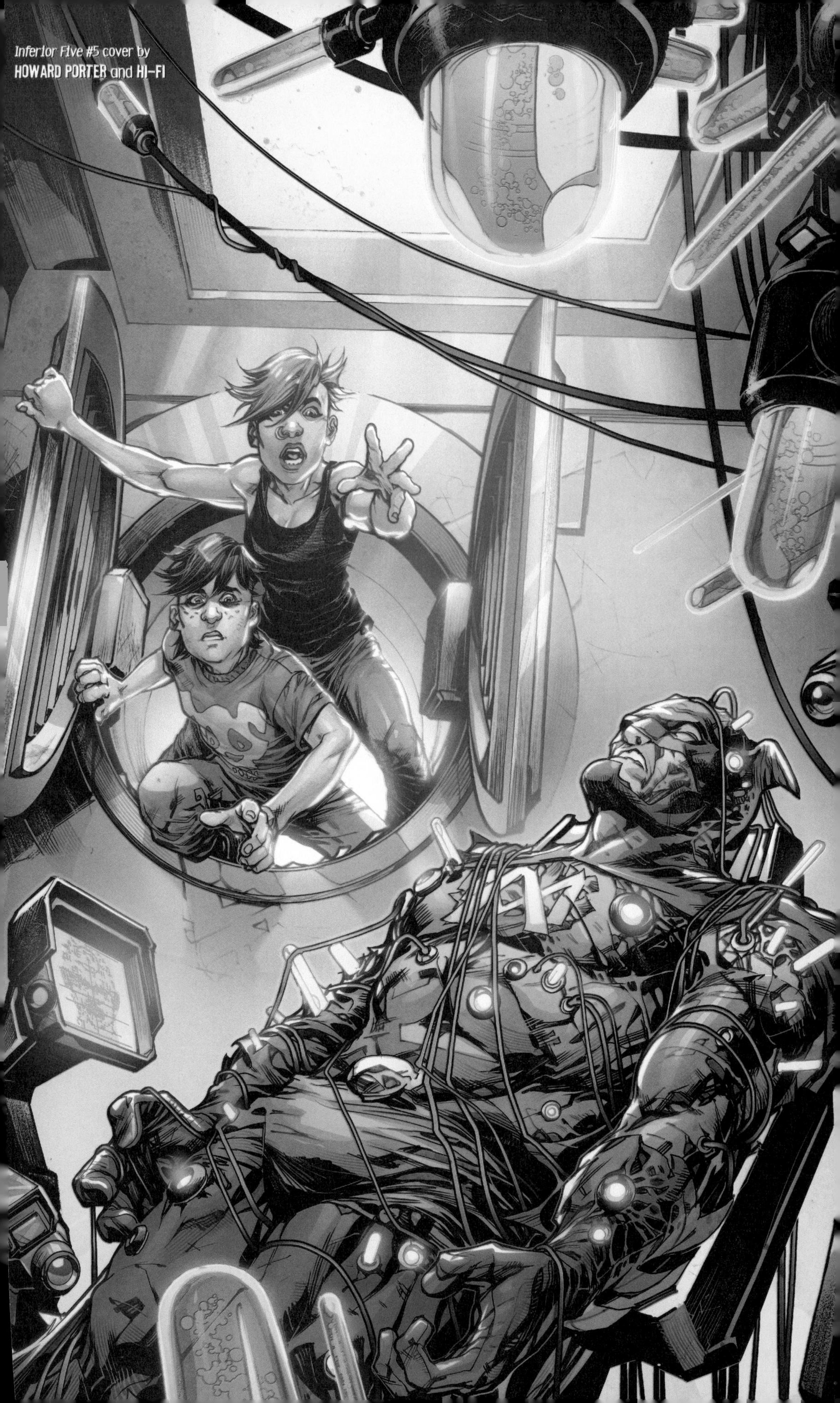

Inferior Five #5 cover by
HOWARD PORTER and HI-FI

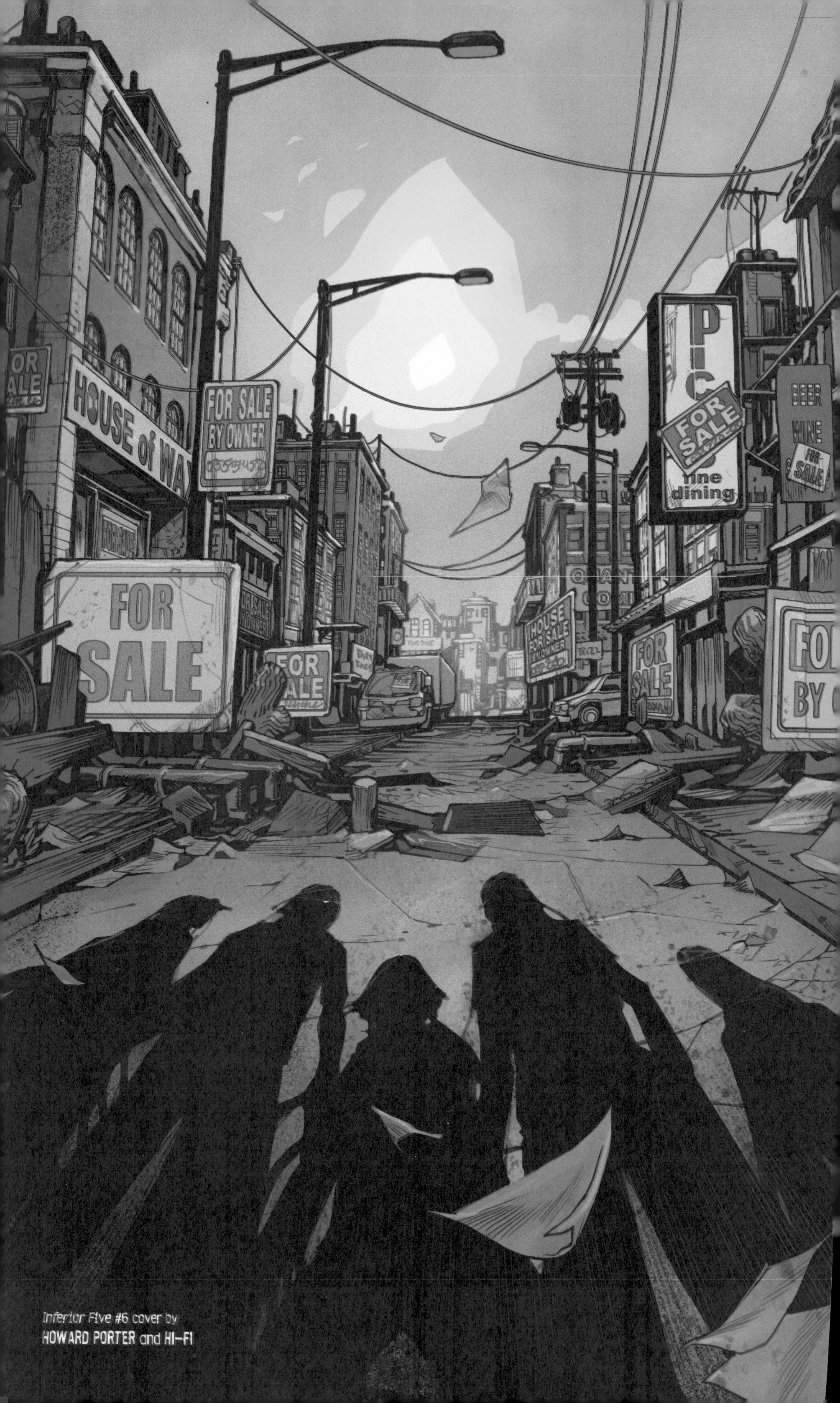
FOR SALE
HOUSE of WA
FOR SALE BY OWNER
FOR SALE
FOR SALE
BEER
WINE
FOR SALE
HOUSE FOR SALE BY OWNER
FOR SALE
FOR SALE

Inferior Five #6 cover by
HOWARD PORTER and HI-FI